A PRIME MINISTER REMEMBERS

BOOKS BY

FRANCIS WILLIAMS

GENERAL

War by Revolution
Democracy's Last Battle
Ten Angels Swearing, or Tomorrow's Politics
Press, Parliament and People
The Triple Challenge
Fifty Years' March: The Rise of the Labour Party
Transmitting World News
Ernest Bevin: Portrait of a Great Englishman
Magnificent Journey: The Rise of the Trade Unions
Journey into Adventure: The History of the W.T.A.
Dangerous Estate: The Anatomy of Newspapers
A Prime Minister Remembers

FICTION

No Man is an Island
A Provincial Affair
The Richardson Story

FRANCIS WILLIAMS

A PRIME MINISTER REMEMBERS

THE WAR AND POST-WAR MEMOIRS
OF
THE RT HON. EARL ATTLEE
K.G., P.C., O.M., C.H.

Based on his Private Papers and on a Series of Recorded Conversations

HEINEMANN

LONDON MELBOURNE TORONTO

William Heinemann Ltd
LONDON MELBOURNE TORONTO
CAPE TOWN AUCKLAND
THE HAGUE

First published 1961
Reprinted 1961

Printed in Great Britain
by The Windmill Press Ltd
Kingswood, Surrey

Contents

Author's Note

This book bears the same title as a filmed conversation piece between Lord Attlee and myself which was broadcast on B.B.C. television on 3 January 1959, on the occasion of his seventy-sixth birthday. The success of this programme, which won wide appreciation and was quoted and commented on all over the world, led to my suggesting to Lord Attlee that similar conversations reviewing his long period of office as Deputy Prime Minister and Prime Minister throughout twelve of the most momentous years in British history might be of great interest if incorporated in a book of memoirs drawing upon many of his private papers covering these years.

He agreed. My writing of this volume was preceded by many hours of conversation between Lord Attlee and myself spread over many days. Verbatim extracts from the tape recordings of these conversations have been used where they throw new light on the events in which Lord Attlee played so major a part and on the personalities involved in them. Lord Attlee also placed at my disposal all his records and private papers. These we went through together and discussed before I started writing and he subsequently made a number of emendations and additions to the draft of the manuscript which I sent him.

This book is, therefore, in part a history, approved by Lord Attlee, of these critical years based on contemporary sources, on hitherto unpublished private papers and on Lord Attlee's own records and recollections, and in part a retrospective comment on events and people by Lord Attlee as he looks back on judgments, achievements – and mistakes. I hope that this combination of narrative and conversation may be found by many to bring fresh insights, not only into recent history, but also into the character of Lord Attlee himself.

Most of the conversations recorded took place at Lord Attlee's home, Cherry Cottage, Prestwood, Great Missenden, Buckinghamshire, and I am deeply grateful to Lady Attlee for the charm and goodwill with which she bore my many intrusions and for her hospitality on so many occasions. Thanks are also due to Sir Norman Brooke for the assistance he gave Lord Attlee in tracing a number of telegrams to President Truman and others of which Lord Attlee himself had not kept copies; and to Mr Arthur Moyle, M.P., Lord Attlee's P.P.S. during the great part of his period at 10 Downing Street, for his helpful guidance in those passages concerned with the internal affairs of the Labour Party.

I must also thank Mr Jack Hill for his invaluable assistance with the tape recording, my secretary, Mrs R. Wyer, for the skill and patience with which she dealt with a difficult manuscript, and my wife, as always, for her unfailing advice and help.

I

The King's Commission

At 7.30 on the evening of 26 July 1945 a small family car drove through the gates of Buckingham Palace: Mr Attlee, Leader of the Labour Party and until two months previously Deputy Prime Minister in the War Cabinet, was going to see the King.

The King had previously seen Mr Winston Churchill at seven o'clock that same evening and accepted his resignation as Prime Minister. It had been a melancholy meeting. Mr Churchill, although calm and unshaken, was both saddened and surprised by the electoral results which had been pouring in throughout that day and which now showed that, with 392 seats to the Conservatives' 189, Labour would have an overall majority in the new House of Commons of 180: the previous day Mr Churchill had told the King that he confidently expected a Conservative majority of between 30 and 80. Nor, as he recorded in his diary quoted by Sir John Wheeler-Bennett in *King George VI: His Life and Reign*, could the King himself avoid sadness at this unexpected dismissal of his great war Prime Minister by the British electorate. They seemed to him 'very ungrateful.'

Mr Attlee, who had been enjoying a late tea with his family at the Great Western Hotel, Paddington, when the King's summons reached him, was hardly less surprised by the result of the General Election than Mr Churchill. He had not wanted an Election at this time. He would have preferred it in the autumn, when a more complete and effective register would have been in force and when those in the Services, very large numbers of them still overseas, would, he considered, have had more opportunity to acquaint themselves with the issues: he underestimated the extent to which they had already been thinking about and discussing the political future.

During the Election he had conducted a vigorous campaign, speaking at seven or eight meetings a day in a tour of the Midlands, Lancashire, Yorkshire and the Eastern Counties. He had also carried on a sharp and acrimonious correspondence with Mr Churchill, who, after an opening broadcast in which he made a violent attack on his former Labour colleagues and declared that they would institute a Gestapo to maintain their politics if returned, had seized on a characteristically maladroit statement by Professor Harold Laski, Chairman for that year of the Labour Party National Executive, to suggest that a Labour Prime Minister would be a mere tool in the hands of a non-parliamentary body to which he might be compelled to divulge the most vital Cabinet secrets.

At all his meetings Attlee had had large and enthusiastic receptions, although not so enthusiastic as those accorded to Mr Churchill. He felt too that he had got the better of his written exchanges with the Prime Minister, as did others, including many not of his own party, like Professor Sir Ernest Barker, who wrote to him from Cambridge on 16 June, sending 'sincere congratulations on the statesmanship and magnanimity of your reply to Mr Churchill' and on 'your assertion of the rights of the parliamentary leader of your party against any challenge *ab extra*', adding: 'It is what Gladstone asserted against Joseph Chamberlain and Salisbury against Randolph Churchill a few years after I was born. They both won.'

Nevertheless although he had fought a good Election Attlee did not believe he had won it. At Potsdam in the interval while the Services votes were returned and counted he told Molotov that it would be 'a close thing', much to that Soviet leader's suspicious bewilderment when the actual result was announced. ('But you said it would be a close thing and now you have a big majority,' he said over and over again when Attlee returned as Prime Minister, making it clear that he thought there had been some inexplicable slip-up on Mr Churchill's part in allowing such a thing to happen and that a necessary deference to the appearances of democracy had been carried altogether too far.) Privately Mr Attlee's views had been even less optimistic than those he expressed to Molotov. He had expected 'the Tories to pull it off'.

Nor, as Mrs Attlee drove him to the Palace, could he help but be aware that even at this moment of triumph there was a movement afoot by some in his party to replace him as Leader by Mr Herbert Morrison.

A letter to which he had returned no more than a formal acknowledgment had been delivered to him from Harold Laski arguing that under the Constitution of the Parliamentary Labour Party the Leader was subject to election at the opening of each new session and that Attlee ought therefore to refuse to accept the invitation to form a Government until the new Parliamentary Party, which was of course very much larger than, and different in composition from, that at the dissolution and contained a considerable number of new M.P.s who did not know Attlee personally, had met and voted on who it wished to lead it: Morrison, not Attlee, Laski and his friends believed. Ellen Wilkinson and Maurice Webb, one of the best-known of the new M.P.s and later Chairman of the Labour Parliamentary Committee, were also canvassing this view among Labour M.P.s. Both were intimate friends of Morrison.

This so called 'constitutional case' (under the Parliamentary Labour Party's Constitution, that is) had also been pressed by Morrison himself at an informal meeting between Attlee, Bevin, Morrison and Morgan Phillips, the Party Secretary, in Ernest Bevin's room at Transport House that same afternoon as it became clear from the results already in that Labour had won. Morrison received during this meeting a telephone call from Sir Stafford Cripps, who, he said, shared the view that Attlee ought not to accept the King's Commission until the Parliamentary Party had met to elect a leader. At this meeting Morrison made it plain that if there were an election he would feel free to stand against Attlee. 'I recall,' says Attlee, 'that he expressed reluctance to serve under me as he thought the Party might want him as Prime Minister.'

But although aware of the attempt to unseat him Attlee was not perturbed by it. Indeed he was a little amused. And he was quite certain that it was right to ignore it on constitutional grounds if no others. His view was: 'If you're invited by the King to form a Government you don't say you can't reply for forty-eight hours. You accept the commission and you either bring it off successfully or you don't, and if you don't you go back and say you can't and advise the King to send for someone else. It used to happen often in the nineteenth century. Queen Victoria couldn't stand Gladstone, so she sent for Granville and Hartington and they had to come back and tell her they couldn't manage it. The constitutional position is quite clear. People like Laski who knew all about the theory of politics and nothing about its practice just didn't understand it.'

Attlee was also quite clear in his own mind that if the King sent for the Leader of the Labour Party and, after leading the Party's campaign throughout the Election, the Leader said he could not say yes or no until he had first called a meeting of the whole of the new Parliamentary Party and put himself up for election, the effect on public opinion in the country would be appalling, particularly as it was known that an immediate return to the Potsdam Conference was essential. He wasted no time, therefore, listening to what seemed to him to be political nonsense of an altogether unrealistic kind, but got ready to try to form a Government if invited.

Nor did he have any doubt that he would be able to do so. He knew he had the support of Ernest Bevin, who had already made it plain to him that his dislike of Morrison was such that he would in no circumstances agree to serve under him, and of most of the more prominent of the other Labour leaders, with the possible exception of Cripps. And he was well aware that the 'old guard' of the Parliamentary Party was solidly behind him.

Looking, as the King later remarked to him, 'still very very surprised', he therefore accepted His Majesty's Commission without any hesitation and explained that he had not yet had time to discuss the offices of State with any of his principal colleagues. According to a note in his diary quoted by Wheeler-Bennett, the King expressed the hope during this brief conversation that Attlee would appoint Mr Bevin rather than Mr Dalton Foreign Secretary. But, if so, Mr Attlee took little note of this remark in his somewhat preoccupied state of mind and did not subsequently remember it. It played no part in his final decision, although, as it turned out, this coincided, after some initial hesitation, with the King's hopes.

However, the morning after he had seen the King, Attlee was still of the opinion that it would be best to send Dalton to the Foreign Office and Bevin to the Treasury and shortly before lunch on that day told Dalton, who had been advancing his own claims for this office, that this was provisionally what he had in mind. It was only after further thought that he decided to reverse this arrangement.

He was guided in so doing by two principal considerations. One was his conviction, even at this early stage, that now that the war in Europe was ended (the war with Japan was still, of course, proceeding and seemed at that time likely to continue for a long period) Soviet Russia would become tough, aggressive and unco-operative and that Bevin was the more suited of the two by temperament and experience to meet such a situation. The other was that he proposed to invite Morrison (who himself had some hopes of the Foreign Office although Attlee never considered him for the post) to be Lord President of the Council and Leader of the House of Commons and he thought it better to keep Bevin and him apart as much as possible: 'Ernie and Herbert didn't get on together. If you'd put both on the home front there might have been trouble, therefore it was better that Ernie should operate mainly in foreign affairs.'

It was not an easy decision. Bevin and Dalton were both equally strong candidates for either office and their personal preferences were exactly opposite to Attlee's final decision. Dalton in fact had intimated to Attlee when he saw him on the morning of the 27th in a room in the Cabinet offices in Great George Street, where he had retreated to get time for quiet thought, that although he would naturally go where the Prime Minister wanted he hoped it would be the Foreign Office, for which he felt he was particularly suited and which he knew well as a former Under-Secretary under Arthur Henderson and as the main Labour spokesman on foreign affairs in the 'thirties. And although Bevin had spoken forcefully on foreign affairs at the pre-Election Party Conference at Blackpool, he told Attlee that he would like to go to the Treasury and have an opportunity to put into effect economic ideas which he had long been turning over in his mind, some of which, indeed, had been present ever since his membership of the Macmillan Committee on Finance and Industry in the late 'twenties.

After his brief talk with the King on the evening of 26 July, Attlee was driven by his wife to a Victory Rally at the Central Hall, Westminster. Here he was given a tumultuous reception.

There had been in the interim some canvassing of new M.P.s by Laski, Webb and other Morrison supporters in an attempt to get backing for a demand that the leadership should still be regarded as open. But it had not made much progress and when Attlee announced that he had just arrived from the Palace and had accepted the King's invitation to form a Government no more was heard of it – indeed with a quick change of front Laski himself bowed to the unavoidable and led the cheering.

Events in fact had moved altogether too quickly for those who wished to unseat Attlee and put Morrison in his place. Not anticipating that Mr Churchill would concede the Election while results were still coming in and tender his resignation to the King immediately, they had calculated on several hours, possibly twenty-four or more, for manœuvre, during which new M.P.s with little personal knowledge of the leaders involved could be persuaded that a more 'dynamic' Leader than Attlee was needed to carry through 'the socialist revolution'. They did not get them and there was nothing more they could do.

'So you are now Prime Minister,' said Herbert Morrison at

the Rally. As for Harold Laski, not only did he demonstrate the most marked if unlikely enthusiasm at the Central Hall, but when Attlee returned from Potsdam (to which he flew with Bevin on the Saturday, leaving Herbert Morrison in charge at home) he found awaiting him a second and very different letter from this indefatigable correspondent who after being for a brief but unsuccessful period his Personal Assistant during the war had subsequently worked so hard to try to prevent him from becoming Prime Minister.

'My dear Clem,' wrote Laski in a letter dated 2 August, 'let me, first of all, wish you the strength and power to carry through your immense task. I have often criticised you. However I think you know that this has been the unpersonal judgment of political difference. Here I want only to say what I said at the National Executive on Tuesday, that whatever support my loyalty can bring to aiding the Government I will give gladly and proudly. No one knows better than I that if we all stand firm we may open a great epoch in the history of civilisation.

'I hope when you come to consider these things that you will find a way of using me at the Embassy in Washington. I do know America with a quite special intimacy; I have a great many friends all over the country; and I think I could do, not least with ordinary people, the kind of job of interpreting Great Britain to the United States which Bryce did in his day. I venture to feel that, after twenty-five years of service in the Party, it is not unreasonable, especially after this election, to hope that you will make it realised that the Party has not regarded my efforts on its behalf as insignificant. I know I could do a good job in Washington; and I care for that more than for anything else. But at least I want the Beaverbrooks and the Brackens to know that my own party does not regard me as a leper it would not touch . . .'

To Laski's earlier letter Attlee had replied briefly: 'Dear Laski, thank you for your letter, contents of which have been noted.' He similarly noted the contents of this, but took no further action.

For the rest, the only permanent result of this abortive attempt to evoke the formal electoral procedures of the Parliamentary Labour Party to prevent Attlee from at once accepting the King's Commission was, whether justly or not, to deepen Bevin's long-seated idiosyncratic suspicion of Morrison as 'a slick wire-puller'. Thereafter he would periodically warn those he believed to be in Attlee's confidence to 'watch 'Erbert', adding massively, 'If you find him getting up to any of his tricks you tell me.' To Attlee's own relations with Morrison it made no difference ('I don't mind these things'). He found Morrison a loyal and hard-working colleague. He recalls however that Ellen Wilkinson 'looked a little surprised' when he wanted her to be Minister of Education with a seat in the Cabinet. No doubt she had not expected such magnanimity from one against whom she had been campaigning so actively.

Whatever may have been the personal disappointments of a few of those at the Victory Rally on that July evening, in the minds of the majority there was no feeling but one of unity behind the man who had been their leader in so great a triumph and had now become the Prime Minister of the first Labour Government in British history with real power. It was in the same mood of elation and taut expectancy that the 392 members of the Parliamentary Labour Party, many of them young men straight from the Services entering politics for the first time, gathered at the Beaver Hall in the City on the morning of Saturday 28 July to elect the Party Leader. All thought of other nominations had been abandoned. Attlee was elected unanimously. All Ministers, he told them, were on trial. He would not hesitate to replace any who were found unequal to the task.

Why did Labour get so unexpectedly large a majority? This is Attlee's assessment: 'I think, first of all, people wanted a positive new policy and not an attempt to go back to the old. Secondly, there was by that time a good deal of feeling among many people against what was felt to be the one-man business Churchill was running. And there was a great deal of suspicion of the forces behind him – Beaverbrook in particular. I always thought Churchill was led away by Beaverbrook and Brendan Bracken in the Election. He had a great opinion of Beaverbrook, who had brought down two Governments, and he listened to him and Bracken on how to fight the Election and they completely misjudged the public mood. All that talk about a Labour Gestapo and the relations between the Parliamentary Party and the National Executive which Churchill didn't understand at all – a miscalculation and quite contrary to the general mood of people; a frightful mistake. And even those who would have liked Churchill weren't prepared to have him if it meant having the Tories too. They remembered Munich and they remembered pre-war unemployment. They didn't want the Tories again. I remember one good woman who came to the committee rooms in my constituency and said she wanted to vote for Churchill. They told her he wasn't standing there. So she said, 'Oh, who is standing?' They told her, 'Mr Attlee,' and she said, 'He's all right, I'll vote for him. I'm not going to vote for any Conservatives.' There was a lot of that feeling.

Immediately after the Beaver Hall meeting Attlee flew to Potsdam with Bevin for the resumed meetings with Stalin and Truman.

He had been Leader of the Labour Party for ten years, five in Opposition, five as Deputy Prime Minister in the War Cabinet. Before turning to the immense tasks that now faced him it may be appropriate to look briefly back on these years, for they provide the setting against which those that followed have to be judged.

2

The Wasted Years

Whatever the totality of the causes that produced so large a swing to Labour in 1945, there is no doubt that one of the major reasons was popular anger against the Conservatives for their pre-war policy of weakness towards Nazi aggression. Yet there are many, Sir Winston Churchill among them, who believe that, although the major responsibility lay with the Baldwin and Chamberlain Governments, the Labour Party's share cannot be disregarded because its opposition to rearmament helped to keep Britain weak.

In retrospect Attlee agrees that in some respects Labour's policy may have been ill-judged. But looking back on the constant parliamentary battles of these years and his own visits to Spain during the Civil War and elsewhere, he believes that not only is there still a great deal of misunderstanding and misrepresentation of Labour's attitude, but that the policies it urged might have averted war if only the Conservative group in Parliament which distrusted Chamberlain could have been brought to vote against him before 1940.

Williams: Wouldn't you agree that Labour was traditionally uninterested in defence?

Attlee: That was certainly so at one time. Many Labour people in fact seemed to be of the opinion that an inefficient army was less wicked than an efficient one. Having served in the First World War, I did not share that view. I tried to interest Ramsay MacDonald in defence questions in the 'twenties, but he didn't take it very seriously and when I went to India on the Simon Commission the matter was dropped. Under Lansbury, a pacifist, it was impossible to do anything and I think it's true that up to 1935 the Parliamentary Party as a whole took little interest in defence problems beyond agreeing that the United Kingdom must contribute to armed forces of the League of Nations for collective security – and there was a pacifist minority that was opposed to that.

However, when I became Leader in 1935, I determined that we must look at the matter more realistically. I set up a Defence Committee, with people who'd had experience at the Service Ministries and some, like Dalton, who'd served in the First World War, and we started to look pretty seriously into things. We didn't like what we found.

I thought the state of air defences was pretty bad; there was no real co-ordination and I hadn't much confidence in the Chiefs of Staff at that time. They weren't a very bright lot, and they hadn't any particularly strong people on top in the Ministries either. Those who were there just stood out for their own show. It was said at that time, you know, that the Chiefs of Staff weren't on speaking terms, which was rather important if you were trying to plan a unified defence system.

As for the Cabinet, most of them hadn't the slightest idea what to do. We wanted combined thinking on defence problems: not just a naval doctrine, an air doctrine and an army doctrine, but a combined doctrine with a proper allocation between the Services based on a co-ordinated plan and not just on which particular Service had a pull on the Chancellor of the Exchequer at the time.

It is true they had the C.I.D., the Committee for Imperial Defence, but that was not an instrument of decision. They had lots and lots of committees. But I don't think they really got down to serious thinking. I spoke in the House and urged that a Ministry of Defence should be set up, but they wouldn't have it. Afterwards I was invited to lecture to the Imperial Defence College. It was a good show, one of the best shows we had, and bore very useful fruit in the war, because we had British people from all three Services and people from the Commonwealth, and not only from the Services but from the Civilian Departments, and one could get together a number of people who understood the civilian background as well as the actual fighting Services.

These younger people were very good indeed, and very useful when war came. They wanted to co-ordinate. They were trained to think on these lines. But there it stopped in those years. It didn't go any further. It never got to the top.

Williams: How far do you think it was still possible to depend on the League of Nations as an effective organisation after the march into the Rhineland and after Abyssinia?

Attlee: Well, Germany was out. And Russia had more or less gone when Litvinov dropped out of favour. After that I don't think there was much chance.

Williams: But you went on opposing British rearmament just the same?

Attlee: Yes. Because it was quite obvious by that time that there was no longer any such thing as effective national defence. One must have collective defence. It was sneered at at the time by people like Neville Chamberlain, who called it midsummer madness, but now, of course, it's orthodox doctrine. We said to him: 'If you get a co-ordinated defence policy against aggression, then we will support it. As long as you go merely on national armaments and as long as we're doubtful on which side you are' – because after all they'd first condoned the Japanese aggression, and then the Italian aggression in Abyssinia, and they won the '35 Election on a speech of Sam Hoare's saying they were going to support collective security and immediately afterwards threw it over – 'we can't go along with you.'

We had no trust whatever in Neville Chamberlain's Government. There was always the possibility that they would prefer the evil dictators to democracy.

What they ought to have done when the League was no longer any use was to try to get a line-up with all the other peaceable powers – what Winston used to talk of as the Grand Alliance. That's what we wanted. As long as people went on the lines of purely national defence, things simply didn't make sense. But

Chamberlain wouldn't do it because a Grand Alliance would have had to include Russia.

Williams: Whom else would you have hoped to see in it?

Attlee: Well, besides France and Russia there were, of course, the Succession States, the Czechs, the Jugoslavs, the Poles and the rest. Whether you would have had help from Scandinavia is a question. You wouldn't have got much, but you might have got something. But if we'd aimed at a defensive alliance of that kind we would have been getting somewhere. The Germans had always expressed their fear of encirclement and if they'd known they could be attacked by air from bases all around Germany it would have been very awkward for them. But there was no attempt to do that.

Williams: If there had been could it have deterred the Germans?

Attlee: Yes.

Williams: Even at a fairly late stage?

Attlee: I think so. Of course, it's very difficult to make out how much confidence you can place in the talks of German generals after the war as to what they would have done if there had been any sign of a real attempt to stop Hitler. Whether they would have done anything I don't know. Even if they had they might have made a mess of it, because they always made a mess of everything in that line. But there was at least a chance.

The trouble was that Chamberlain was always trying to make up to the wrong people, to Mussolini for instance. He wouldn't see that Mussolini wasn't any use anyway. He was even afraid of the Italian Navy, which in view of subsequent events was quite absurd.

Williams: Do you think the Spanish Civil War marked a turning point after which Hitler and Mussolini felt they could get away with anything?

Attlee: I am sure it encouraged them. I think it was a succession of getting away with things. First of all Japan, then Mussolini in Ethiopia, then the Spanish Civil War. They came to the conclusion that no one was going to try to stop them and there was really nothing they couldn't do.

Williams: But you supported non-intervention in Spain.

Attlee: Well, Léon Blum fell for it and the French were much closer than we were, and provided it could be made effective it seemed the right policy. There was an extraordinary amount of xenophobia in Spain and trying to intervene might just have set Spain against us. But once the thing had broken and it was clear Franco and his rebels were getting all they wanted from Italy and from Germany it was frankly a deception. I was discussing this over the air with Strang of the Foreign Office the other day and he admitted it was a complete deception, a lie on most cynical grounds.

Williams: Did Blum recognise that it was a lie?

Attlee: I think he did.

Williams: Well, why did he hold on to it?

Attlee: It's difficult to say. It depended to some extent, I think, on his support, which was very doubtful. He hadn't really a solid majority. In France, they never have. And he probably had all the Catholic weight against him, so that from a domestic political angle non-intervention was the policy easiest for him. He began by believing it would be effective and then had to hold on to it, even when it stopped being.

Williams: What did you find when you went to Spain?

Attlee: One heard a great deal about Communist intervention and Communist intrigue and I have no doubt it was going on all the time, but the leaders, as a matter of fact, were liberals and socialists. And I was impressed by the lads I saw in their newly-raised battalions, just like our New Armies in 1914, you know. President Negrin was a scientist. I thought him a very well-balanced and a democratically-minded man.

Of course it was difficult. You must remember the Government was supported by a strange collection of people. There were the Catalans, more or less separatists. There were the Basques, devoted Catholics. There was the mass of liberals and socialists, and there were anarchists and all kinds of people. It wasn't an easy people for him to drive.

They had a good general in Madrid, Miaja – I was very impressed by this man. I had a long talk with him. I thought their training wasn't all that bad: I saw their training manual. They were doing pretty well considering the paucity of resources and I think they would certainly have won but for the mass of intervention on the other side. Not that the Italians did very much there. They weren't awfully good. But still they had all the stuff, and of course they had the air. They tried to shoot us down when we were flying in Negrin's plane, as a matter of fact. And a lot of things were tried out which came into their own in the Second World War.

Williams: Do you feel, looking back, that you tried hard enough to get a changed British Government policy on Spain?

Attlee: It was pretty adamant, you know. I think the majority in the Commons was pretty solid behind Chamberlain. Winston! I don't think he really judged the Spanish show rightly. If he had come out strongly he might have turned a certain number, you know – possibly enough to have made the Government think again. I don't know.

He didn't really see the significance of the Spanish Civil War, probably because of his anti-Communist bent and his general objections to a revolution – after all he is a Tory. He wasn't very much perturbed about Abyssinia either. As an old imperialist I don't think he objected much to a backward country being taken over by Italy.

Williams: You went to Czechoslovakia?

Attlee: I did. I went there to see Benes. Benes was always extremely confident. It was always difficult to get a word in edgeways, in the matter of the Spanish Civil War for instance. He seemed convinced that he was so clever that he could manage everything. But if you suggested it needed a pretty long spoon to sup with the devil he always thought he could pull it off. He thought so right up to the end, first with the Nazis and then with the Russians.

And I went to Russia and saw Litvinov and had a long talk with him. Litvinov was, broadly speaking, a Westerner. He knew a good deal of the outside world, much more than Uncle Joe and the rest, because he had lived in England for a longish time. I think that, given adequate support from us, he could have kept Russia behind the League of Nations. That was his policy and he was backed by Uncle Joe. But what went astray was that the League didn't act anywhere and they had a growing suspicion that Chamberlain and Co. would give way all the time and wouldn't mind throwing them to the wolves.

As a matter of fact Chamberlain was prepared to throw anyone to the wolves. He was a peace-at-any-price man. He was totally unacquainted with war and he must, at the back of his mind, have known that he would be no use in war-time as a Prime Minister. And I think he had quite a genuine horror of war, which of course we all had.

He clearly was the weakest of all the three Chamberlains. I can't imagine Joe not making up his mind. And Austen was always critical of him, thought him very much the younger brother. He came into politics late in the day, of course. Was it Lloyd George or Winston who said he looked at foreign affairs through the wrong end of a municipal drain-pipe? But he always thought he knew everything.

Williams: Do you still feel, as you suggested then, that offers of economic co-operation or development in the Colonies or anything of that kind might have kept Hitler from war?

Attlee: No, I don't think so. I think he would have had to show something worthwhile. But if we had made it quite clear that we were coming in with Russia he wouldn't have tried it on, I think. But Neville had a violent anti-Communist bent, naturally, and he didn't know anything about foreign affairs at all. So he wouldn't agree.

Williams: What about the French?

Attlee: I shouldn't have thought there was much opposition there, not in Léon Blum's time anyway, or even Flandin's. They were quite prepared to make a line-up. They had a tradition of friendship with Russia, whether it was Czar Nicholas or Uncle Joe.

Of course it was a very divided country, not so much pacifist as 'don't care'. There didn't seem to be any spirit in the French people when I was there. I went to see Blum several times and the other leaders of the socialist parties. They had a very strong pacifist section, of course. On the whole I found them defeatist. Except for Blum. Blum was never defeatist. It was difficult for him to take effective action, though – a lot of unreliable Communists and a whole lot of Fascists, and I don't know how far he could rely on his generals. They'd never got over their losses in the First World War and they always felt their weakness, for all their big talk. Still, I think they'd have stood firm if we'd been ready to have the Russians in with us.

But Chamberlain wouldn't have that, wouldn't discuss it. I didn't see him much, you know, he wasn't a person who ever talked with you at all. He spoke to me before the flight to Germany, otherwise we didn't talk much. He never tried to get *our* opinions. He gave us no information even when Russia later proposed a Triple Alliance with ourselves and France to defend Czechoslovakia – simply sent over to Moscow Strang, who was then a comparatively junior Foreign Office official.

Williams: What about Roosevelt's proposal in January 1938 for a conference in Washington to try to ease international tension?

Attlee: Chamberlain never told us about that either. He turned it down out of hand on his own: an odd thing to do. Never even told his Foreign Secretary, Eden, I believe. There was no consultation at all, no information given to the Opposition that this had come forward. We knew nothing about it until it was all over.

Williams: What would you have done if you'd been in power?

Attlee: Accepted right away. America was the great uncertainty everywhere. If Hitler had realised that there was also America, and America was going to stand-in, he would have thought twice about it, or his generals would.

Williams: What was Chamberlain's mood when you talked to him before the first flight to Berchtesgaden?

Attlee: Apprehensive. But he said he thought there was a chance of doing something. I wouldn't stand in the way of anything that was a chance. I said, 'Well, don't give way' or words to that effect. I think he still thought he could pull something off.

Of course he wasn't used to international affairs and was quite ignorant of the nature of people like Hitler. He thought they were all reasonable people he could talk to like businessmen. And it's obvious he got a good reception over there from the mass of people. They didn't want war. But whether, if he'd stuck out, the generals would have seen the red light I don't know. Or whether they were strong enough to do anything. They'd given away so much.

Williams: When did you regard war as inevitable?

Attlee: As soon as we allowed Czechoslovakia to go. I don't think it was absolutely inevitable before that. I suppose Hitler had some regard for his military people; they'd always regarded Czechoslovakia as a key front in Europe and he wasn't anything like as ready as he was a year later. Later of course it was claimed that the year was also to our advantage. It may or may not have been. I doubt if it was. But that wasn't Chamberlain's policy anyway. He thought he could avoid war altogether.

Williams: All the same doesn't the Labour Party share some of the blame? You went on voting against conscription even after Munich. Wasn't that a mistake? Didn't that mislead the public?

Attlee: Well, it probably wasn't awfully wise. But, you see, there'd always been in the House of Commons the consideration that voting against Estimates did not mean that you refused to supply the stuff, but that you were voting against the policy. There was a wangle of John Simon's quite early on, when he claimed that we were against any provision for the armed forces because we voted against the Estimates, although of course he'd done the same thing himself in the past. It was always the custom.

But we ought to have realised that it would be misunderstood. The French of course were always thinking in terms of numbers of divisions in the field. But there was a case for concentrating on a highly efficient professional army even at that stage. There was a good deal of expert opinion that thought conscription a mistake, just as there was in 1914.

It's not always a good idea suddenly to change your system just approaching a war. It's quite a difficult proposition. And there was no real attempt at co-ordination. All we could see was wasteful duplication and no clear idea what we were providing for.

Williams: Whom do you regard as most responsible for the weakness of British policy?

Attlee: I think four people were mainly responsible: MacDonald, Baldwin, Simon and Chamberlain.

MacDonald put a kind of woolly shield over the whole thing and never advocated real action anywhere. Baldwin just pottered and let things slide. He wasn't interested at all, not the least bit interested in foreign policy, just let everything drift. Simon – well, Simon could always find an argument to support the wrong policy. He had the best brain of the lot of them and he could always supply the reasons – lawyer's reasons. Chamberlain thought he could run things himself but he knew nothing about how things go in the world. Stubborn and narrow and always convinced he was right, he wouldn't listen to advice.

Williams: What about Halifax?

Attlee: I never understood Halifax's line. He seemed to be in full agreement with Chamberlain. It was curious. You wouldn't have thought it with his background. He acted as a kind of shield for Chamberlain because of his reputation for morality. But he came in at a late stage. You can't blame him as much as the other four.

Williams: What about Labour's responsibility? I remember your writing in 1937 that you wouldn't rule out a Popular Front as an impossibility if a world crisis was imminent. But in fact you went on opposing it right to the end.

Attlee: Well, first, I had no trust in going in with the Communists. You couldn't rely on them and it would obviously put off everybody else. Secondly, the Liberals were a fairly weak lot.

They didn't pull much weight. And then you could never get the revolting Tories up to scratch. There was the root of the trouble. You couldn't get them to vote against the Government. They wouldn't vote on your amendment. They'd say, 'Of course if it's just a matter of voting on the adjournment . . .' and then you'd vote and they ran out. You could never get them to stand. It was the surprise of my life when eventually I did see some of them marching into our lobbies in 1940.

For an effective Popular Front you wanted Labour and the Liberals and a considerable section of the Tories. But it was an absolute necessity that there should be a substantial body of Tories. You had to have that because you couldn't get beyond the House of Commons, and it was full of Tories at that time. And one couldn't get it. There were talks with various people but they never came to anything. It wasn't a question of asking them to put Labour in. We were quite ready to go in with other people if there had been enough Tories to join with us and the Liberals, and we would not necessarily have expected to be the leaders. Probably the Tories would have had to lead a new Government to be sure of support in the House.

But even when Eden resigned and there might have been a chance, he refused to do anything very effective against the Government, you know, or even link up closely with Churchill. Sign of weakness, I think. He was too anxious not to break with the Conservative party organisation. Of course his resignation was mainly due to the fact that Neville was intriguing behind his back and treating him like an office boy, running a foreign policy against him.

Williams: Was there ever any chance of throwing out Chamberlain?

Attlee: There would have been if the Tories who saw the way he was going had acted up to it. About forty or fifty Tories would have had to take it very seriously. That would probably have been enough, especially if they'd included, as they would have done, a number of their ablest people. Worked like that, it might have thrown him out. But an awful lot of the Tories were safety-first people. They used to say they were all adventure-minded, you know, but in fact they didn't want any risks. They wanted to have a comfortable time.

You must remember what the position was in Parliament. The Conservatives had a complete majority, they could do anything they liked. We didn't stop them rearming. With their majority they could have done anything they wanted about armaments and putting our defences in proper shape – if they'd had the will.

We criticised them on policy and we also criticised them on the way they were trying to build up defence. But it does not mean that we weakened our defences in the slightest degree – we didn't.

We couldn't throw them out. To do that we needed Conservative help. We needed Tories ready to vote as well as talk. And that we could never get.

3

'The Country Won't Have You'

When war came at last, Attlee was ill. He had known for some time that he would have to have an operation for prostate trouble but had put it off as long as he could because of the pressure of international affairs. He was seriously ill when the Labour Party met in Southport for its Annual Conference and could only address the delegates briefly, leaving Hugh Dalton to present the main report on labour and defence.

From Southport he went into hospital, where it was found necessary for him to have not one but two operations, followed by a long period of recuperation at Nevin in North Wales. The leadership of the Parliamentary Party was left to Arthur Greenwood, the Deputy Leader.

Greenwood rose to the responsibility so ably that a number of Attlee's critics in the Party decided in comradely fashion to set going an intrigue to oust him from the leadership while he was away and put Greenwood or, as some, activated by Ellen Wilkinson, preferred, Morrison in his place. The move came to nothing. Greenwood himself refused to have anything to do with it and the majority of the Parliamentary Party soon showed themselves firmly opposed to any change. On this occasion, as in 1945 and yet a third time in 1947, when a small group sought to persuade Ernest Bevin to make a bid for the leadership during a low point in the Government's fortunes and was sent packing with a blistering rebuke by that tough, loyal man, Attlee's best defence against intrigue proved to be the loyalty of those who had worked closest with him and knew him best.

Although he had never got on well with Chamberlain and

politically the two of them were poles apart, it is pleasant to record as an example of the courtesies of parliamentary life that on the eve of his first operation he received the following personal note in Chamberlain's handwriting written from Laverstoke House, Whitchurch, Hants. 3 June 1939:

'Dear Attlee,

'I was extremely sorry to see that you have to undergo an operation very shortly. Although we differ on politics I hope that does not exclude sympathy on other subjects. I am one of the fortunate ones who have never had any operation but a minor dental one. But even that was enough to make me very sorry for anyone who has to go through a more serious ordeal.

'I sincerely trust that everything will go according to plan and that your recovery will be speedy and complete.

Your sincerely,

Neville Chamberlain'

Attlee was touched by this letter from a man he had never liked, but it did not make him any more ready to trust Chamberlain as a politician, least of all in war, and when an invitation was transmitted to him through Greenwood on the outbreak of war asking if Labour would be prepared to join the Government he replied with a brusque rejection.

'We had no faith in Chamberlain,' he says. 'We felt that if there was to be a change, and there would have to be before long, it would have to be a pretty drastic one.'

On the day after war was declared he received from Paris a letter from another Prime Minister, Dr Negrin, whom he had last talked to among the falling bombs in Madrid:

Paris 3 September 1939

'Dear Mr Attlee,

'Upon the declaration of war today my first thought is to serve the democratic countries in their struggle with Germany and I learned something in doing so. I have no desire to be in the public eye or to occupy any position. I want to embarrass no one. But as a Spanish Republican and in the interests of my country I wish to do my best against totalitarianism. I would appreciate a word from you in this matter.

Yours very truly,
J. Negrin

24 Avenue Charles Floquet, Paris.'

Alas, there was no place for the defeated leader of the democratic forces in the Spanish Civil War against Fascism in this new war for democracy and Attlee was unable to persuade anyone in authority at the time to take advantage of his offer.

It was not until late autumn that Attlee was well enough to return to London to resume his responsibilities as Leader of the Labour Party and to broadcast to the nation on the moral issues involved in the war as he saw them.

'During the last nine years,' he said in his broadcast, 'the world has, step by step, moved towards war until it has reached the present position. I believe this has been due to the failure to act on moral principles. When aggression and the use of armed force began again, a stand was not taken. The evil was condoned. Peace was destroyed. Successful violence bred more violence. Ruthless cruelty became rampant.

'We are now faced with the danger of the world relapsing into barbarism. Nazism is the outstanding menace to civilisation not only because of the character and actions of the men who are in absolute control of a great nation but because of their ideas, which are openly in conflict with all the conceptions upon which civilised life is based. . . . It is essential to remember that civilisation takes long to build and is easily destroyed. Brutality is infectious . . .'

He went on to elaborate for the benefit of his own supporters in the country his view of the true nature of the Labour Party – a view from which he has never varied – and of its position in this struggle.

'The Labour Party', he said, 'owes its inspiration not to some economic doctrine or to some theory of class domination. It has always based its propaganda on ethical principles. We believe that every individual should be afforded the fullest opportunity for developing his or her personality. . . .

..'The struggle for the freedom of the individual soul takes different forms at various periods. Here in Britain we have achieved freedom of speech and action within the law, freedom for workers to combine together. They are victories which we will not allow to be reversed.

'But the fight for freedom continues. The Labour Party is the expression of the revolt of men and women against a materialist system of society which condemns to a narrow and stinted life the majority of our citizens and gives rewards to the greedy and acquisitive. . . . During its existence it has done much to preserve and extend the rights won by its predecessors. It has done much to modify and humanise the capitalist system itself. It has seen many of its ideas accepted by those who formerly scoffed at them.

'All this achievement of the workers is threatened by the rule of the Nazis. The German workers, who built up a great structure of trade unionism, co-operation and social services, have seen it destroyed. Wherever there is Nazism there is cruelty, tyranny and the rule of the secret police. Therefore the Labour Party takes its stand with the rest of the country to stop this evil spreading.'

Then he laid down what he considered to be the principles Britain ought to affirm as an evidence 'that we are fighting for something greater than the safety of our own country' – many of them to be put into effect by his own Government:

'We must press forward the policy of extending self-government wherever that is practical. We must abandon any claim to special rights. We must be prepared to bring all our colonial territories under the mandatory principle and to extend and widen the scope of international control. We must rid ourselves of any taint of imperialism.'

And at home: 'If we really believe in the supreme value of

every human individual, and this is the core of our democratic faith, we must change a system of society which does not express this in its institutions. We still live in a class society. . . . If we really wish to build a new world wherein justice, mercy and truth shall replace brute force, wherein equality and good neighbourliness shall take the place of violence, aggression and domination, we must also build a new Britain.'

But the war was still to be won and victory was still a long, long way off. When Attlee visited the front as the guest of the Commander-in-Chief, Lord Gort, early in the New Year he found himself becoming increasingly depressed. Gort he found 'a first-class fighting regimental soldier, just the man to hold out in a tight place; but without strategical ideas.'

And he was worried by the dependence upon a static defence line and the absence of any mass of manœuvre. He asked, 'Where are the reserves?' and was told that there weren't any.

'I was afraid of a knock-through. They told me to remember the Ardennes: "They can't get through Ardennes, it's difficult country." But I didn't like the look of it at all, although Gort seemed perfectly happy at the time.'

When he got back to London, after a long talk with Gort at his headquarters at Habarcq which in no way lifted his depression, he reported to some of the General Staff that he had found the troops themselves very keen but was worried about the general strategy of the defence and by what he had learned both of our own military thinking and that of the French Higher Command, in whom he had no great confidence. He again asked about the lack of adequate reserves to meet a break-through on one sector of the line and urged the need for a greater mass of manœuvre. But he found the generals, who were presided over at this time by Ironside, Gort's successor as C.I.G.S., content and not much interested in the view of an ex-major and politician.

The depression brought on by his visit to Gort's headquarters and his realisation of the complete Maginot Line mentality of the French General Staff was not lightened by a trip to Paris to see French Socialist leaders. He found them even more pacifist, or defeatist, than they had been in the months immediately before the war – with, as always, Léon Blum the shining exception. He came back convinced that there was very little confidence to be put in the majority of either French generals or French politicians and more than ever persuaded that greater decision and vitality were needed in British leadership.

This was confirmed not only by the poor impression made by Ministers in the House, but by the experience of the trade union leaders who were in constant touch with Departments on industrial and man-power problems. The only Minister he found capable of prompt and decisive action, said Ernest Bevin, was Churchill – an old enemy for whom he now developed a new respect, as did Churchill for Bevin – and in private and public he bitterly attacked the 'obstruction, lack of drive, absence of imagination and complacency' he found in most Government Departments and 'the middle-class mind which actuates those responsible for strategy and government and which has little knowledge of the psychology and organising ability of the people in charge of the totalitarian States'

Attlee and Bevin were not at this time so close as they were later to become. They had disagreed on the Parliamentary Party's decision to vote against the Defence Estimates up to 1937, which Bevin considered unrealistic and bound to add to the difficulty of rousing public opinion to the international danger. But they had worked in close collaboration during the abdication (Attlee wrote to Bevin, particularly thanking him for the influence he exerted on the *Daily Herald* against the pressures brought by Beaverbrook and others during that time) and on many questions of economic policy, and had developed a high regard for each other. Bevin paid Attlee the high complement of not considering him as 'an intellectual,' and Attlee, in his turn, had immense respect for Bevin's commonsense and shrewdness of judgment.

The reports of Bevin and other trade union leaders on their dealings with the Government added, therefore, to his deep distrust of the Chamberlain Administration, which had been strengthened but not basically altered by the accession of Churchill, John Anderson and Eden. And he was very conscious of the sense of anger and frustration that was growing in the country and in Parliament. The need to get rid of Chamberlain seemed to him more and more urgent. But how?

At this stage he was approached by 'the other Clem', Mr Clement Davies, later Leader of the Liberal Party, who came to him as an intermediary from a group of prominent Conservatives headed by an esteemed elder statesman of great influence, the late Lord Salisbury, whose house had become a meeting place for Tory critics of the Government like Duff Cooper, Harold Macmillan, Amery, Boothby, Lord Cranborne (the present Lord Salisbury) and several others who had grouped themselves behind Winston Churchill before he joined the Government. Lord Salisbury was deeply disturbed by the way the Government was going and anxious to find if there was sufficient possibility of agreement between Conservatives, Liberals and Labour to have some chance of bringing a change. A series of confidential meetings was held – largely devoted on Attlee's part to trying to find out what hope there was of the Tory rebels being ready to vote against the Government if the issue arose; a course which the critics of Chamberlain had always previously refused to take when it came to the point.

As these discussions proceeded the storm broke: the Phoney War was over. On 8 April the Germans launched their long-prepared attack on Norway and Denmark – both countries with socialist Governments whose leaders Attlee knew well; his last pre-war holiday had been spent in Denmark, where he had been enchanted by the general sense of happiness and democratic well-being and had made many new friends, so that the thought of its being overrun by the Nazis came to him with all the force of a personal as well as an international tragedy. Two days later the Germans had occupied all the Norwegian ports; within another few days British troops had landed at Narvik, and had then landed at Namsos, north of Trondheim, and Andalsnes, south of it. But already it was too late.

When on 7 May the House of Commons debated the Norwegian campaign on a Labour Motion for the Adjournment, British troops had already been forced to withdraw from both Namsos and Andalsnes and it was clear that the whole of Norway must soon be lost.

In the House of Commons the tide was rising against Chamberlain. To Attlee it seemed plain that he could not last much longer and that Labour must show itself prepared to join a new Government. He had already discussed the possibility with the Parliamentary Executive of the Party on 9 April, the day after the Germans invaded Norway, and had proposed that if this situation arose the Parliamentary Executive should feel itself free to join a reorganised Government without considering it necessary to call a special conference of the Party, although subsequently asking a special conference to approve its action. In the event this was very much what happened, although the procedure of a special conference was not necessary, as the normal Annual Conference of the Labour Party was already in session at Bournemouth in May when Chamberlain was at last compelled to resign, and it approved the Executive's decision without further ado.

On 7 May the debate on the conduct of the war called for by the Opposition opened. From the appearance of the House and the attitude of Members it was immediately plain that discontent with the Government was nearing its climax and that the revolt against the Chamberlain Government on the Tory benches had now reached a gale force much greater than Attlee, remembering past experience, had believed likely even at this stage, or than had emerged in his conversations with Lord Salisbury and others. Many Members serving in the Forces and with direct and bitter experience of the inadequacy of British equipment had returned to take part, several of them straight from the withdrawals in Norway. Admiral of the Fleet Sir Roger Keyes, the hero of Zeebrugge, who had pressed unavailingly for the chance to command a naval attack on Trondheim, took his seat wearing his uniform of an Admiral of the Fleet, his breast covered with ribbons, the better to demonstrate, as he said in the opening sentences of his speech, that he spoke for many naval officers who were deeply critical of the Government's handling of affairs.

It was a tense and moving scene, nor was the distress and anger of the House lessened by Mr Chamberlain's opening statement, which was unimpressive and without sense of the seriousness of the occasion. He was frequently interrupted. When the House adjourned it was clear to very many, although not apparently to Chamberlain himself, that, in the imperious words of Cromwell to the Long Parliament, quoted with biting passion by Mr Amery amid cheers from both sides of the House: 'You have sat too long here for any good you have been doing. Depart, I say, and let us have done with you.'

The following morning at 10.30 Attlee met the Parliamentary Executive of his party. When the Opposition had originally called for this debate it had not been intended to press it to a division, because of the undesirability of suggesting a split in the country at a grave moment, unless it could be made the prelude to decisive action. Now Attlee and Morrison both recommended that this should be done. In view of the mood of the House on the previous day Attlee was convinced that at long last a moment had arrived when it might be possible to drive Chamberlain from office. Although he was still not wholly confident that enough Conservative M.P.s could be brought to the point of actually voting against the Government, he thought it essential in the national interest that the chance should be taken.

The recommendation that there should be a vote was opposed by several members of the Executive, including, surprisingly, Hugh Dalton and Wedgwood Benn. They argued that a division might consolidate the Government's majority and play into Chamberlain's hands. However, they were in a minority. Attlee's and Morrison's view that the Motion for the Adjournment should be treated as a Vote of Censure with all the consequences that might flow from it was endorsed by the Committee: if the vote brought the Government down, then Labour must, if necessary, be prepared to accept responsibility for putting an effective new Administration in its place, although Attlee was clear in his own mind, as he had already made plain to his colleagues, that the head of the new Administration would have to be a Conservative acceptable to the Conservative majority in the House, since he could not otherwise be sure of a stable majority. He was ready to serve under almost any Conservative leader other than Chamberlain, although he did not share the view, held by Dalton and some others, that Halifax would be the best choice, with Churchill as Minister of Defence. Nor in any event did he believe that the Conservatives would choose Halifax. He thought they would have to turn to Churchill, much as many of them disliked him, and he did not consider that the former suspicion of Churchill in the Labour Party and among the trade unions because of General Strike and other memories was any longer of importance.

The decision to force a division reached at this private meeting on the morning of 8 May sealed the fate of the Government. Without it and the concrete demonstration of distrust in Chamberlain's leadership which it was able to evoke in the one form he could not, in the final reckoning, ignore – a vote – the Government might well have ridden the storm, heavy though it was. Chamberlain had no intention of resigning. Indeed he told the King on the evening of 7 May that he had not come to offer his resignation but still hoped that he would be able to reconstruct his Government as a National Coalition with Labour Party participation. Without a vote he would probably have stayed on – with terrible consequences to the nation and the world.

It was agreed that Morrison, who was to speak first in that day's debate, should state the Opposition's intention to force a vote at the outset of his speech. This he did. The decision surprised Chamberlain, who was to an amazing degree out of touch with the mood of the House and the country, for it was his habit to believe that opinion in the country was what *The Times* said it was, and that of the House of Commons what the Conservative Chief Whip told him.

His response, now historic, had a devastating effect upon his own position and reputation, for he made the grave, yet characteristic, mistake of immediately intervening to say: 'I accept the challenge. I ask my friends, and I still have some friends in this House, to support the Government tonight in the lobby." To this appeal Mr Lloyd George in the last major intervention he was ever to make in the House of Commons gave the right and devastating reply: 'It is not a question of who are the Prime Minister's friends. It is a far bigger issue. He has appealed for sacrifice . . . I say solemnly that the Prime Minister should give an example of sacrifice because there is nothing which can contribute more to victory in war than that he should sacrifice the seals of office.'

That night when the vote was taken Attlee saw to his pleasure and surprise something he had long hoped for but had feared might never come to pass: Conservative M.P. after Conservative M.P. crowding with Labour and Liberal Members into the same lobby. Altogether forty-three Conservatives, among them Amery, Admiral Sir Roger Keyes, Duff Cooper, Boothby and most of the Conservative M.P.s in the Services, voted with the Labour Party. Another seventy abstained. The Government had a majority of eighty-one. It had not been defeated, but it had suffered a crushing and fatal moral reverse.

Yet even at this stage Chamberlain was not prepared to accept what had happened.

The following morning, Friday 10 May, he invited Attlee and Greenwood to call at 10 Downing Street. Attlee has a lively remembrance of the impression then made.

Attlee: He appeared calm. He was hardly worried and still seemed to think he could carry on. He had Winston and Halifax with him. He told us he believed there was now a paramount need for a National Government and asked us if we would join it and serve under him. Then Winston joined in and urged us to come under Chamberlain. Halifax did not speak, he said nothing all through, so far as I remember. I could understand Winston's loyalty, but I thought it best to be frank. It is not pleasant to have to tell a Prime Minister to his face that he must go, but I thought it the only thing to do. I said: 'Mr Prime Minister, the fact is our party won't come in under you. Our party won't have you and I think I am right in saying that the country won't have you either.'

Until that moment I think Chamberlain believed it would be possible for him to remain as Prime Minister. It was necessary to make it plain that he could not. Then they asked whether we would serve under someone other than Neville. I said I thought yes, but of course I could not answer for my party without consultation. The Party Conference was meeting at Bournemouth and the Executive would be in session there. In order that there should be no doubt I said I would put to them two questions 1) Are you prepared to serve under Chamberlain? 2) Are you prepared to serve under someone else? and would wire or telephone back. On that we parted politely.

Next morning, the morning of 11 May, as Attlee prepared to go to Bournemouth with the two questions he had offered to put to his colleagues, grim news arrived. The German Army in the West was on the move. Holland and Belgium had both been attacked and the frontiers crossed at several points. The invasion of the Low Countries and of France had begun.

Hard on this news Sir Archibald Sinclair, Leader of the Liberal Party, arrived to see Attlee in his room at the House of Commons. He suggested that in view of that morning's events it might, after all, be desirable for Chamberlain to remain Prime Minister for a time. As subsequently became known, this was an opinion Chamberlain also held. Attlee could not share it. On the contrary, he believed a change was now more urgent than ever if the nation was to be united. This was made plain in a call to Labour Party members in the new crisis which was issued over Attlee's and Greenwood's signatures: 'The Labour Party, in view of the latest series of abominable aggressions by Hitler, while firmly convinced that a drastic reconstruction of the Government is vital and urgent in order to win the war, reaffirms its determination to do its utmost to achieve victory. It calls on all its members to devote all their energies to this end.'

Having signed this, Attlee and Greenwood accompanied by Dalton, who used the journey in a taxi to Waterloo to impress upon Attlee his own passionate anxiety for direct involvement in the war effort, preferably at the Ministry of Economic Warfare, left immediately for Bournemouth, where the National Executive of the Party was meeting in a basement room of the Highcliff Hotel. As it met, a report was brought in that the Germans were bombing Canterbury. The report was, as it turned out, untrue, but it quelled any lingering doubts that may have existed among members of the Executive in less close touch with the political situation than Attlee and the other parliamentary leaders. A resolution that Labour should take its 'share of responsibility as a full partner in a new Government which under a new Prime Minister commands the confidence of the nation' was unanimously approved.

This done, Attlee and Greenwood prepared to return to London. As they were leaving, a message was brought that the Prime Minister's secretary was on the telephone from 10 Downing Street wishing to know whether Mr Attlee was yet in a position to give Mr Chamberlain a reply to the two questions. Attlee went to the telephone and replied: 'The answer to the first question is, no. To the second, yes.' He then read over the Executive's resolution and asked that this should immediately be conveyed to the Prime Minister in order that there should be no doubt in his mind as to the Labour Party's attitude. It was five o'clock.

When Attlee and Greenwood arrived at Waterloo they were met by a naval officer with a message that Mr Chamberlain had resigned and that Mr Churchill had accepted the King's Commission to form a Government and was anxious to see Mr Attlee as soon as possible. He at once drove to the Admiralty with Greenwood.

Chamberlain had met his Cabinet immediately after receiving Attlee's message, which compelled him to accept the fact that he could not hope to continue, and had driven to see the King shortly before six o'clock. He had at first hoped to recommend Halifax as his successor (a choice to which the King himself would have been very sympathetic), believing, quite wrongly, that the former Labour animosity to Churchill was still too strong for him to be able to command complete Labour co-operation and knowing also that many of his own supporters in the House would prefer Halifax to Churchill, whose pre-war attacks upon him and them they had not forgotten. However, Halifax himself made it plain to both Chamberlain and Churchill before the final Cabinet that, other reasons apart, it was in his opinion impossible for the Prime Minister to be a peer in war-time.

When Attlee arrived at the Admiralty, Churchill was waiting. This is Attlee's recollection of their meeting:

'He at once told me that he had been commissioned to form a Government and asked if we would come in. I said yes. Then we discussed positions. I was very conscious that in the First World War there had been a lot of haggling over places. It seemed to me that this was the reason for some of the failures of the military show then, and I determined we would not haggle this time. Winston proposed that we should have rather more than a third of the places in the Government, seven Ministers, I think, and some Under-Secretaries, and that there should be a small War Cabinet of five or six, something I'd always urged, in which we should have two seats. I at once accepted.

'We then discussed names. He mentioned Bevin, Morrison Dalton and A. V. Alexander as among those he would like, in addition to Greenwood and myself. I said I thought there should be no difficulty, although I must of course speak to them and have a talk with Ernie, who was not in the House. He also asked me to let him have a list of suggested offices and we discussed the general composition of the Government. Winston said he had asked Chamberlain to lead the House. I said I was absolutely opposed to that. I didn't think the House would stand it and certainly our people wouldn't. So it was dropped. Otherwise there was no disagreement. You get to know the measure of people in the House even if they are on the other side from you, and there were no differences between us on what was needed. We talked for some time, and then I telephoned and told the people in Bournemouth what had happened and went home to bed.'

In the morning Attlee rang Bevin, who had taken no part in the discussions of the previous day, and asked him what he thought of Labour's joining the Government. 'You helped to bring the other fellow down,' said Bevin, 'and if the Party refuses to take its share of responsibility now they will say we are not great citizens but cowards.' Attlee asked if he himself would come in. At first Bevin hesitated: 'You have sprung it on me,' he said. His next reaction was that others already in the House had a prior expectation of office, but he agreed to come over to see Attlee, who then told him that what was proposed was the Ministry of Labour. To this his response was: 'If it remains what it is now, a glorified conciliation board, it will be a waste of time.' However, when Attlee assured him that something much more central to the whole war effort was contemplated he agreed to take it on if the T.U.C. and his own union approved: he wanted his own people behind him.

The following day the composition of the War Cabinet and the Defence Committee was agreed on and, this settled, Attlee returned to Bournemouth to report on what had been done to overthrow a Prime Minister and put in his place a man more suited to the desperate situation of the nation.

As is his wont in such matters he said what he had to without rhetoric. Greenwood followed his example. 'I feel', said Laski, 'as though the cook and kitchen maid have been telling us that they sacked the butler.'

The delegates to the Annual Conference on Monday felt otherwise. They did not doubt what the issues were, as in his quietest tones Attlee concluded his speech to them: 'Friends, we are here today to take a decision not only on behalf of our own movement but on behalf of Labour all over the world. We have to stand today for the souls in prison in Czechoslovakia, in Poland, yes, and in Germany. We have to stand for those whose freedom is threatened all over the world. We have to fight for the freedom of the human spirit. . . . Life without liberty is not worth living. Let us go forward and win that liberty and establish it for ever on the foundation of social justice.' By a majority of 2,450,000 votes to 170,000 (the congenital pacifist minority) they approved what Attlee and his colleagues had done.

The new Government whose composition was completed a few hours later continued without major change until the war in Europe was won: an example, almost without parallel, of men of diverse views and political attitudes working together in complete harmony without conflict or party tension. Here is what Attlee has to say of it:

'I can remember no case where differences arose between Conservatives, Labour and Liberals along party lines. Certainly not in the War Cabinet. Certainly not in the big things. We applied ourselves to winning the war. When one came to work out solutions they were often socialist ones, because one had to have organisation, and planning, and disregard private interests. But there was no opposition from Conservative Ministers. They accepted the practical solution whatever it was. For instance our drastic taxation programme was put forward by Kingsley Wood. It was the same with the Emergency Powers Bill, which gave us complete control over persons and property; not just some persons but all persons, rich and poor alike, not some property but all property. I moved it in the House, but all sides in the Government joined in working out the terms and all agreed equally on its necessity: a great tribute to them. We had no quarrels.'

He has this to say of the part played by his old enemy Chamberlain in the new Administration:

'He was Lord President. Very able and crafty, and free from any of the rancour he might well have felt against us. He worked very hard and well: a good chairman, a good committee man, always very businesslike. You could work with him.'

The time for disputation was over. Everyone was now in it together.

4

War Commanders and War Policy

Only two men, Churchill and Attlee, served without break in the War Cabinet from the first day of the National Government until the end of the war in Europe; only these two were members of the Defence Committee all through: Churchill as Chairman, Attlee as Vice-Chairman. During the whole of the time Attlee also acted as Deputy Prime Minister, at first *de facto* and later with the formal title. It was a unique association in the higher direction of war between two men dissimilar in almost everything except tenacity.

The record of these years, of the ebb and flow of battle, the decisions taken, the mistakes made and the strategy and determination that eventually won the war, has already been told in detail by Sir Winston Churchill himself, by Alanbrooke, Montgomery and other generals, by several politicians in relation to their own parts in the tremendous story, and by official historians. There is no point in retelling the story here. What follows therefore is a glance at some of the chief personalities, events and problems of that time as they seemed to Attlee from his position at the centre of affairs, and as they seem now in retrospect.

Williams: How grim did things look to you when you came in?

Attlee: Pretty grim. I didn't take so gloomy a view as some about our chances at Dunkirk. Dill, who'd been made C.I.G.S., thought we'd get practically none of our men away. Having served through the evacuation of Gallipoli I thought we would. But after Dunkirk there was the danger of invasion: a very real menace. If we hadn't held the air, the Straits of Dover would have been open because the Fleet couldn't have moved in narrow seas without air protection. It was a tight business.

Williams: If they had landed, do you think we would have been able to throw them back?

Attlee: It would have been a grim affair. We should have fought, of course, right across the island. Whether we would have held them or not, I don't know. We hadn't an awful lot of stuff at that time. Most of our stuff had gone at Dunkirk and we were only very slowly re-equipping.

Williams: Was there any idea that the Government or some part of it should move to Canada?

Attlee: We never entertained that view. Our minds were made up from the start that the Government would stay and that we would fight it out on the island. We wouldn't have gone unless we were driven out.

Williams: Was there ever any expectation that the Government might have to move out of London – then or during the heavy bombing or later when the V.1s and V.2s started?

Attlee: Oh no. We were quite sure that that would be absolutely fatal. All arrangements had been made for it by the Chamberlain Government; they had a most elaborate place in the country. We never used it. We were determined from the beginning that we would stay in London whatever happened. In the same way we took early steps to see that if the Houses of Parliament should be destroyed, Parliament should still carry on in London. Some people thought it was nonsense when we got Church House ready, but the day came and we had a home. If we'd gone to a funk-hole somewhere else, it would have had a very bad effect. It was essential for us to stay, just as it had a good effect when the King stayed at Buckingham Palace in the bombing. To bomb Buckingham Palace was a tactical error, of course, on the part of the Germans. If they'd only bombed the poorer parts, some people might have said, 'Ah, well, the rich are getting off all right.' But when the King was bombed as well, then everyone felt, 'He's just like us.' The Germans never understand psychology.

Organisation of Government

Attlee: I had long been persuaded that a small Cabinet was essential in time of war. Winston took the same view. We started with five members and although it increased a bit later we never let it get above eight. But it isn't enough to keep a Cabinet small, you've got to prevent it being snowed under, leave it free to deal with the big issues and get on with the urgent jobs. So I started by taking a look at the organisation of the Government under the old lot, with Greenwood to help me. We found a mass of committees. Each committee had two branches, there was a Ministerial committee and a Civil Service committee, and every committee seemed to have that fellow – what was his name? – Neville's man – on it.

Williams: Horace Wilson?

Attlee: That's the fellow. He ran everything. Dominated the show. We pushed him off the whole lot of them and started afresh. We began with a Lord President's Committee. It had about five top-ranking Ministers with power to act, and it relieved the Cabinet of an immense amount of the civil work of government. Neville Chamberlain was chairman first of all and I succeeded him, or was it Anderson? It was Anderson, an excellent chairman, one of the few Civil Servants to make a success as a Minister. A bit heavy in the hand at times and couldn't always quite get out of the Civil Servant's way of looking at things, but most able. Turn his hand to anything. I remember the only time Winston and I were going to be out of the country together, in Italy, saying, 'And who carries on now?' 'Ah,' says Winston. 'We hand over to the automatic pilot.'

Later I took over this committee. We decided differences between Ministers and acted on a whole range of matters that needed a serious decision but weren't big enough to come to the Cabinet. It made for rapid business. We kept it small, a sort of counterpart of the Defence Committee for home affairs. Below that we set up functional committees to deal with particular aspects of business or for special jobs. It all worked very smoothly. Everyone wanted to get on with the job, you see, and didn't waste time thinking about their political positions or pushing an individual line. We all worked as a team. There were some clashes between Ernie and Beaverbrook of course, mostly outside the Cabinet on the Supply Committee. Beaverbrook thought he could take what he wanted without consulting anybody. He was highly mistaken.

Williams: Did these clashes of personality bring any crisis?

Attlee: I shouldn't think so. There was occasional friction but it never came to much.

Williams: Did Churchill back Beaverbrook?

Attlee: He couldn't back him against the rest of the Cabinet. Beaverbrook was a lone wolf. He bucked things up in the first few months of the war when getting aircraft out was very important. Thereafter he hadn't any great influence.

Williams: What about Churchill and Bevin? Bevin had been antagonistic to Churchill in earlier days.

Attlee: Oh, they got on very well. They were both pretty tough guys, you see. You had to understand that Ernie wouldn't stand any nonsense in his own line. Winston understood that. He held together the whole of that job of organising Labour. It was a tremendous job.

The Fall of France

Less than three weeks after the formation of the National Government it became plain that France might soon be out of the war. At the Bournemouth Conference of the Labour Party Léon Blum, who had flown over from Paris, made a rousing speech expressing determination to fight alongside Britain. Unfortunately it was his own emotions, not those of most of his countrymen, he expressed. After his speech Attlee saw him and told him of the private reports reaching London of demoralisation in Paris and advised him to get back as quickly as he could. Blum took the advice. But it was already too late. He had no power to halt the decay.

On 31 May, as the news from France became darker and more ominous and the position of the British forces in France more and more precarious, Churchill and Attlee flew to Paris in an eleventh-hour attempt to put heart into the French Government. They flew in two planes, Churchill and General Sir Hastings Ismay in one, Attlee and General Sir John Dill, who had succeeded Ironside as C.I.G.S., in the other, with a fighter escort of Spitfires. When they reached the British Embassy in Paris, where they were to stay, the staff were already burning the archives in the garden. They went immediately to see the heads of the French Government in Reynaud's room in the War Office in the Rue Saint-Dominique. This is Attlee's impression:

'They were pretty much at the end of their tether. They had decided they would rather lie down than fight. It was a terrible thing. They had no one to take hold of them this time, no Clemenceau, and the country was infested with Communism and riddled with Fascists and a lot of defeatists. Weygand looked like a little rat caught in a trap: a Staff Officer put in command who didn't know what to do. Pétain looked like a great old image, past everything. Darlan was trying to show that he was a bluff sailor. Paul Reynaud – a little man doing his best but no one to depend on. And the rest of the politicians snatching at anything. The only man you felt meant anything was de Gaulle, glowering at the back. I thought they were a hopeless lot. For twenty-four hours Winston put a bit of heart into them and then it wore off. Afterwards I drove round Paris with Spears.[1] One felt an atmosphere of utter hopelessness.'

Sixteen days later, by which time the disembarkation of most of the British forces from Dunkirk had been miraculously accomplished and Paris had fallen, a last effort was made to keep France in the war. Throughout these days the War Cabinet had been sitting almost continuously, with Attlee presiding while Churchill made two further visits to France to try to stiffen French resistance and co-ordinate plans between the Allies. M. Monnet, M. Pleven, members of the French Economic Mission, and General

1. Major-General Sir Edward Spears, British Liaison Officer to the French Prime Minister and Minister of Defence.

de Gaulle were in London, and together with Lord Halifax, Sir Robert Vansittart, M. Corbin, the French Ambassador, and Major Desmond Morton, one of Churchill's personal assistants, they produced a plan for a Franco-British union which it was believed might give Reynaud, who almost alone among the group now in control of French affairs wanted to go on fighting, some ammunition with which to stiffen the morale of his colleagues.

On 16 June, Mr Churchill brought the draft of their suggested declaration to the Cabinet. Attlee and the others studied it silently. The difficulties were apparent, but the need for a gesture of high drama even more so. As they read, the imaginations of all the members of the War Cabinet were caught by the possibilities inherent in a proposal that went much further than anything before in the history of war-time alliances, offering, at this moment of extreme French weakness, that Britain and France should be not two nations but one, with joint organs for defence and for foreign, financial and economic policies, with common citizenship, and with joint plans for carrying on the war under a single War Cabinet directing the forces of both countries wherever they might be and from wherever they could best fight. Unanimously, after only a brief discussion, the War Cabinet approved. The declaration was at once handed to General de Gaulle, who was returning to France that night, for him to deliver personally to M. Reynaud, who believed, as did de Gaulle, that with such an undertaking in his hand he could even yet hold the position.

This done, a telegram was dispatched to the British Ambassador, Sir Ronald Campbell, then at Bordeaux, with instructions to inform M. Reynaud that a proposal for a complete union between the two countries was on its way and that Churchill and Attlee, accompanied by Sir Archibald Sinclair as Leader of the Liberal Party (so as to demonstrate that the idea of union was one to which all parties adhered) and by the Chiefs of Staff, would that night leave for France from Southampton in a cruiser and be at Concarneau by twelve noon the following day for a meeting with the French Cabinet.

From the Cabinet room Churchill, Attlee and the others drove to the station.

Attlee recollects how they took their seats and waited: 'The special train to take us to Southampton was at Addison Road station as I recall, a curious place I'd never been to before – or since, and I remember it seemed a long time moving. We were anxious to get on, for there seemed a chance that if we could get there we might still do something. Then there came a message to say the Foreign Office had telephoned to ask for the train to be held. After that a private secretary arrived from Downing Street with a telegram from Ronald Campbell at Bordeaux to say that it was no use our coming, there'd been a fresh Cabinet crisis in France and no one was prepared to meet us. We knew then it was all over and Reynaud had lost. We got out of the train and drove back to Downing Street and went back to work.'

That was the end for France and for those who wished to keep her faithful to her alliance. Of all those at Bordeaux only de Gaulle, who flew out with Spears, tricking at the very last minute those of his enemies who hoped to hand him over to the Germans, continued the fight. Blum, who was no longer at the centre of affairs but of whose absolute fidelity to the cause of freedom Attlee had long been assured and with whom he had been in close contact during so many critical times, was not so fortunate. He was handed over to the Nazis and brought to 'trial', there to confront the German conquerors with a superb and insolent courage that heartened all who were still determined to fight for the greatness of France. From prison he managed to send a brief unsigned undated note to his old friend:

Mon cher Attlee,

Je profite d'une occasion sûre pour vous faire passer ces quelques lignes.

Ma vie n'a pas changé sauf que je suis pratiquement passé sous garde allemande.

Je travaille et réflechie de mon mieux, pendant cette fin de guerre, aux problémes que la paix posera pour chacun de nos pays et pour l'humanité entière.

Je suis et j'admire l'effort britannique – quant à la France, elle vit dans la revolte et dans l'attente anxieuse.

Soyez mon interprète auprès de mes amis et de mes camarades du Labour *et aussi auprès du Premier Ministre, de Monsieur Eden et de Lord Cranborne.*

Bien affectueusement à vous.

THE DEFENCE COMMITTEE

Williams: At one stage I think Menzies of Australia made a criticism that Churchill had too much personal control over the strategic planning of the war. Some others made the same criticism and it's been heard since. Do you think it has any justification?

Attlee: No. Winston was the driving force, a great War Minister. No one could have done the job he did. But there was quite a lot of discussion at the Defence Committee. We surveyed the whole strategic field.

Williams: Was there much disagreement?

Attlee: Occasionally, yes.

Williams: But Churchill usually had his way?

Attlee: Pretty often. Very often. But there were quite a lot of occasions when he didn't. He'd get some idea he wanted to press, and after we had considered it the rest of us would have to tell him there was no value to it. But you needed someone to prod the Chiefs of Staff. Winston was sometimes an awful nuisance because he started all sorts of hares, but he always accepted the verdict of the Chiefs of Staff when it came to it, and it was a great advantage for him to be there driving them all the time. Your advisers always tend to say 'It can't be done', and it's as well to have someone who'll tell them it can. There were sufficient checks and balances. And Winston always took the big view: very essential. Alanbrooke was good for him. What Winston requires is some strong people round him saying 'Don't be a fool over this.' He has big ideas, but every now and again he gets a perfectly futile one and he doesn't always know. I remember Lloyd George saying to me once, apropos of something, 'There's Winston there. He's got ten ideas and one of them is right, but he never knows which it is.' A certain amount of truth in that. Alanbrooke used to sort out which was right. Winston was always in a hurry. He didn't like to wait for the pot to boil, you know.

Williams: Were there many quarrels between politicians and generals?

Attlee: No. A very large proportion of us in the Government had served in war, so we understood something about it, understood the military mind. I think, also, we had much more intelligent heads of the Services than in the First World War. They worked very well as a team: very unusual – it seldom occurred in peace-time. We always accepted their professional advice. Even Winston did after a struggle. We never moved on a professional matter against them.

The Generals

Williams: Who do you consider was the best strategic brain on our side?

Attlee: Alanbrooke undoubtedly. Portal was good too, but I'd say Alanbrooke was the real master. A very cool judgment and decision; he knew his own mind. He was much better than Dill as C.I.G.S., although Dill was a tower of strength with the Americans when we sent him to Washington. Dill was extremely able, rather pessimistic, a worried man. He hadn't the self-confidence of Alanbrooke. A charming person but not such a strong personality. Alanbrooke was prepared to stand up to Winston if he thought he was wrong – there were plenty of disagreements between them – and he had considerable patience in dealing with our Allies, who weren't awfully easy. I didn't know MacArthur, of course, though everyone says he was very good. Alanbrooke himself put Marshall as the biggest man on the Allied side. He had the appearance of a big man. His lines were sound and he had a good knowledge of strategy, but I don't think he was as good a strategist as Alanbrooke. Alanbrooke was unlucky in not having the top command in the field. There's every indication from what he did when he had a command in the field earlier that he'd have been first-class. We originally wanted him to take command of the combined forces in the attack on Europe, but there we had to yield because the Americans were providing a bigger number of troops. I think it was unfortunate myself.

Williams: In what way?

Attlee: Well, I think Alanbrooke would – I don't say that Eisenhower did not do well, but I think Alanbrooke was better. I was surprised when the Americans put in Eisenhower. He was fairly junior and he'd never commanded in the field. But it had to be an American and I suppose they thought Marshall was too important at home. Ike was a very good fellow: an extremely good diplomat, the man to get 'em all working together, a man of courage, who took important decisions without hesitating; but not a great soldier, not in any sense a major strategist. He hadn't a very good strategical background or conception.

Williams: What about Alexander?

Attlee: Alexander was extraordinarily good at working with everybody. He had people of twenty-two nations, I think, on the Italian front who all worked perfectly harmoniously. And he had a broad strategy of the war; he didn't look just at the battle, he looked ahead at what was going to happen. Rather more than Montgomery would and with a broader conception of things. He was the man for a campaign, Montgomery for a battle – an operation. Monty was a brilliant commander of a task force, but, of course, he came in at a time when he was able to get what he wanted, more or less. Very different from people like Wavell. Wavell had to make do. Bill Slim had to make do.

When Monty took over, he was able to get what generals he wanted and the supplies he needed. He was always pretty well in a strong position. Well, good luck to him. Having got them, he knew how to use them. He understood how to create morale.

There was no doubt about it, when he took over the Desert Army its tail was down. It had been defeated when it probably oughtn't to have been. There was a good deal of grousing and so on. Monty took over the whole show and got their tails right up, made them a fighting force. His so-called theatricality was a realisation that men wanted to know their generals. We didn't know any of the top people in the First World War. The Divisional Commander was as far as it went. The Corps Commander was a name, you might possibly just see him, but I never remember seeing anyone higher up. Monty's personal plan was to see that every man knew him by sight and if possible had heard him. He didn't confine this to the troops either, he took great care to go round the factories to get everyone keyed up in one unity – make them see they were all in the show and not merely pawns moved on the chessboard.

It makes all the difference. The First World War conception of a general was someone entirely remote, right behind the line. Remember the books that were written at that time. The general was always someone far in the background, officiating from a distance while the battle was on. It may have been a result of the South African War, in which it was said Buller was so soft-hearted that he failed to press forward when he saw some of his men killed. So we swung the other way and kept our generals at a distance where they wouldn't see blood. But Monty had the idea that a general must be a general who led. He made himself as well-known to his troops as was Napoleon or Marlborough. I think he was right.

Williams: What about Wavell?

Attlee: I think equally good. He had a very, very difficult job. We were always making demands on him. He seemed to me to be overwhelmed with a multitude of tasks in the end, but he did a great service in the early stages when he had very little to use, and he made that great push against the Italians which came at a time when it was very necessary to have something to buck us up. But in the end I think he got tired.

Williams: And Auchinleck?

Attlee: The Auk was a good fighting general. I don't think he selected his commanders well: that was one of his failures. And certainly the criticism of the Germans was that he didn't use the troops he had as a mass and so they were able to destroy bits in detail. That's probably true. Now I think Bill Slim was first-class. Again, everybody knew him just as they did Monty. Extraordinarily practical. He had the hardest task of anybody. He had enormous guts to carry that through. And he was able to work with 'Vinegar Joe', the American, which took a lot of doing. Oh, I think he was one of the very best that anybody had. Mountbatten was a good choice as a Supreme Commander. He did very well in South-East Asia. There again, he understood how to talk to the troops – he had all sorts from all countries and had to talk their language. He impressed me greatly. That's why I remembered him later. Of the Americans, leaving aside Marshall, whose work was in the background, I thought Bradley pretty good. Then there was that startling fellow Patton: too much of an individualist, out for his own show all the time, but a good fighting man.

Williams: What about the air?

Attlee: Oh, I think Peter Portal was first-class. So was Tedder. They had to understand warfare in three elements, where and how to use their forces. Tedder had a very calm, cool, collected judgment and a good deal of ability to co-operate with people. Now I never thought Bomber Harris was frightfully good at the time, though I may well have been mistaken. I had the impression that he was, so to speak, very much a man for not wanting to waste his bombs on small and difficult targets such as oil installations, but preferred mass targets such as big cities. Of course the ultimate responsibility for bombing policy lay with the Cabinet and I don't seek to evade it, but I thought that concentration on strategic targets such as oil installations would have paid better. That at any rate was my impression at the time though there were technical difficulties involved which were only solved later and which I hadn't fully realised. But how much was effected by the bombing of the cities – which contained armament factories of course – is a question. The German morale stood up to it pretty well. I fancy that Lord Cherwell also doubted the efficacy of mass bombing.

Williams: And on the naval side?

Attlee: Well, Dudley Pound was very old at the time I first saw him and very deaf. A. V. Alexander always swore by him – said he was awfully good. He didn't say very much. I think towards the end he was getting a bit of a passenger. It was a good thing when he was replaced as Head of the Chiefs of Staff by Alanbrooke. But he was a very tough naval fellow. Andrew Cunningham was excellent. I never saw a lot of Ramsay but I think he was pretty good too. And there were plenty of others. We were very well served, and with no intriguing as there was in the First World War.

Not that it was always easy to get everybody to see eye to eye, especially after the Americans came in. The Americans rather took it for granted they knew best, didn't believe they could learn from our experience. It's an odd thing, for instance, but shipping losses in the Atlantic rose almost to their climax when they came in because they wouldn't accept our view of the need for convoys. They're a wonderful people but they have to learn for themselves – can't believe anyone else can tell them anything. And like the Russians they didn't at first realise in the least what it meant to invade the Continent. Marshall came out with his plans, asked us to do everything within a very short time. We couldn't. It was a long-term job to working it out – getting the landing craft and adequately trained forces. The Americans were pretty raw at that time; naturally they didn't realise how long it would take, they were impatient.

Williams: Did you get the impression Roosevelt understood the strategical side much?

Attlee: I think he did, although he wasn't in as continuous contact with his Chiefs of Staff as Churchill was. He'd issue a direction and then leave it alone for several days, weeks almost. But he had a clear conception and a long view. I remember talking to him in Washington back in 1941 and his pulling out a map and putting his finger on Algiers and saying, 'That is where I should like to have American troops.' He had grasped the essentials of attack and assault, how to deploy your troops to advantage and get ready to punch where the enemy is weakest. I don't think Roosevelt really understood European politics. I don't think any American did. And he had that hangover about British imperialism. He'd always been brought up to think of us as a colonial imperialist power – couldn't get it out of his head.

AMERICAN ATTITUDES

Williams: When it came towards the end do you think Eisenhower let the Russians come much further into Western Europe than was really necessary?

Attlee: Yes. I think he took the view, 'Well, we've got to win this war and I've got to do it as cheaply as I possibly can in life', and therefore he was not closely concerned with the future of Europe. He was the American commander looking after the American troops. Neither he nor the bulk of the Americans understood the position in Eastern Europe at all. I don't mean giving the Russians a zone in Berlin – at that time we had to. It was earlier the mistakes were made.

Williams: When?

Attlee: I think if Alexander had been allowed to go on in Italy, he would have joined hands with the Yugoslavs and moved across into Czechoslovakia and perhaps right over Germany before the Russians got there. But the Americans were obsessed with the idea of this attack in the South of France, partly because of the general American outlook, which is to put all your stuff in together. It's always mass they believe in – mass production, mass attack, a lot of men.

Ike's idea was to have every available man fighting. He never thought much of strategy, or of coming round and taking the enemy from behind – which I think we could have done both with Alexander in the South and if we'd followed the plan of sending Monty through in the North. This American attitude was a sort of hangover; the kind of thing one got in the 1914 War when generals could think of nothing but plugging away at the point where the enemy was strongest.

Williams: Do you think the war would have been shortened if Alexander had been allowed to go on?

Attlee: I think so. And of course it might have altered the political face of Europe immensely. It would have meant, for example, that we, rather than the Russians, liberated Prague. But the Americans didn't understand the political situation in Europe, and when we advocated anything in the East of Europe they always fancied we were following some strange imperial design of our own. It took them a long while to learn the facts of life – especially the facts of European life. They had an idea that we were just an obsolete old imperialist colonial power and that they understood Russia much better than we did. That was Roosevelt's line at Yalta. It was two to one against us. We had to agree to many things we oughtn't to have agreed to.

Williams: Such as?

Attlee: Giving Russia far too great a predominance in Eastern Europe.

Williams: But would it have been possible to stand out against Russian expansion at that time? Hadn't the situation developed so that one really couldn't prevent it?

Attlee: I think we could. It was rather gratuitous to hand over Eastern Europe to the Russians. They weren't in much of a position to resist if we'd taken a stronger line, you know. They were in a pretty difficult situation by that time.

Germany

Williams: Looking back, do you think the unconditional surrender declaration was wise?

Attlee: Roosevelt more or less blurted it out and after he'd said it we had to agree. It may have been referred to in some document earlier on, but if so I don't recollect it. It was certainly never discussed. I don't think it was very wise, but I don't think it necessarily did much harm.

Williams: You don't think it lengthened the war?

Attlee: I should doubt it. If we hadn't said it we might have encouraged the German generals to kick over the traces. But it was pretty hopeless to expect much from them. A futile lot, lacking in will and lacking in execution. How they failed to bump off Hitler with the opportunities they had I don't know. There wasn't any real anti-Hitler movement that we could have got going at that time. They had an ineffective one very late, but even then they bungled it.

Williams: You were a good deal concerned with the preliminary planning for the future of Germany.

Attlee: Yes, I was. Our feeling at that time was that it would be possible to have a divided Germany. There were suggestions that one might have a sort of sub-Catholic Germany in Austria, Bavaria and Württemberg, as against Prussia. There was a strong view that we didn't want a united Germany again. The idea was that we'd have a division into zones as a temporary step for the occupation and then a further consideration of the actual shape of things. But once the zones were in existence the Russians refused to go on from there, and further ideas for Germany just fell to the ground.

Williams: Do you think a divided Germany of that kind would have worked?

Attlee: Very difficult to tell. Probably German nationalism would have turned out too strong. But it seemed a possibility at the time. After all, the union of Germany was comparatively recent.

Williams: What about Berlin? Were the zones absolutely necessary?

Attlee: I think so, yes. Of course the belief was that we were going to work together. But in any event we couldn't have avoided the quadripartite scheme without a complete breach. When you have an alliance you have to work on the assumption that it'll stay one.

The Commonwealth

Williams: Were the Commonwealth countries satisfied with the central direction of the war?

Attlee: There was difficulty with the Australians for a time. They wanted a greater share in the direction of the war and that their representative over here should sit in on everything. That was Bruce. It wasn't received awfully well by Winston. I used to bring Bruce in where I could, but what they were really after was someone permanently in the War Cabinet, which you couldn't have done without bringing in everybody else. Winston was against having a sort of Commonwealth Cabinet. I agreed with him. It would have been a very difficult thing to arrange and it would have meant having their own Prime Ministers, or someone with equal authority, there all the time.

However we kept in very close touch when I was Secretary of State for the Dominions, following the usual practice. I saw the High Commissioners every day and told them everything and the Commonwealth Prime Ministers themselves sat in with us when they were in London. Peter Fraser[1] for instance was there when the Atlantic Charter idea blew up. I got a telephone call at two o'clock in the morning from the ship where Winston and Roosevelt were meeting in Placentia Bay, Newfoundland. I was still up – never got to bed very early. I called a Cabinet at three o'clock in the morning, and by four we were able to send our reply with a new clause on social security which we wanted among the Allied aims. Peter Fraser was helpful on that. On the strategical side Smuts was exceptional. He had a complete grasp of the situation not only when he was in London but from a distance when he got back. You could see it in all his letters. They were most helpful.

Williams: What about the Canadians?

Attlee: The Canadians weren't worried about the higher direction of the war in the way the Australians were. What they worried about was that they had to hang around so long before they got in on anything. They were in this country waiting and it

1. Prime Minister of New Zealand.

was pretty hard. There was a feeling generally about what was called delay, of course, but we couldn't hurry the cross-Channel adventure regardless of logistics. Anyone who knew what it was like to invade a fully defended coast realised the danger that we might bash ourselves to pieces. The solution came with our artificial harbour, which enabled us to attack where they didn't expect us. But without it invasion would have been a most hazardous thing to try. Dieppe showed the difficulties.

Governments in Exile

Williams: You spent a good deal of time with the Governments in Exile in London.

Attlee: Yes, quite a lot. I used to see the Czechs fairly often, and a good deal of the Czech Social Democrats. Benes unfortunately never had confidence in them. He was always bringing in other people over their heads. He was jealous of them. It was a great weakness in the long term because after the war the Russians made him give all the plums, all the key positions, to the Communists, and then they cut his throat. He thought he could manage them. The Social Democrats saw the danger but he wouldn't work with them. If he had, he might have been able to form a strong enough Government to ride the storm. Jan Masaryk was more flexible.

Williams: Was Masaryk a strong person?

Attlee: Not very. Charming. His father was a great man. Benes was the stronger character, but he was obstinate. Strong but narrow. He thought he could do everything by his own brand of finesse.

Williams: And de Gaulle. Did you see much of him?

Attlee: Yes, very often. He was very difficult but I sympathised with him. After all, as far as he could see he was the only asset France had. He had to try to set himself up as a great power. You can quite understand his being difficult. He wasn't awfully sensible in dealing with other Frenchmen, he didn't work happily with other people in exile, and he wasn't very wise in his dealings with us or the American Government.

Williams: He wasn't given to conciliation?

Attlee: No. He was damned awkward. He always had to assert himself. Partly his nature, I suppose. I think he's mellowed since but he was very angry at that time. But he's a good fellow. I've got a great admiration for him. And he's got a nice wit. I reviewed a book of his after the war. I said, 'General de Gaulle is a very good soldier and a very bad politician.' So he wrote back to me and said, 'I have come to the conclusion that politics are too serious a matter to be left to the politicians.' A good jest on his part. Clemenceau would have liked it.

The Norwegians and Danes were very good. So were the Dutch. I remember with the Dutch East Indies there was the question whether we should put something into Java. We got together something as a gesture. But the Dutch said, 'No. You can't do any good. Don't waste your resources.' It showed sense and toughness. You never got that in the French Government – the original lot, I mean. They would have wanted us to put in everything, whatever was happening. They tried to pull in every bit of our Air Force for France when they already knew they were unlikely to carry on. They wanted every drop of blood from us.

Williams: Did you find the Poles bitter because we hadn't given them much aid when they were attacked?

Attlee: No, they never raised that with me, although we certainly hadn't. Sikorski was a big man. So was Anders, who commanded their troops in the field, a nice chap. I reviewed their troops in training – a fine fighting lot. Excellent fighters but very bad politicians.

The Beveridge Plan

Williams: How did the Beveridge Plan start?

Attlee: Arthur Greenwood was in charge of the post-war reconstruction plans. He conceived the idea of a committee to consider necessary changes in National Insurance and so on. It was originally a committee of high-powered Civil Servants, but somehow or other they all went and Beveridge remained as the Beveridge Reporter.

Williams: Beveridge claims that the Beveridge Report was cold-shouldered by the Government when it came out.

Attlee: It wasn't cold-shouldered, but it wasn't immediately put into force. I think the real reason was that Winston planned to come in as the first post-war Prime Minister and he thought it would be a nice thing to have the Beveridge Report to put through as an act of his Government. He didn't want it done by the war-time Coalition. Also he was always a bit wary of wicked Socialists pulling the wool over the eyes of innocent Tories. But the Beveridge Report was endorsed by the whole Cabinet in its broad lines – there may have been one or two minor points of disagreement.

Williams: Both sides of the Cabinet?

Attlee: Oh yes. There was no dissension on that. There was the question of when it should come in, of course, which was not very easy. Beveridge seemed to think the war ought to stop while his plan was put into effect. He wanted it right away. A lot of other people pressed for that too, possibly as a help to morale. But in the event it was just as well it was held up till we came in, as part of a broad scheme.

Williams: Beveridge himself has since claimed that because his plan got such a big public response the War Cabinet turned against it.

Attlee: He is a little bit elevated there, I think. He seemed to imagine he was going to be a leader of the nation or of the House of Commons. Always a mistake to think yourself larger than you are.

5

The End of the Grand Coalition

When the European war ended and on Lüneburg Heath the German armed forces, which had for so long menaced the peace of the world, laid down their arms in unconditional surrender, Attlee was in San Francisco, to which he had flown in the middle of April for the conference which was to establish the United Nations.

It was the latest of a series of war-time flights which had taken him to Canada, to Washington for talks to Roosevelt, to New York for a meeting of the International Labour Office, to Newfoundland (which proved very useful when he had later as Prime Minister to deal with the future constitution of that island), to Algiers to meet the French National Committee, to Naples, where Harold Macmillan was British Minister of State at Allied Headquarters, to Rome to see the Pope and talk with a group of leading Italian politicians (among them the Socialist leader Nenni, whom he warned, unavailingly as it turned out, not to put his faith in the 'firm agreement' he thought he had negotiated with the Communist Party, who would, Attlee told him, stab him in the back at the first opportunity), to Siena for meetings with Alexander and General Mark Clark, to Normandy for a trip to the American forces under Bradley, beyond Bayeux, and to British H.Q. for talks with Montgomery, who told him everything was working out exactly according to his forecast, and then, on the eve of his American journey, to Paris, Aachen, Brussels, Antwerp (on which the V.1s were still falling) and Walcheren Island to prepare plans for sending food supplies to the liberated territories, particularly in northern Holland, where the food situation was critical.

His visit to San Francisco produced a small scene in the House of Commons. The announcement that Eden would lead the British delegation, not Attlee, who, as Deputy Prime Minister, was the senior Minister going, brought protests from some Labour Members who considered their Leader had been altogether too modest in keeping himself away from the limelight throughout the war and that this reticence might soon prove an electoral liability. Attlee considered the protest silly. As Foreign Secretary Eden had been much more concerned than he with the preliminary work on a United Nations Organisation and it was therefore right as a matter of practical efficiency that he should lead the delegation. Attlee had no patience with those who put questions of status, their own or other people's, before the most sensible way of getting a job done.

He first flew to Washington to meet the new President, Truman. He had last been there for talks with Roosevelt in the White House and on his yacht on the Potomac, and like most others was a little apprehensive as to how this new, almost unknown, President would wear the mantle of his great predecessor. But Truman and he took to each other immediately, forming a firm and easy friendship that was to be of the greatest importance to the world in the following years.

Williams: What was your first impression?

Attlee: I thought he was one of the best. Of course he'd just come new to things. He didn't know much. But his instincts were right and he was learning fast. A very courageous fellow and a good friend. You could always talk to him. I was much encouraged when I met him.

Arrived at San Francisco, Attlee also met Molotov for the first time.

Attlee: He was doing his best to be pleasant then, but I never liked him. He laughed with his mouth not his eyes. A hard creature. Later Ernie Bevin used to say he always hated meeting him because he knew he had murdered hundreds and thousands of innocent peasants. He could never get over this hatred of meeting him. But at San Francisco he was pretty genial at first, slightly frosty underneath but trying to show he was a really pleasant fellow. But he had no humour. I tried to pull his leg once or twice. He couldn't take it, not like Stalin. At San Francisco he learned to say 'Okay'. We used to sit there and old Senator Vandenberg would say 'Okay' and Molotov would say 'Okay' and I would say 'Okay' and everything would go as merrily as a marriage bell – until we came to something that mattered, or that the Russians thought did. He showed his real hand for the first time over the Poles, and over the veto. There was no doubt in my mind that once the war was over the Russians would be difficult friends.

Williams: Were you satisfied with the San Francisco Conference?

Attlee: Yes. There was the veto, of course. One had to have it in the Security Council, but the idea was if one behaved there it wouldn't be used habitually, only in the last resort. And at that time on the basis of sovereign independent States one couldn't have got anything through unless the U.S.A. and the U.S.S.R. and we ourselves, I think, had a power of veto in reserve. But it wasn't expected to be used except in extreme instances. Procedural matters for instance – we didn't expect it to be used in those, but the Russians decided to make a habit of it.

Williams: But on the whole you felt the Conference was a success?

Attlee: Oh, it was on the whole. It was absurd of course to have China as a permanent member of the Security Council at that time, and it brought nothing but trouble afterwards. China wasn't a Great Power then: hopelessly divided and in odd bits and pieces. We were very much against it, but Roosevelt and the Americans had always looked on China as their pet. They insisted on bringing her in – as a kind of balance, they claimed. We all thought it a piece of folly.

But otherwise – yes, I thought things had gone very well. We'd got a very good preamble based on a draft by Smuts. We'd got all the people in and we had established a new League of Nations with various organs that might work. Of course, our smaller parts of the Commonwealth were very strong against the veto, Peter Fraser and the rest of them, but it would have been quite unrealistic to try to make a United Nations in which the vote of the big Powers had no more significance than the small ones. You couldn't have had that. In fact, we went too far in giving a vote to every little Power. We had to do it at that time.

Williams: Do you think, looking back, you might have had a better organisation?

Attlee: If we could have got an organisation with a cession of sovereignty, then we'd have got somewhere; and power to act. But it would have required a different conception altogether – a conception of world government which I suppose we weren't prepared for at that time. We did provide for a permanent International Police Force, but it never came off, largely because of the Russian attitude, which began to show itself, of course, very soon after Potsdam. But I don't think we did too badly over all. And the British delegation worked admirably together. It was very harmonious. Not many party splits, although it was getting obvious that at home everybody was beginning to get very election-minded.

Before leaving for San Francisco Attlee had discussed the question of an Election with Churchill; it was already clear that the European war was nearly over and some decision would then have to be taken. He had been given a firm promise that nothing would be done until he returned. However, conjectures about an Election were brought to a head by the German capitulation, which the British delegation celebrated looking across the vast panorama of the San Francisco Bay to the Golden Gate from the top of the Mark Hopkins Hotel, feeling rather solitary and far from home in a city whose eyes were on the Pacific and which was concerned more with the war with Japan than victory in Europe.

Moving the prolongation of Parliament six months earlier, on

31 October 1944, Mr Churchill had expressed his firm belief that it 'would not be prudent to assume that a shorter period than eighteen months after the destruction of Hitler would be required for the final destruction of the Japanese will or capacity to fight.' He had gone on to declare, 'Therefore it seems to me that unless all political parties resolve to maintain the present Coalition until the Japanese are defeated we must look to the termination of the war against Nazism as a pointer which will fix the date of the General Election . . . I have myself a clear view that it would be wrong to continue this Parliament beyond the period of the German war.'

However, amid general agreement that the announcement of the dissolution would necessarily mark the close of the Administration and, in view of its clear majority in the House, it would fall to the Conservative Party to make arrangements for the inevitable General Election, he had added: 'I cannot conceive that anyone would wish that Election to be held in a violent hurry. . . . There must be an interval. . . . It may therefore be taken as certain that from the moment the King gives his consent to a dissolution a period of between two and three months would be required.'

What had seemed certain to the Prime Minister in October seemed less so to Conservative Ministers and organisers in May with victory in Europe already secured. They were now pressing for a quick Election in June or at the very latest the beginning of July. Seeking the views of his senior Conservative colleagues in the Cabinet, Mr Churchill found all but two plumping for a June Election. On 11 May he sought Eden's opinion in San Francisco, telling him of the consensus of view among Conservatives that a June Election would be to their party advantage, but pointing out also that against this must be set the fact that 'the Russian peril, which I regard as enormous, could be better faced if we remained united.' The Foreign Secretary replied promptly that he was in favour of June.

On the same day Attlee received a long telegram from Herbert Morrison, who had been made Chairman of a Special Campaign

Committee to prepare for the General Election. In this Morrison reported that he had talked over the situation with Churchill and had gathered that Conservative opinion was pressing strongly for an early dissolution of Parliament. His own firm opinion was that Labour ought to be making ready to withdraw from the Government but should press for an October Election fought on the new register coming into force on 15 October.

It was plain that the political situation at home made it impossible for either Attlee or Eden to remain out of the country any longer. The Annual Conference of the Labour Party was due to meet at Blackpool on 21 May and some decision as to the future must be reached by then. Fortunately the main business of the San Francisco Conference had already been accomplished, and on May 15th Attlee, Eden and other principal delegates, including Ellen Wilkinson, that year's Chairman of the Labour Party, departed for London, leaving Lord Halifax in charge.

Arrived in London, Attlee first saw Morrison, Bevin, Dalton and other principal colleagues, and then shortly after midnight on the 17th (the war-time habit of private discussions in the small hours persisted) had a long talk with Churchill at 10 Downing Street. As they talked it became plain that they were very much of the same mind in wanting the war-time Government to continue until the end of the war with Japan (which they both then anticipated would be some time ahead). Ernest Bevin and A. V. Alexander, First Lord of the Admiralty, also shared his view.

Both Attlee and Churchill, however, had to recognise that there would be considerable pressure from large and influential groups in their own parties to terminate the Coalition earlier. The arguments for this had already been forcibly presented to Attlee by Morrison, while on the Conservative side Beaverbrook and Brendan Bracken, Churchill's closest personal intimates, were both urging him to ask the King for an immediate dissolution in order to hold a General Election while victory emotion was still strong. Neither Churchill nor Attlee was in favour of a coupon Election – they remembered too well what had happened after the First World War. If there were an Election it would have to be fought on normal party lines.

They finally separated after a long and friendly talk, recognising that they saw eye to eye on the desirability of keeping the Government in being until victory in the Pacific had crowned the national effort, but conscious that the political pressures might be too strong for them. This proved to be the case.

When the Labour Party National Executive met, Attlee reported on his conversation with Churchill and read a letter he had subsequently received from him. This put the case for a continuation of the Coalition until the end of the Japanese war and made a new proposal, that of a national referendum to sound public opinion on the prolongation of Parliament for this purpose. The letter made clear, however, that, failing an agreement, Churchill was determined to have an early Election and rejected as against the public interest the suggestion that the Coalition should be continued until October.

Attlee recommended that the Party should stay in the Government until after the defeat of Japan. Bevin supported him. However, they were unable to persuade their colleagues, the majority of whom, led by Morrison, argued that the political mood of the country was such that it would be quite impossible to persuade the delegates to the Annual Conference to support the continuance of the Coalition for an unspecified period during which questions of national reconstruction were likely to become increasingly important. They were prepared to stay until October but no longer.

In these circumstances Attlee had no option but to write to Churchill telling him that a continuation of the Coalition beyond October was unacceptable to the Labour Party.

Clifton Hotel, Blackpool

'My dear Churchill, May 21 1945

'I thank you for your letter of May 18th. I have with my colleagues given the most careful consideration to the proposals which you make that we should continue together until the end of the Japanese war, and seek a further extension of life for the present Parliament.

'The Labour Party on entering the Government gave no particular date for the termination of the partnership.

'It has however been recognised that a General Election must necessarily bring the partnership to an end, if the electors were to have a full and free opportunity of expressing their views on future policy.

'The need for bringing to an end, when conditions allowed, a Parliament the life of which has been prolonged year after year, has been recognised by all of us, and by no one more emphatically than yourself. You stated that the prolongation of the life of the existing Parliament by another two or three years would be a very serious constitutional lapse.

'The increasing success of our arms warranted you, when personally introducing the last Prolongation of Parliament Bill, to assume the probability of the defeat of Germany. As you said, "We must look to the termination of the war against Nazism as a pointer which will fix the date of the General Election."

'Political parties and the country generally shared your justifiable faith in victory this year, and have therefore accepted from you the end of the present Session as the terminal date for a General Election.

'It has been the view of the Labour Party, which I think you share, that a rushed election like that of 1918, before the electorate and especially those serving overseas have had a fair opportunity of considering candidates and policy, would be utterly wrong, and would gravely weaken the authority of any Government resulting from such an election at a time when public confidence would be especially necessary.

'It is for that reason that my colleagues and I have always held that there should be an interval between the time when conditions permitted an election to be held and the election itself. Recognising the possibility of prejudice to the party holding power during this interim period, we have been prepared to share the responsibilities of Government up to the time when an election was declared.

'An autumn election would provide a more complete and effective register than that now in force, and would give to the Service electors the opportunity of more fully acquainting themselves with the candidates standing, and the issues involved in the election, than would be available in July. Service candidates would also have a fair chance of making themselves known to the electorate.

'My colleagues and I do not share your view that the country's interests would be prejudiced by a continuance of the present Government until the autumn. On the contrary, we think that there would be great advantage in the Government which has successfully brought the nation through the war continuing for a short time in order to deal with the immediate problems in the international field, and especially to help to bring to a successful conclusion the San Francisco Conference. We can rely on our Members in the House to do all they can to maintain this unity.

'We therefore consider that the fair and just solution of the problem is an election in the autumn.

'You suggest as an alternative that we should continue together until the end of the Japanese war. It is unnecessary for me to assure you that whether in or out of the Government, the Labour Party will give its fullest support to the war until Japan is defeated. But when this will be is uncertain. We hope it may be soon, but, if it were to be prolonged, we see arising in a much more acute form all those difficulties which you apprehend at the present time in the domestic sphere, and which you give as an objection to continuing to the autumn.

'It is precisely on the problems of the reconstruction of the economic life of the country that party differences are most acute. What is required is decisive action. This can only be forthcoming from a Government united on principle and policy. A Government so divided that it could take no effective action would be a disaster to the country.

'My colleagues and I do not believe that it would be possible to lay aside political controversy now that the expectation of an election has engaged the attention of the country. To give a guarantee of agreement to carry on for an indefinite period is not in my power, nor, I suggest, in yours.

'I do not think that it would be either right or possible to obtain from Parliament another prolongation of its life. I could not consent to the introduction into our national life of a device so alien to all our traditions as the referendum, which has only too often been the instrument of Nazidom and Fascism. Hitler's practices in the field of referenda and plebiscites can hardly have endeared these expedients to the British heart.

'For the reasons which I have given, your present proposal is unacceptable.

'It has been my desire, publicly expressed, that the long and honourable association of the parties in the Government which has brought the country through so many perils to victory under your leadership, loyally supported by your Labour colleagues, should be brought to an end by common agreement and without controversy. I am sure that this would be your own wish, but I am bound to state that the reasons for rejecting an autumn election seem to me to be based not on national interests, but on considerations of party expediency.

'It appears to me that you are departing from the position of a national leader by yielding to the pressure of the Conservative Party, which is anxious to exploit your own great services to the nation in its own interest.

'I would earnestly ask you to reconsider your decision to hold an election in circumstances which are bound to cause bitter resentment among the men of the fighting services.

'Should you, however, decide on an election in July despite all the disadvantages to the electors set out in this letter, with which you are familiar, the responsibility must and will, of course, be yours.

C. R. ATTLEE'

By now, however, election fever was burning too strongly within the Conservative Party and the pressure of his most intimate colleagues for an early Election was too great for Churchill to be ready any longer to entertain those arguments for a pause of some months between the end of the war in Europe and the holding of a General Election which he had put so cogently to the House of Commons the previous October and which had been restated in detail in Attlee's letter. Instead he replied brusquely that he could not accept an October election but proposed to tender his resignation to the King without delay. He therefore requested that Attlee and the other Labour Ministers should at once place their offices at his disposal. To this letter Attlee replied briefly and formally.

'Heywood, Stanmore, Middlesex

'My dear Prime Minister, May 24th 1945.

'I thank you for your letter of May 2nd. I am in accordance with your invitation placing my office at your disposal but will continue to act till Monday.

'I shall be glad to discuss the points you mention and shall be available at any time. I shall be in town tomorrow.

Yours sincerely.

C. R. ATTLEE'

The Grand Coalition was over.

6

Warning at Potsdam

Attlee had little time to share in the Labour jubilation that followed the counting of the votes on 26 July. Within forty-eight hours of accepting the King's Commission he had filled the first six key posts in his Administration and was in the air on his way back to Potsdam for a resumption of talks with Stalin and Truman. He was accompanied by Ernest Bevin, the new Foreign Secretary.

He had invited Churchill to return to Potsdam with him in the same capacity as he himself had gone there in the pause between the election campaign – which Churchill had fought with such unexpected and, as it turned out, ill-advised acrimony ('The voice we heard was that of Mr Churchill but the mind was that of Lord Beaverbrook' was Attlee's own comment) – and the counting of the votes. This was, in the words previously used by Churchill, an invitation 'to come as a friend and counsellor and help on all the subjects on which we have been so long agreed.' This arrangement had seemed to Attlee at the time, as he said in his reply, to have 'great public advantage in preserving and presenting to the world at large that unity on foreign policy which we maintained throughout the last five years,' and would provide a means whereby, although the responsibility for decision was naturally the Government's, the leaders of the two parties could keep in constant touch at this decisive stage of peacemaking 'in order to present a policy consonant with the views of the great majority of the people of the country'.

This need seemed to him no less now and he hoped Churchill would be ready in the same way to lend his intimate knowledge of events and incomparable authority as a war leader to the final discussions at Potsdam. However in the light of Election results so contrary to those he had anticipated Churchill felt differently. To Attlee's regret he refused, and Attlee and Bevin went without him, although much to the surprise of some of the Americans they took the same advisers and Attlee even had the same principal private secretary as Churchill, Leslie Rowan.

They arrived by air late in the evening of the 28th and after a call at the 'Little White House', where the American delegation was staying, to meet Truman and introduce Bevin, proceeded to the 'Stock-Exchange-Gothic mansion' (Attlee's phrase) of Cecilienhof, once the residence of the German Crown Prince, for a late-night meeting. There they took the seats at the round conference table occupied until three days before by Churchill and Eden. 'A dramatic demonstration,' noted President Truman, 'of the stable and peaceful way in which a democracy changes its Government.'

Truman had by now come to know Attlee well and had, as he says in his memoirs, developed a great respect for 'his deep understanding of the world's problems'. He felt happy there would be no break in Anglo-American understanding. Stalin and Molotov were less pleased. Relying on British Communist Party intelligence, no more accurate in this than in other matters, Stalin had prophesied that the Conservatives would have a majority of about eighty seats and made no secret of his chagrin when the result proved him wrong, nor of his dislike of the British Labour Party. Indeed when, the day after Attlee and Bevin arrived, the Conference was temporarily held up by Stalin's indisposition Truman confided in a private letter to his mother and sister that he thought Stalin was 'not so sick but disappointed over the English elections.'

This Soviet coolness towards a Labour Prime Minister, although it surprised some of the Americans, neither surprised nor affected Attlee himelf. His first impression of Stalin was this:

'He was clearly a pretty ruthless tyrant but a man you could do business with because he said yes and no and didn't have to refer back. He was obviously the man who could make decisions, and he was obviously going to be difficult. It was plain to me from the beginning at Potsdam that the Russians were going to ask for everything on the grounds of their immense sufferings and so forth. Stalin was genial enough. He could make jokes and take jokes. But I was under no illusions as to his readiness to co-operate or as to his liking for us.

'Bevin at one time thought the Russians might be more friendly to a Labour Government than to a Conservative one. Personally I never believed that. I knew from experience that the Communists had always fought us more vigorously than the Tories because they thought we offered a viable alternative to Communism. They regarded the Tories as the advocates of a dying cause while they thought we were a rival in the new life. Naturally Stalin didn't like the British Election results. I wouldn't have expected him to. But despite that we did try very hard to get alongside him. It proved perfectly impossible.'

For the moment, however, everything was correct and courteous, if formal. But Stalin had a surprise. Before proceeding with the agenda on that first night he announced that the Soviet delegation had just received a communication from the Japanese Ambassador in Moscow asking whether the Soviet Government, which was not yet at war with Japan, would be willing to receive Prince Konoye as an emissary from the Emperor to discuss the possibility of Russian mediation in bringing the war to an end – although not on the terms of unconditional surrender demanded by America, Britain and China in their ultimatum of two days before. There was, said Stalin, nothing new in this, and although the Soviet delegation had not been officially informed of the terms of the Anglo-American ultimatum he proposed to reply to the Japanese request in the negative. President Truman thanked him. With this the question of Japan was dismissed from further consideration by the Conference.

Despite its brevity this was a moment of high, if unacknowledged – perhaps not wholly appreciated – drama, for most of those present were by now aware that preparations were far advanced for the dropping of the first atom bombs in history on Japan.

The news of the successful detonation of an atom bomb at the top of a pylon 100 feet high at Alamogordo, New Mexico, had been received by Truman at Potsdam eleven days previously. He immediately informed Churchill and later Attlee. Until then, although he knew of the combined work on the bomb by British and American scientists, Attlee had deliberately refrained from seeking to acquaint himself with the extent of the progress made, since it was important that the secret should be confined to as narrow a circle as possible of those who were actually working on it: indeed even Churchill had not known the date of the decisive test. When informed of the successful outcome of the test both Churchill and Attlee agreed that the new weapon should be used against the Japanese if they refused to surrender. The actual decision as to time and place was left to Truman, who had himself known nothing of the work on the bomb until told of it a few hours after Roosevelt's death by Stimson, the U.S. Secretary for War.

Truman waited seven days before telling Stalin, and then deliberately gave him the informaton rather casually at the end of the afternoon session on the day Churchill and Attlee were returning to London. Stalin appeared delighted but asked no questions. Nor, Truman told Attlee later, did he make any comment that indicated he understood the significance of the news.

Yet he can hardly have failed to do so. Although no one on the American or British side was aware of the fact, the Soviet Intelligence Service had been informed eight weeks before by Fuchs and Greenglass, one British, one American, both secret Communist agents working on the atomic bomb project, that the test was to be made. And they also knew a good deal about the atomic project from information passed through Colonel

Zabotin, the Military Attaché in Ottowa, by the scientists Nunn May and Pontecorvo.

When he reported the Japanese request for Soviet mediation Stalin made no reference to the bomb. Nor did Truman or Attlee. They passed on to other matters. Eight days later the first atom bomb was dropped on Hiroshima.

A decade and a half later Attlee's opinion remains that it was right to drop it.

Attlee: Of course at the time we knew nothing, I certainly knew absolutely nothing, about the consequences of dropping the bomb except that it was larger than an ordinary bomb and had a much greater explosive force. If we are going back you must look at the situation as it then was. The Japanese were scattered over wide areas and we had no knowledge – I hadn't anyway – that they were likely to collapse. Knowing how they had fought in Burma, the odds were they would fight it out wherever they were with immense loss of life on both sides unless we could get a rescript from the Emperor ordering them to stop. The bomb was a way of getting such a rescript. And in fact we did get it.

Without it there is no evidence that there would have been an immediate Japanese collapse. Indeed, taking into account the Japanese idea that it's rather better to die than surrender, we might have had to winkle the Japanese out over half Asia. We did not know how far they were materially down and how far they were morally down. It is difficult to know for certain even to this day. What we did know was that, failing an Imperial rescript, they were likely to go on fighting right to the end wherever we found them and that the casualties would be enormous – far more than from the atom bomb.

Williams: Couldn't they have been warned?

Attlee: We did warn them against bombing raids bigger than anything known before. We gave populations notice to quit. But they wouldn't and didn't quit.

Williams: But couldn't there have been a specific warning

about the atom bomb – a demonstration of power instead of a massacre?

Attlee: No, I don't think so. We could hardly have invited them round to see an explosion in New Mexico or something like that. And there were only two bombs in existence, I understand. On the knowledge we had we were right. You can't make judgments retrospectively. We knew nothing whatever at that time about the genetic effects of an atomic explosion. I knew nothing about fall-out and all the rest of what emerged after Hiroshima. As far as I know, President Truman and Winston Churchill knew nothing of these things either, nor did Sir John Anderson, who co-ordinated research on our side. Whether the scientists directly concerned knew, or guessed, I do not know. But if they did, then, so far as I am aware, they said nothing of it to those who had to make the decision.

Certainly there was nothing in the discussions at Potsdam to indicate that any of those present, including President Truman and his closest advisers, were fully aware of the nature of an atomic explosion. Thus although – had they but realised it – the bomb had created a situation in which the only effect of a Russian declaration of war could be to bring the Soviet great advantage at no cost, President Truman was still determined to bring Russia in.

Only seven days before the first bomb was dropped, he angrily informed Attlee that Stalin was trying to back down by stipulating that before Russia came in she should be sent a formal note by the United States, Britain and the other allies in the Far Eastern war asking her to do so in order to shorten the war and save lives. To both Truman and Attlee this seemed an obvious manœuvre by Stalin to make Russia's entry seem the decisive factor in securing victory, although under the Moscow Declaration of October 1943 she had already agreed to do so not later than three months after the end of the war in Europe. This obligation had been reinforced by the Charter of the United Nations. In this talk with Attlee, Truman made it plain that he and his military advisers still regarded Russian intervention as essential to neutralise the large Japanese forces on the Chinese mainland. A note was therefore sent to Stalin on 31 July, insisting that he should honour his obligation without further formal request. Neither Truman nor Stalin would seem in the light of this to have had any clear idea at this time of what the atom bomb would do. Certainly Attlee did not. They knew they had a weapon whose explosive power far exceeded anything previously known and that it might shorten the war considerably. But even at this late stage they did not realise that the bomb's material and moral effects were such as to make it capable of bringing the war to an end in a matter of days. This only came after the first bomb had been dropped and it was only then that Russia came in– without even waiting for the signing of a Mutual Assistance Pact with China which Stalin had previously declared necessary.

Meanwhile it was with the future of Europe and specifically, in these closing sessions, with that of Italy, Germany and Poland, that the Potsdam Conference was concerned, and it was to these matters that the three national leaders turned on that first late-night meeting after Stalin had completed his short statement on the Japanese request for mediation and after Attlee had modestly apologised for the fact that 'domestic occurrences' in Britain had interrupted the work of the Conference.

Differences at once made themselves felt. Attlee was shocked by the size and nature of Soviet demands on Italy. After expressing his full sympathy with the Russian people in the sufferings they had undergone, he reminded Stalin that Britain had also suffered and declared firmly that the British people could not be expected to agree to Russian claims which seemed to envisage taking from Italy, in reparations, supplies which America and Britain had provided in order to keep Italy alive.

To this, Stalin, after remarking rather pointedly that he had no wish to ignore the interests of *America*, said they would be willing to take equipment as reparation. Then it must, Attlee insisted, be military equipment having no peace-time usefulness and it must be in the form of once-and-for-all removals and not levies on production. Somewhat reluctantly Stalin finally agreed in principle to this. With this first evidence that the change in British personnel meant no change in British determination this first session ended shortly before midnight. Next day Stalin announced himself temporarily indisposed.

This was the first of several such revelations of the difference between Soviet and Anglo-American attitudes to the peace settlements, differences which reached their height with the discussions on the Polish frontier and on German reparations.

Attlee: The Russians had the Lublin Poles in tow and Bevin and I went to see them. I never saw such a collection of shifty-looking individuals in my life. But we'd had to agree that these Lublin Poles and the Poles with us in London should get together to form a Government, and very soon, as you know, the Russians saw to it that the Communists had the upper hand – the first example of that settled Soviet technique they later employed in Czechoslovakia. In Czechoslovakia, at the time of Potsdam, things seemed to be going satisfactorily. Little Benes was quite sure he could fix everything – he only found out too late that he couldn't trust the Communists after they'd made him think they were faithful yes-men to him. He was too clever by half.

When it came to the Polish frontier the line of the Oder and Eastern Neisse had been agreed at Yalta, but now they wanted the Western Neisse. We never agreed to that, but there was a kind of vacuum from which the Germans had been driven between the Eastern and Western Neisse and they'd already occupied it. We couldn't escape from that. We refused to agree to a final line, we told them it must wait until the Peace Conference. But of course when it came to the point we were faced with a *fait accompli* and nothing could be done about it.

Williams: What about Germany?

Attlee: At first it didn't look too bad. The quadripartite arrangements seemed likely to work all right; we were quite hopeful about co-operation there. There didn't seem to be much difficulty – not at that time. The quadripartite scheme was, in any case, quite inevitable if we were to stay together at all – and we were very anxious to do that if the Russians would play. The main difficulty was over reparations. Stalin wanted the lot. He constantly emphasised the immense losses Russia had sustained. This of course was quite true and he was entitled to say so. But I had to remind him that we had suffered also. He wanted to reduce the Germans to complete impotence. So far as he was concerned they could all starve. He wanted to take everything. But, of course, we knew that, whatever Stalin thought, you couldn't do that and we and the Americans would have to look after the Germans if the Russians were allowed to bleed them white. Bevin was very good on all this. Sound and tough. The difficulty was that when you tried to get down to details Stalin would become vague and say he wasn't ready. A slippery customer. You couldn't pin him down. In the end we did get an agreement. It wasn't as precise as we would have liked and we had to concede more on reparations from Germany to Russia than we thought either just or feasible. But it could have worked with goodwill. Only the goodwill was lacking.

The Conference ended with a somewhat more friendly exchange on war criminals after Stalin suddenly snapped that he would like to know why Hess wasn't being handed over instead of being 'kept in comfort' in England. To this Attlee replied 'You needn't worry about that,' and Bevin interjected, 'You can have him if you want him but we'll charge you his keep for two years' – a remark which put Stalin in good humour. 'I want advance delivery,' he said. 'You've already got it on some of them,' said Attlee. 'You've got Goebbels. What more do you want?'

Stalin took with a chuckle, too, Attlee's crisp intervention during some rather pointless bickering over the order in which the final protocol should be signed: 'I propose we do it alphabetically. That way I would score over Marshal Zhukov.'

But this show of geniality deceived no one, certainly not

Attlee. When the Potsdam Conference finally adjourned at three o'clock in the morning of 2 August, it was possible to look back on some achievements and to hope that the establishment of the Council of Foreign Ministers would keep co-operation of some kind alive in the future. But on the wider issues Attlee's mind was clear. This was his conclusion as he flew back home with Bevin:

Attlee: The Russians had shown themselves even more difficult than anyone expected. After Potsdam one couldn't be very hopeful any longer. It was quite obvious they were going to be troublesome. The way the war had been conducted had left them holding positions far into Europe, much too far. I had no doubt they intended to use them.

7

The Making of a Cabinet

Immediately on his return from Potsdam Attlee set about completing his Administration and preparing for the task of post-war reconstruction. This he knew would inevitably invoke many controversies and could hardly help but bring hardship and disappointment to many who had believed that somehow life would return to normal once the European war was over. In his Election broadcast he had concluded with the words: 'I do not seek to conceal from you that the post-war years will not be easy. They will require from the nation in peace the same resolute spirit as was shown in war.'

He had just concluded nearly five years of heavy labour, usually for long hours and often far into the night, as Deputy Prime Minister in the War Cabinet, bearing grave responsibilities throughout. But his powers of resilience were great and he felt fresh and eager for the tasks ahead.

Williams: Didn't you feel in need of a rest after the long haul of the war?

Attlee: I'd had a bit of rest at San Francisco, you know, if you could call it a rest. Change of air and scene anyway. I felt quite fit. I usually do.

Williams: How do you manage it?

Attlee: By not worrying. Clearing off every day's job before the end of the day. You take a decision and then have done with it. No good to keep on asking yourself if you've done the right thing. It gets you nowhere.

Williams: Is that an acquired talent or did it come naturally?

Attlee: Oh, I think I probably acquired it. As you come to a more responsible position you take decisions and there you are. No good going over them. You come to a decision as carefully as you can and that's that.

Williams: What sort of a life was it as Prime Minister?

Attlee: Probably busy during the week, get a bit of time off at week-ends if you're lucky. As a matter of fact I read the whole of Gibbon when I was Prime Minister, just at week-ends, at Chequers. You live on the job, of course, which is a great advantage. I saw more of my family when I was at Number 10 than ever before or after.

Williams: Was it usually a long day?

Attlee: Fairly long. I had breakfast and then I had a walk round the Park, with a dog, my wife and sometimes a child or two. I was generally on the job in the Cabinet Room by 9.30 or earlier. I then worked right through the day and generally got upstairs about eleven or twelve at night – intervals for lunch and dinner, of course; not very long and often part of the job, official lunches and so on. I usually got to bed round about midnight. Not always of course. But then I'm attuned to a long day. In the old days I had to get back after the House rose and I lived out of London, so I was very seldom in bed until after twelve. I was used to it.

Williams: When you got down to completing your Administration what sort of principles of Cabinet-making did you have in mind?

Attlee: Well, first of all, you must try to keep the Cabinet small – as small as possible. Then you have to look at your key posts and consider first of all the fitness of the person for the post and secondly his status in the party. You may have a man who is admirably fitted for one post but you may want him for another. Chuter Ede was eminently fitted to be Minister of Education, but a Home Secretary is a particularly difficult job and he was far the best man for that. He had therefore to leave Education, which was his special thing, and go to the Home Office. Again nowadays, if you can, you should have some women in and there are certain jobs like Education or National Insurance where a woman will fit better than others. Then you have to consider how far those you want are likely to work as a team. You've got to balance the personalities, the weight of the responsibility of the particular office, and perhaps, also, standing in the country. It's a blend of things. You can't always depend on the office. Normally I wouldn't have put the Ministry of Fuel and Power into the Cabinet, but we were nationalising mines, electricity and gas, so in goes Shinwell.

And then you've got to have a certain number of solid people whom no one would think particularly brilliant, but who between conflicting opinions can act as middle-men, give you the ordinary man's point of view. I'll tell you who was an ordinary man and a very useful man. You remember little George Tomlinson. He was Minister of Education after Ellen Wilkinson. A Lancashire man. I can remember a thing coming up which looked like a good scheme, all worked out by the Civil Service. But I wasn't quite sure of how it would go down with ordinary people, so I said: 'Minister of Education, what do you think of this?' 'Well,' says George, 'it sounds all right but I've been trying to persuade my wife of it for the last three weeks and I can't persuade her.' A commonsense point of view like that's extremely valuable. Another very valuable man in all sorts of ways was old Christopher Addison. Great experience you see. An excellent conciliator.

A Prime Minister has to know when to ask for an opinion. He can't always stop some Ministers offering theirs, you always have some people who'll talk on everything. But he can make sure to extract the opinion of those he wants when he needs them. The job of the Prime Minister is to get the general feeling – collect the voices. And then, when everything reasonable has been said, to get on with the job and say, 'Well, I think the decision of the Cabinet is this, that or the other. Any objections?' Usually there aren't. I didn't often find my Cabinet disagreeing with me. I was always for getting on with the job, you know. To get through the agenda you must stop people talking – unnecessary talk, unnecessary approval of things already agreed, pleasant byways that may be interesting but not strictly relevant. You have to be pretty stern because business is very heavy. And you shouldn't talk too much yourself however good you are at it, in my view. We used to have very good talk from Winston in the War Cabinet of course. Excellent talk. I remember he complained once in Opposition that a matter had been brought up several times in Cabinet and I had to say, 'I must remind the Right Honourable Gentleman that a monologue is not a decision.'

Williams: And you don't take a vote.

Attlee: You don't take a vote. No. Never. You might take it on something like whether you meet at 6.30 or 7.30, I suppose, but not on anything major. In the same way you never take a vote at a Commonwealth Meeting of Prime Ministers. The presiding Prime Minister collects the voices.

William: What's the right size for a Cabinet?

Attlee: Probably about, at the most, sixteen.

Williams: Yours was bigger.

Attlee: Yes, but I planned to reduce it by moving the Service Ministers from the Cabinet to the Defence Committee and winding up as soon as possible one or two dying Ministries such as the Ministry of Information. You find it hard to keep it down these days, though. You have to consider the importance of the man and the importance of the job at the time.

Broadly speaking, you don't want to include in the Cabinet purely administrative jobs; an obvious example is the Postmaster-General, or normally, as I said before, Fuel and Power. But sometime, the personality of the Minister will outweigh the secondary importance of the job. Of course, you've got to have some administrative people. You can't have a Cabinet entirely of people operating in a vacuum. But you must have a certain number with leisure to look around and think. It's a mistake to have just a collection of hardworking Departmental Ministers.

What one needs in a Cabinet Minister is decision and a sense of priorities, ability to make up his mind. He must be able to select and absorb the necessary amount of information and not cumber his mind with a whole lot of unnecessary stuff. The fellow who goes wrong is the laborious fellow who reads everything in great detail and is quite unable to get any sense of priorities. He needs to be able to talk clearly in the House, too. Sometimes people say of a fellow, 'He's not much at explaining a case but he's a good administrator.' I don't set much store by that. If a man can't explain himself he hasn't got enough clear thinking.

And he mustn't get too big for his boots and lose touch with the rank and file. That applies particularly to Prime Ministers. It's fatal if a Party Leader depends on a few intimates. He mustn't have favourites. It's very dangerous to be the centre of a small circle.

Williams: What other qualities are needed for a Prime Minister?

Attlee: Ah! A sense of urgency, of dispatch. A sense of the time and the occasion and the atmosphere of the country. He must be ready to labour and wait sometimes; it's no good thinking you can thrust something through when the country isn't ready for it. That doesn't mean you've got to sit back, because you may have to press things through at times, but you must have a sense of timing, judgment of what will go and what won't and when. It isn't the same thing as intellectual power, often quite divorced from it. A lot of clever people have got everything except judgment.

A Prime Minister's got to be even more of a co-ordinator than a Cabinet Minister. He ought to have a reasonable historical background and a reasonable degree of toleration. He need not necessarily have a charming personality, but it helps. And he should remember that you don't necessarily think the other fellow's a dirty dog. You are good friends, but you hold opposite views. That goes for all M.P.s of course. Another thing: a fairly egocentric Cabinet Minister can get along, but an egocentric Prime Minister can't. He must remember he's only the first among equals. He necessarily has, if he's any use at all, a good deal of experience and authority. Some people may think he has a certain amount of wisdom. His voice will carry the greatest weight. But you can't ride rough-shod over a Cabinet unless you're something very extraordinary. What you do generally is give guidance. A Prime Minister ought to keep his hand on the pulse and know how Ministers are doing, of course, but he mustn't go and interfere and overrule a Minister, he must always work through the Minister. He should keep in touch and see what he's doing, but if he's picked the right man he should trust him. If he finds he can't he should get rid of him.

I was lucky, of course. When we came in in 1945 there hadn't been a Labour Government for fourteen years and in the normal way of things there wouldn't have been many people with Ministerial experience to draw on after such a lapse of time. But during the war the number of Labour Ministers had steadily increased. Several, like Cripps and Dalton and George Hall, who'd only held junior office previously had enormously enlarged their experience in senior jobs, and others, like Ellen Wilkinson, Chuter Ede, Tom Williams and George Tomlinson had done sound administrative work. They provided me with a good cadre when I came to form a Government.

You must take care over Junior Ministers too. It's generally best to have a talk with the Minister concerned in choosing an Under-Secretary, not just foist someone on him. But you can't necessarily accept the man a Minister wants. He's the only one who doesn't usually know his own deficiencies. You may have picked a Minister who is awfully good but, although he doesn't know it, rather weak on certain sides, so you must give him an Under-Secretary who fills in the gaps. For instance, if you have a rather obvious member of the intelligentsia it's quite useful to give him a Trade Unionist to correct his outlook. In the same way, it may be useful to a Trade Unionist to have someone who's got a different background. The fatal mistake is to select only people you think are docile yes-men. You must put in people who are likely to be awkward – I did. And you must always warn Ministers: 'If you don't turn out all right I shall sack you.' I did with all my Ministers.

Williams: And it's essential that the Prime Minister shall pick the Ministers himself?

Attlee: I thnk so. You may talk it over with other senior Ministers. As a matter of fact, my general experience was that where I accepted advice it wasn't very good. I did once or twice have people foisted on me. People don't always understand why a man who seems clever may not turn out particularly good as a Cabinet Minister.

Actually in 1931 there was a movement in the Labour Party, because of the feeling about MacDonald, to set up some sort of group that would have a say in choosing Ministers. They were to be elected by the Parliamentary Party – a body of three or four senior men to advise. Well, it fell by the wayside, partly because most people soon forgot about it, partly because of the time factor. The fact that I had to get over to Potsdam at once meant there was no time for lengthy confabulations or for going through a process of electing various people who admired each other. It wouldn't have worked. The Australian Labour Party do something of the sort, you know. Awful business. They elect a certain number of people as Ministers, and then they're handed over to the Prime Minister and he's told to fit them into the jigsaw. It's quite possible that someone with particular technical qualifications may get left out because he doesn't happen to be the popular man. I don't believe in that at all. You must have confidence in the judgment of the man in charge. If he hasn't got that confidence, he's not fit to be Prime Minister.

Williams: What if you pick wrongly?

Attlee: It's awkward to have to sack a man and tell him he doesn't make the grade. But I always think it's best to tell him so frankly, not rush around looking for some sort of a cushion for him, like telling him it isn't his fault but you happen to need a man with some other sort of experience and you'll try to fit him into some other job later. I don't think that's playing straight with a fellow. If he doesn't measure up to the job, you should tell him. It's unpleasant, but it's a job a Prime Minister must do for himself. As a matter of fact most of the people I had to get rid of took it very well. In a good many cases, of course, it was age. They were getting on and I wanted to make way for younger men. They were very nice about it. People don't think politicians are like that. They are. What struck me was not the selfishness of Ministers but their unselfishness.

Williams: In your book *The Labour Party in Perspective*, written some time before the war, you said a good deal about more efficient organisation of the Cabinet. How far did you, in fact, change the organisational structure of the Cabinet when you became Prime Minister?

Attlee: Well, of course it was too big and I reduced it in various ways, the most important of which was setting up a Ministry of Defence with a Defence Minister, and removing the First Lord of the Admiralty and the two Secretaries of State, who from the time I could remember had always been members of the Cabinet, and reducing them to non-Cabinet Ministers. This was quite a big step, substituting one for three. It had one other result too. You must remember in earlier times with a smaller Cabinet people were put into the Service Ministries not because they had the slightest interest in military affairs but because they were people of a certain status. Once you got rid of that you could put in people who really understood the Services and not, for instance, the sort of people who were sometimes Service Ministers in the Chamberlain Government and knew nothing about it whatever. It was the same in the MacDonald Government. Walsh and Tom Shaw knew nothing about the War Office, but because of their status in the Party they had to be given Cabinet office.

Williams: In *The Labour Party in Perspective* you also suggested that there ought to be a small group of Ministers with a general functional supervision over a number of areas of policy. How did that work out in practice?

Attlee: Well, in effect, one had that. We had a committee dealing with social services. Arthur Greenwood presided over that. It didn't take away from the responsibility of individual Ministers, but it co-ordinated education, health and all those things. In the same way we got co-ordination on the economic side at first under Morrison and then under the Chancellor of the Exchequer. Broadly speaking, while I don't believe in a Cabinet of people with no administrative function, I think it's necessary to have a committee system in which, under the guidance of senior non-departmental Ministers, you can get co-ordination. And although we didn't have a special committee for overseas affairs, Ernie at the Foreign Office was always in close contact with the others. He didn't confine himself to foreign affairs – he took a full part in everything. A very wide knowledge, a capacious mind, and a mind fertile in suggestions. I'd discuss something with him and he'd come rolling in on Monday morning and say, 'I've been having a look at this, been going through the statistics, and it occurs to me that this might be a way out.' Generally it was a very good suggestion, something you mightn't have thought of.

Defence I kept myself. I was Defence Minister until the war with Japan ended. During war the Prime Minister must be actual Chairman of the Defence Ministry. After that I put in A. V. Alexander as Defence Minister and later Shinwell, but I continued as a rule to preside at all major meetings on defence. And we introduced the Defence Committee, which was not like an ordinary Cabinet committee that comes and goes according to circumstances and need. This was a new piece of governmental machinery that has lasted to this day.

And then Herbert Morrison co-ordinated the Home Front; considering the legislation and when to bring forward this or the other and working out the details of various nationalisation schemes. He did a great deal of work there. A good administrator and a good co-ordinator. And there was Cripps. Stafford was first of all at the Board of Trade, where he had a big say in the whole of economic planning. Later he became the chief economic co-ordinator and eventually as Chancellor of the Exchequer had general supervision in the economic field, which was a logical development but required rather special qualities in the Chancellor. It wouldn't have done to have had a Chancellor who was entirely in the hands of the Treasury and looked at everything from a narrow Treasury point of view, as used to be the case with the Budget in the old days, which was really just a financial business. But we brought in the economic survey; we looked at finance in terms of our broad economic position and had to bring in our finance measures as part of our general planning economy for the country.

Williams: Had you a complete working pattern of policy already in mind when you became Prime Minister?

Attlee: Certainly. I was definitely determined to go ahead with plans of nationalisation. I expected some trouble over the Bank of England, but it caused no difficulty; rather odd when you think of all the row and trouble there used to be about it. Cable and Wireless caused no difficulty either. There was very little difficulty over gas and electricity – they were fairly well over already. And there wasn't much with the mines. Transport was much more difficult and iron and steel had not been worked out by the time we came in.

There were a lot of post-war problems to clear up of course, but I thought that we must push ahead. Fundamental nationalisation had got to go ahead because it fell in with the planning, the essential planning of the country. It wasn't just nationalisation for nationalisation's sake but the policy in which we believed: that fundamental things – central banking, transport, fuel and power – must be taken over by the nation as a basis on which the rest of the re-organisation of the country would depend. It was also obviously essential in the socialist sphere to drive on towards social security. There was the Beveridge Report to which all parties were committed. There was the making of the Health Service and the co-ordination of all the various social services and the advance in education. All this didn't really, as they say, brook delay. And then there were the practical things – housing, largely a matter for working through local government, and the building of many new factories.

All this had to be worked out having regard to the materials and the man-power available, and while this was going on there was the enormous task of demobilisation and resettlement. It wasn't possible to demobilise without a clear idea of where people were to go. You had to have some control. The available labour might have gone into the less essential industries if you hadn't. We had to see that the essential industries were keyed up. We also had to see – and be pretty drastic about it – that essential building went up before luxuries. If we had left that to the free play of private competition it would have gone where the profit was greatest, and there might have been a far more profitable showing in non-essential industries, amusements and things like that, especially in the sort of conditions we were dealing with at the end of the war. We had to have the power to determine our national future. Nye Bevan once said government was a matter of priorities. There's a lot of truth in that.

We were armed of course with very big powers – war-time powers, but quite obviously we couldn't get rid of them. The Tories made a great howl about them, although, as a matter of fact, we got rid of the non-essential ones. The others we just had to keep. We were still in a state of siege, still short of everything we wanted.

Williams: What about the non-nationalised industry, the private sector?

Attlee: Well, there had to be some control there too. We had to have an allocation of building labour, for example, and materials and so on. The whole thing had to be seen as one. I don't think people realised, you know, the extent to which this sort of planning was essential, irrespective of the point of view you had. A great deal of industry had been practically destroyed, knocked down; it had to be started again. Other industries had to switch back to civilian output. Their labour had been dispersed. They had to collect their old teams. It was all a tremendous mess. You couldn't get out of it without planning.

Williams: How large a part of your thinking was specifically directed to a more equal society?

Attlee: A very considerable part. And there we had a great advantage because no Government had been so vigorous in applying egalitarian policies as the war-time Government – profit taxes, and so on. These policies were quite ruthless, both under Kingsley Wood and Anderson. Very properly so. You might have said, 'The war's over. Relax them all straight away.' Well, we didn't. We couldn't afford to. It was also not our policy to try to re-create an un-egalitarian society but to work steadily towards a greater equality. Not a dead level, but fewer great differences, more opportunity and more social justice.

Williams: One criticism made at the time was that you went ahead with nationalisation and other things without due regard for the international economic situation in which the country found itself, and that the pace was altogether too fast.

Attlee: We had to work fast. We had to rebuild the export trade, and you can't build an export trade in a vacuum. You've got to have the fuel and power, transport, finance and all the rest to do it. And of course, because of the export situation, there had to be control of masses of things that were forbidden to our own people at home. Shops would have lovely china, for export only. Very frustrating, but you couldn't avoid it. It was often easier to sell in the home market than the foreign market. To get back into export markets that were essential for our survival we had to insist that what would sell abroad went abroad, and we had to think not only of our economic situation, which was bad enough, but of our voice in international policy, which was vital. We had to get back our international markets. We had to be back on our feet as an international power in order that our voice could count where it was most needed. And it was badly needed.

Williams: There's a good deal more formal machinery of party decision in the Labour Party than in the Conservative Party. Did this reduce your freedom of action?

Attlee: No. Naturally as the leader of a party any Prime Minister has been sent in to carry out a party programme. That is what electors have voted for. He wouldn't be leader if he didn't believe in it. But he must always remember that he is more than a party leader. His Government is responsible primarily to Parliament and through Parliament to the nation. If you begin to consider yourself solely responsible to a political party you're halfway to a dictatorship. You must always have in mind what is in the best interests of the country as a whole at a particular time.

In the Labour Party the Annual Conference passes resolutions which are party policies. It is for the National Executive to interpret these on a national sphere. But as far as work in the House goes they must always be interpreted and dealt with in the light of circumstance by the Parliamentary Party. They are a guidance to the Parliamentary Party, not an absolute mandate. They couldn't be. You can't have a non-parliamentary body arranging things, saying, 'You must do this. You mustn't do the other.' What you do must depend on the circumstances. The National Executive is useful in giving a consensus of opinion, keeping you in touch with feeling, but there can never be any question of orders being issued by the National Executive to a Labour Government. That would be quite out of the question. You must always remember you are the Government of all the country and act accordingly. It is the same with the trade unions. Trade union resolutions are things to take account of, they show the way an important body of opinion is going, but they're not binding on the Parliamentary Party, and still less so, of course, on a Labour Government.

Williams: In earlier days many people used to suggest that a Labour Government with a socialist programme would run into trouble with right-wing Civil Servants. Did you have any of that difficulty?

Attlee: Never. I always found them perfectly loyal. So did all the others as far as I know. I never had complaints. That's the Civil Service tradition, a great tradition. They carry out the policy of any given Government. If they think it's silly, of course they'll tell the Minister so. If he decides to go ahead, then they carry it out. There may have been some whose advice to Ministers was coloured by their own personal attitudes. I never encountered them. They were all anxious to do the best they could by a Labour Government.

Williams: What about relationships with industrial leaders, employers and businessmen?

Attlee: I generally found them pretty helpful, I must say. If I had to talk to industrial leaders on national issues, I always found them co-operative.

Williams: Of course there was some criticism from the Labour side that too many industrial leaders, too many from the employers and management side, were given top jobs in the nationalised industries.

Attlee: Well, one had to put in people who understood the techniques. It's no good thinking a lot of amateurs can run a complicated business. You want a mixture from both sides of industry.

Williams: Do you think you could have used more trade union people?

Attlee: We used what we could get. They weren't always willing to cross over, nor were their men always willing for them to go in: a curious contradiction, because they talked of Labour running the show and yet when you put a trade unionist in to help run a nationalised industry they tended to regard him as a bosses' man.

Williams: Did you ever feel that industrialists appointed to run nationalised industries might not have their hearts in it, might be glad for them not to do too well, in the interests of private enterprise?

Attlee: I've never had an instance of anything like that, nor a complaint of it. I think they did a very good job on the whole.

Williams: Looking back, do you think the pattern of nationalised industry you chose, the public corporation not directly accountable in detail to Parliament, is the best pattern?

Attlee: On the whole, yes. Of course, we based our ideas on experience to some extent. Herbert Morrison was very strong on that, learning from the Transport Bill and so on. And we took the line that these were businesses which should be run in a businesslike way and it would be wrong to have perpetual parliamentary interference in detail. We put that forward and curiously enough it was also stressed by the Tories, but as soon as we'd done it all the Tories began to demand parliamentary control. They were entirely inconsistent.

Williams: There was a different criticism from your own side that still comes up among some workers in the nationalised industries, that nationalisation ought to have meant a bigger share in control by the workers.

Attlee: We tried to get it, I can't say with an awfully good response. We tried hard to establish more joint consultation and things of that kind, but not with much success. A hangover from the past, I'm afraid. Some of them still had the old feeling of opposition to any administration. Others frankly said, 'Well, look, management isn't our job."

Williams: But many did complain that nationalisation simply meant the same old bosses with different hats on.

Attlee: Inevitably, it did. You couldn't suddenly create a whole lot of new mining engineers, for example. You couldn't sack all the old mine managers and put in people who knew nothing about it. There was a good deal of difficulty here and there, I've no doubt, because a lot of the older dogs couldn't learn new tricks. They're working it out now, giving more and better opportunities for able people to come up.

Williams: Was there as much sense of participation by workers in nationalised industries as you'd hoped to see?

Attlee: No, I don't think so. It's one of the big problems, at any rate in the initial stages. And there were a lot of people who demanded change and when they got it started looking backwards, didn't want people messing about with 'our show'. Curiously enough, I think in some ways it was most difficult in the railways because there were a lot of old loyalties there. A Great Western man was a Great Western man and he resented being pushed in with the other lot, so to speak. You've always got to allow for human nature. The miners played up awfully well, trying to get increased production and voluntarily going back for longer hours and so on.

Williams: They were conscious of a bigger change than in any other industry, of course.

Attlee: Also, of course, they're so much more a community, being a localised industry. One problem with mining was that a lot of the mines were more or less worked out. There had been no provision for extensions during the war and the mines had been thoroughly let down. They hadn't got the young men coming in either and we ran very short. On top of that, with our drive for full employment there was a big increase in demand. Many people didn't realise the extent to which you must have development going on all the time.

Also with the large increase in industrial activity that we had as compared with pre-war, and with no reserves, we required a good many more electricity stations. You can't make those in a day and we were constantly having difficulties, especially when we had that extremely severe winter on top of it all, which I don't think we could have foreseen. That was bad luck. We'd had very gloomy forebodings from all our experts on fuel, power, transport, food, almost everything, while there was still a Coalition. It was only to be expected. You can't fight a war and scrape right down to the bottom of the barrel, throwing in everything you've got, and then start up again after it as if nothing had happened. We had a shortage of man-power, of equipment, of raw materials. We had to get back our export trade and build it to a larger scale than ever before. Quite a business, you know. I don't think the workers did too badly when you look at the size of the job. Or the managements. Or the millions of ordinary people who had to knuckle down to austerities none of us wanted. And I don't think the politicians did too badly either, when you come to think of it.

8

The Atom Bomb

Although he had acquiesced in the decision to drop the atom bomb and remained convinced that it was right at the time, Attlee was very conscious that during the brief discussions at Potsdam neither he nor any of the others concerned had fully grasped the consequences of doing so.

A week after his return to London, therefore, immediately following the bombing of Hiroshima and while the surrender of Japan was still six days off, he sent the following personal telegram:

'Prime Minister to President Truman. 8.8.45

'When we were at Potsdam the potentiality of the atomic bomb had not become actuality and the pressure of immediate problems was too heavy to give us the opportunity of discussing the implications of success.

'The attack on Hiroshima has now demonstrated to the world that a new factor pregnant with immense possibilities for good or evil has come into existence.

'Thoughtful people already realise that there must be a re-valuation of policies and a readjustment of international relations. There is widespread anxiety as to whether the new power will be used to serve or to destroy civilisation.

'The economic effects of the discovery will probably not reveal themselves for some years: the influence on international relations is immediate.

'I believe that our two nations are profoundly convinced that if civilisation is to endure and progress, war must be banished for ever.

'I consider, therefore, that you and I, as heads of the Governments which have control of this great force, should without delay make a joint declaration of our intentions to utilise the existence of this great power, not for our own ends, but as trustees for humanity in the interests of all peoples in order to promote peace and justice in the world.

'The problems of control and the effect of the existence of this power on the new World Organisation will require careful consideration, but I believe that a declaration of intentions made now will have great value.'

Truman had just arrived home on board the U.S.S. *Augusta* when this telegram reached him. He replied immediately that he proposed to make a broadcast to the American people covering the points Attlee had in mind and was also sending recommendations to Congress for making atomic energy 'a powerful and forceful influence towards the maintenance of peace.' This delighted Attlee and he cabled back:

'Prime Minister to President Truman. 11.8.45

'I have read the admirable statement which you included in your broadcast on 9 August, which in fact amounts to a declaration of intentions of the kind I had in mind. In these circumstances I think that any joint declaration should wait until the means of control and the implications in the field of international relations have been more fully considered between those concerned.'

He followed this with a public statement from 10 Downing Street:

'Since I issued a statement on the day of the release of the first atomic bomb nearly a week ago, the vast and terrible effects of this new invention have made themselves felt. The last of our enemies has offered surrender. The events of these tremendous days reinforce the words in that statement to the effect that we must pray that the discovery which led to the production of the atomic bomb will be made to conduce to peace among the nations, and that instead of wreaking measureless havoc upon the entire globe, it may become a perennial fountain of world prosperity. President Truman in his broadcast of 9 August has spoken of the preparation of plans for the future control of this bomb, and of a request to Congress to co-operate to the end that its production and use may be controlled and that its power may be made an overwhelming influence towards world peace. It is the intention of His Majesty's Government to put all their efforts into the promotion of the objects thus foreshadowed, and they will lend their full co-operation to that end.'

At the same time he instructed Lord Halifax, whom (despite Laski) he had asked to remain on as an Ambassador in Washington, to keep in close touch with the President and to assure him of Britain's great anxiety that there should be early consideration of the international problems brought by the bomb. He also asked Bevin to raise the matter with the U.S. Secretary of State, Mr James F. Byrnes, when he came to London for the first Foreign Ministers' Conference.

By 25 September, Attlee felt the time had come to open his mind more fully to the President. He therefore sent to him privately on that date the following long letter, concluding with a proposal for an early meeting:

'Dear Mr President, 25.9.45

'Ever since the U.S.A. demonstrated to the world the terrible effectiveness of the atomic bomb I have been increasingly aware of the fact that the world is now facing entirely new conditions. Never before has there been a weapon which can suddenly and without warning be employed to destroy utterly the nerve centre of a great nation. The destruction wrought by the Germans through their air fleet on Warsaw and Rotterdam was startling enough, but subsequent attempts to do the same to London were defeated, though without much to spare. Our own attacks on

Berlin and the Ruhr resulted in the virtual destruction of great centres of industry. In Europe the accumulated material wealth of decades has been dissipated in a year or two, but all this is not different in kind from what was done in previous wars in Europe during the Dark Ages and the Thirty Years War, in America by your own civil war. Despite these losses civilisation continued and the general framework of human society and of relations between peoples remained. The emergence of this new weapon has meant, taking account of its potentialities, not a quantitative but a qualitative change in the nature of warfare.

'Before its advent military experts still thought and planned on assumptions not essentially different from those of their predecessors. It is true that the conservative (with a small c!) mentality tended to maintain some of these although they were already out of date. For instance we found at Potsdam that we had to discuss a decision taken at the Crimea Conference as to the boundaries of Poland. These were delimited by rivers although the idea of a river as a strategic frontier has been out of date ever since the advent of air warfare. Nevertheless, it was before the coming of the atomic bomb not unreasonable to think in terms of strategic areas and bases, although here again it has seemed to me that too little account has been taken of the air weapon.

'Now, however, there is in existence a weapon of small bulk capable of being conveyed on to a distant target with inevitable catastrophic results. We can set no bounds to the possibilities of airplanes flying through the stratosphere dropping atomic bombs on great cities. There are possible developments of the rocket for a similar purpose. I understand that the power of the bombs delivered on Nagasaki may be multiplied many times as the invention develops. I have so far heard no suggestion of any possible means of defence. The only deterrent is the possibility of the victim of such an attack being able to retort on the victor. In many discussions on bombing in the days before the war it was demonstrated that the only answer to the bomber was the bomber. The war proved this to be correct. This obvious fact did not prevent bombing but resulted in the destruction of many great centres of civilisation. Similarly if mankind continues to make the atomic bomb without changing the political relationships of States sooner or later these bombs will be used for mutual annihilation.

'The present position is that whilst the fundamental scientific discoveries which made possible the production of the atomic bomb are now common knowledge, the experience of the actual processes of manufacture and knowledge of the solutions which were found to the many technical problems which arose, are confined to our two countries and the actual capacity for production exists only in the United States. But the very speed and completeness of our joint achievement seems to indicate that any other country possessing the necessary scientific and industrial resources could also produce atomic bombs within a few years if it decided now to make the effort. Again, our two Governments have gone a long way in securing control of all the main known sources of uranium and thorium, the two materials at present believed to be of importance for the process. But new sources are continually coming to light and it would not be surprising if it were found that large deposits existed in parts of the world outside our direct or indirect control. Nor may it be altogether easy to defend the measures which we have already taken in this matter when they become known and are considered in the light of such principles as that of the freedom of access to raw materials.

'It would thus appear that the lead which has been gained as a result of the past effort put forth in the United States may only be temporary and that we have not much time in which to decide what use is to be made of that lead. It is true that other countries, even if they succeed in producing atomic bombs, may not, at any rate at first, be able to produce them on the same scale. I am told, however, that, in future, it may be possible for the process to be developed at a far smaller cost in industrial resources than has inevitably been demanded by your pioneer production enterprise, carried through in time of war when speed was the first essential; and in any case, with a weapon of such tremendous destructive power, it is perhaps doubtful whether the advantage would lie with the possessor of the greatest number of bombs rather than with the most unscrupulous.

'A further consideration which I have had in mind is that the successful manufacture of bombs from plutonium shows that the harnessing of atomic energy as a source of power cannot be achieved without the simultaneous production of material capable of being used in a bomb. This means that the possible industrial uses of atomic energy cannot be considered separately from its military and security implications.

'It is clear to me, therefore, that, as never before, the responsible statesmen of the great Powers are faced with decisions vital not merely to the increase of human happiness but to the very survival of civilisation. Until decisions are taken on this vital matter, it is very difficult for any of us to plan for the future. Take the case of this country. During the war we had to shift much of our industry to the less exposed parts of our island. We had to provide shelters for our people. Now we have to restart our industries and rebuild our wrecked homes. Am I to plan for a peaceful or a warlike world? If the latter, I ought to direct all our people to live like troglodytes underground as being the only hope of survival, and that by no means certain. I have to consider the defence forces required in the future in the light of San Francisco, but San Francisco did not envisage the atomic bomb. Its conceptions of security are based on appreciations of a situation existing in June of this year. We considered regional security and a policing of the world by the Powers with the greatest resources in the interests of all so that there should be available the forces to prevent aggression.

'I have only mentioned Great Britain as an example: for every Head of Government must, in varying degree, find himself confronted with the same problems.

In these circumstances, while realising to the full the importance of devising means to prevent as far as possible the power to produce this new weapon getting into other hands, my mind is increasingly directed to considering the kind of relationship between nations which the existence of such an instrument of destruction demands. In your country and ours resort is not had to violence not just because we have efficient police forces but because the vast majority of our citizens are law-abiding and conditions are such that men are not driven to have recourse to desperate measures. Our constitutions allow of peaceful change.

'We have, it seems to me, if we are to rid ourselves of this menace, to make very far-reaching changes in the relationship between States. We have, in fact, in the light of this revolutionary development to make a fresh review of world policy and a new valuation of what are called national interests. We are ourselves attempting to undertake such a review. What was done on American initiative at San Francisco was a first step at erecting the framework of a new world society, but necessarily it could have regard only to the requirements imposed by the technical advances in methods of warfare then known. Now it seems to us that the building, the framework of which was erected at San Francisco, must be carried much further if it is to be an effective shelter for humanity. We have to secure that these new developments are turned to the benefit rather than to the destruction of mankind. We must bend our utmost energies to secure that better ordering of human affairs which so great a revolution at once renders necessary and should make possible.

'I am therefore most anxious, before we proceed much further with our own deliberations, to know how your mind is moving: and it is primarily for this reason that I have set before you at such length my tentative views before they have really begun to crystallise.

'Mr Byrnes has had a preliminary talk with Mr Bevin here on the matter but, later on, I think it may be essential that you and I should discuss this momentous problem together so that we may agree what the next step should be and be in a position to take it before the fears and suspicions which may be developing elsewhere have got such a firm hold as to make even more difficult any solution we may decide to aim at.

Yours sincerely, C. R. ATTLEE'

The President of the United States of America.

There could be no doubt after this letter of the importance Attlee attached to early action to reduce the threat to world civilisation and his realisation of the significance of the news they had first received at Potsdam. Truman, who shared his anxieties, responded and in a statement to Congress eight days later announced that he was proposing to initiate discussions 'first with our associates in this discovery, Great Britain and Canada, and then with other nations, in an effort to effect agreement on the conditions under which co-operation might replace rivalry in the field of atomic power.'

A meeting was arranged for November and on the 9th of that month Attlee flew to Washington. He went straight to the airport from a Lord Mayor's luncheon at the Mansion House, where he explained that his principal purpose was to discuss world affairs with President Truman and Mr Mackenzie King, the Canadian Prime Minister, 'in the light, the terrible light, of the discovery of atomic energy'. It might well be, he said, that many people did not yet realise to what an extent it had now become necessary to readjust our ideas, but science applied to warfare might discover other weapons even more terrible than the atomic bomb and the question that faced them was not so much how they could control this new and devastating force as what kind of society was necessary in a world where a few bombs might utterly destroy great cities, the work of centuries of human endeavour.

'Unless,' he concluded, 'we can devise human relationships other than those which have obtained throughout the ages, destruction on an unbelievable scale may fall upon our civilisation.'

With him to Washington Attlee took Sir John Anderson, who had been put in charge of the British Atomic Energy programme in 1941 as Lord President of the Council in the war-time Government and had more knowledge of the whole background of the joint American, British and Canadian effort that had produced the bomb than any other man in Britain. His knowledge and advice were therefore invaluable.

The party landed in Washington at 9.30 (American time) the next morning after a journey which established a new record for the flight. Dismissing larger problems from his mind for the time being, Attlee passed the flight agreeably in talk about cricket (one of his permanent passions), cross-examining members of his personal staff on *Wisden* ('Always good reading for settling the mind') and musing on the similarities between picking a properly balanced cricket team and choosing a Cabinet.

Arrived in Washington, he was conveyed through the streets of the city with a motor-cycle escort with sirens going (an experience he found odd but entertaining, while the American security people found equally odd his informal relationships with the two unobtrusive plain-clothes detectives from Scotland Yard who accompanied him and whom he treated as old friends) to the White House, where he was to stay.

The atmosphere in Washington was tense and excited. On the one hand, American public opinion, and more especially a large part of American scientific and political opinion centred in the capital, was suffering from feelings of guilt and revulsion because their nation had been the first in the world to drop an atom bomb. These feelings grew with each fresh evidence of what might be the genetic and other consequences of atomic warfare. On the other hand, fear of what might happen if the secrets of the bomb fell into the hands of other countries, particularly of Russia, brought with it a demand for tighter and tighter security measures which Truman could not ignore, especially as at that moment a tough battle was being fought in Congress between those who wanted to put the future development of atomic energy under civilian control and those who wanted it to be left firmly in military hands.

In these circumstances Truman had already found it necessary to declare at a press conference that, although the basic scientific knowledge behind the harnessing of atomic energy should be in the possession of scientists all over the world and he was in favour of full exchange of information at that level, the United States had no intention of sharing the actual technical know-how of the bomb, or even how to use atomic energy for industrial purposes, with anyone.

Attlee himself was anxious above all to force upon the conscience of the world and upon its Governments the realisation that the atom bomb had introduced an entirely new element into world affairs and that in these circumstances the infant United Nations assumed a far greater importance even than that foreseen for it at San Francisco. Potsdam had left him under no illusions as to the difficulty of getting Soviet co-operation, or as to the dangerous extent of Stalin's ambitions, and he was as much opposed as Truman to passing on the secret to the Soviet at this stage. But although he did not doubt that in due course Russia could find means to catch up, he hoped the shock of Hiroshima and Nagasaki and the obvious likelihood of still more destructive weapons might persuade Stalin that international co-operation was the best policy. Therefore, although he believed complete international control of atomic weapons could only be reached by stages and must depend on the development of confidence between nations, he thought it politically and morally imperative for the United States, Britain and Canada to demonstrate that they had no wish to hold on to their monopoly but would pass control to the United Nations just as soon as the development of international confidence permitted.

Meanwhile he wanted to make it plain to President Truman that Britain's contribution to the development of atomic energy left no question in his mind that whatever security measures the United States felt impelled to take ought not to be allowed to stand in the way of the continued exchange of information between the United States, Canada and Britain.

It soon emerged from the talks that, although there were differences on detail between them, Truman, Attlee and Mackenzie King shared the same general approach. Four days later a joint communiqué was issued proposing the setting up of a United Nations Commission on Atomic Energy and embodying most of the principles Attlee had declared to be important, although unfortunately the hopes thus engendered were soon to be vitiated by the developing hostility between Russia and the West.

What appeared to be agreement on the second point was also reached more easily than Attlee and the rest of the British delegation had anticipated. A memorandum covering future relations between the United States, Britain and Canada in the development of atomic energy was drawn up and signed. It stated:

1) We desire that there should be full and effective co-operation in the field of atomic energy between the United States, the United Kingdom and Canada.

2) We agree that the Combined Policy Committee and the Combined Development Trust should be continued in a suitable form.

3) We request the Combined Policy Committee to consider and recommend to us appropriate arrangements for this purpose.

Although this memorandum was in general terms, the talks that it led up to appeared to offer adequate assurances that the U.S. ban on information about atomic know-how would not apply to Britain and Canada. After a speech before Congress, Attlee therefore left well content for Ottawa, where he and the Canadian Prime Minister had talks on other matters and where he addressed both Houses of Parliament. He had not however been long back in Britain when the development of American opinion made these hopes illusory. Within a matter of months he found the United States persistently refusing to divulge information to which he believed Britain and Canada to be properly entitled. He reacted sharply.

To understand why, it is necessary to turn back to the war-time arrangements.

Research into the possibility of releasing energy by atomic fusion had been begun in Britain shortly before the war in Oxford, Cambridge, Imperial College, Liverpool and Birmingham. After the start of the war this work was co-ordinated under the Ministry of Aircraft Production by a committee headed by

Sir George Thomson and information was passed to America, whose scientists were engaged on a similar project – as indeed were German scientists also. By 1941 British research had made so much progress that there appeared solid grounds for the hope that it would prove possible to produce an atomic bomb in time to be of use in the war and, with the agreement of the Chiefs of Staff Committee, the project was given top priority. Sir John Anderson, Lord President of the Council in the War Coalition, was made the Cabinet Minister responsible.

There is little doubt that at this stage British scientists were ahead of American. The drain on scientific man-power and resources was, however, immense, and when President Roosevelt proposed in October of this year that the efforts of the two countries should be co-ordinated and jointly conducted the British Cabinet at once agreed and a number of the British scientists most directly concerned were sent to the United States.

In June 1942 this co-ordination was further advanced when at the Washington Conference of that date Churchill produced evidence of British progress which convinced Roosevelt that, although American scientists were less hopeful than British of getting practical results in time to be of use in the war, the immense expense of building a large-scale research station ought to be undertaken. Had Roosevelt not agreed on this the Cabinet intended to embark on a British project. In view of Britain's vulnerability from air raids and the difficulty of concealing from enemy reconnaissance planes work on the enormous plants required, it was proposed to site these in Canada, which was already vitally concerned because of her sources of uranium and the work of her own scientists.

However, American willingness to undertake the work made a British-Canadian project unnecessary. Instead it was agreed that Britain, Canada and the United States should pool information and know-how and share the results between them as part of the common war effort. The rest of the British team was therefore sent to America, where work at once began on the erection of giant installations in Tennessee and the State of Washington. Thereafter the main expenditure of money and materials was an American responsibility. The British contribution in brain-power and scientific experience continued, however, to be vital.

Despite this, co-operation did not always prove easy. By May 1943, when Churchill paid his third visit to Washington, Sir John Anderson had been compelled to report a growing American reluctance to exchange information and the Prime Minister therefore again raised the matter with the President. Following their talk he was able to telegraph back to Attlee for communication to the Cabinet the satisfactory news that the President had ruled that exchange of information on 'Tube Alloys' (the code name for the atomic experiments) should be resumed and the enterprise be considered a joint one. This ruling was only given in face of strong objections from many of Roosevelt's military and security advisers who were determined to keep the know-how exclusively American if they could. In deciding against them the President held that as an atomic weapon might be developed in time to be used in the war, information regarding it must fall within the general Anglo-American war-time agreement covering the interchange of research and invention secrets.

They capitulated reluctantly and by the time of the first Quebec Conference in August 1943 a further clarification of the partnership had become essential.

This was only one of a number of issues at Quebec on which there was considerable Anglo-American disagreement. Others included Far Eastern strategy and Britain's part in the war against Japan, where Churchill wanted a larger share than the American Service chiefs were ready to give, the South-East Asia Command, for which he got their acceptance of Mountbatten, the distribution of forces between Overlord (the attack on the Continent across the Channel) and the Mediterranean operations, and the recognition of the French Committee of National Liberation, to which the Americans were at first opposed. Britain had to give way on a number of points – it was at this Conference that the Prime Minister withdrew the British claim to the command of Overlord, provisionally promised to Sir Alan Brooke, and accepted instead an American Commander. At the end of the Conference Churchill telegraphed Attlee that everything had gone off well and settlement been finally reached on 'a number of intractable problems'. Among these he listed 'Tube Alloys'. In fact, however, in order to secure agreement on other matters the British negotiators felt it unwise to press too hard on 'Tube Alloys', and although an agreement covering both military and industrial uses of atomic energy was arrived at, it turned out to be capable of several interpretations.

On this Attlee comments: 'It was really rather a loose agreement. Practically Winston said to the Americans, "You can have all the peaceful developments." I think we could have claimed more. We had given a great deal through our experts. We contributed a great deal in fundamental research, although, because of a sensible division of effort, we left the actual development, the know-how, to them. We were fully taken up with other things. But I don't think there could be any doubt of the value of our contribution. Of course at the time of Quebec atomic energy was still only in the advanced research stage. As a practical proposition it was hardly in being, certainly not on the industrial side. We might have had to wait for many years for it. And no doubt it seemed a nice gesture not to bother about industrial use, or even to insist on too much specific exchange on the military side. We were allies and friends. It didn't seem necessary to tie everything up.'

The Quebec Agreement, although not as precise as it might have been in view of the American attitude subsequently, did however set up a Combined Policy Committee with three American and three British and Canadian members. This Committee was given a number of principles to guide it. These were:

'There shall be complete interchange of information and ideas on all sections of the project between members of the Policy Committee and their immediate advisers.

'In the field of scientific research and development there shall be full and effective interchange of information and ideas between those in the two countries engaged in the same sections of the field.

'In the field of design, construction and operation of large-scale plants interchange of information and ideas shall be regulated by such *ad hoc* arrangements as may, in each section of the field, appear to be necessary and desirable if the project is to be brought to function at the earliest moment. Such *ad hoc* arrangements shall be subject to the approval of the Policy Committee.'

By the time Attlee went to Washington in November 1945 it was already clear that the American interpretation of this was very different from that of the British and that under the pressures of Congressional opinion the American members of the Policy Committee were unready to pass over information to which the British thought they had every right. This unwillingness extended not only to the bomb but to the development of plants for the peaceful use of atomic energy.

However, Attlee found Truman sympathetic to the British arguments and when he left Washington both he and Mackenzie King thought that the memorandum the three of them had signed had removed all difficulties in the way of peace-time co-operation. They were soon disabused. Although Truman personally might be sympathetic, the attitude of most members of Congress was very different. They did not want to share anything.

As the McMahon Bill gathered way, Attlee became increasingly apprehensive. Part of the price paid by the Administration for keeping atomic energy under civilian instead of military control, for which the U.S. military machine and its friends in Congress were pressing, was that the Bill was drafted to rule out any exchange of information on atomic know-how, even with those who had contributed hardly less than the United States itself to make the development of atomic energy possible. This seemed to Attlee a breach of faith. Moreover in view of Britain's need of new sources of industrial power he was, on the most practical grounds, anxious to get to work as soon as possible on the development of atomic energy for peaceful purposes.

He therefore informed the U.S. Ambassador in London, Mr Harriman, that if the McMahon Bill was passed Britain would be forced to build her own plants for atomic energy production for both military and civil purposes. At the same time he instructed Lord Halifax in Washington to request detailed information on the construction and operation of atomic energy plants in the United States at the next meeting of the Combined Policy Committee in order that Britain should have the necessary data to begin this work. The request was put at a meeting on 15 April. It met with a blank refusal from the American members.

Attlee reacted forcibly and immediately. As soon as he received Halifax's report he sent a strong personal message to the President:

'Prime Minister to President Truman. 16.4.46

'Lord Halifax has reported to me what happened at the meeting of the Atomic Energy Combined Policy Committee on 15th April and Mr Byrnes has no doubt made a report to you.

'I am gravely disturbed at the turn which the Combined Policy Committee's discussions have taken over the implementation of the second and third paragraphs of the short document which you, Mr Mackenzie King and I signed on 16th November last. I feel that unless you and we and the Canadian Government can reach a satisfactory working basis of co-operation, at least to cover the period until we see the outcome of the discussions in the United Nations Commission on Atomic Energy, we in this country shall be placed in a position which, I am sure you will agree, is inconsistent with that document.

'As you know, the document stated that it was our desire that there should be "full and effective co-operation in the field of atomic energy between the United States, the United Kingdom and Canada"; and it seems to me that this cannot mean less than full interchange of information and a fair division of the material.

Moreover, the interchange of information was implicit in the Washington Declaration, paragraph 4 of which recognised as a matter of principle that our three countries possessed the knowledge required for the use of atomic energy, and paragraph 6 of which stated our willingness, subject to suitable safeguards, to share with other States information about the practical industrial applications. The Declaration contained nothing about the sharing of information among ourselves and the clear indication is that this was already provided for. The war-time arrangements under which the major share of the development work and the construction and operation of full-scale plants were carried out in the United States have naturally meant that technological and engineering information has accumulated in your hands, and if there is to be full and effective co-operation between us it seems essential that this information should be shared. I would therefore urge most strongly that the Combined Policy Committee should make a further attempt to work out a satisfactory basis of co-operation. In the last resort a solution might be that the heads of the three Governments should each issue instructions for the interchange of information, including, in particular, the technical information which each of us requires for the implementation of immediate programmes.'

He also sent a personal telegram to Mackenzie King informing him of what he had done and asking for his support:

'Prime Minister to Mr Mackenzie King. 16.4.46

'Pearson will have told you what happened at the meeting of the Atomic Energy Combined Policy Committee on 15th April. I am very gravely disturbed at the turn which the discussions took for I feel that if we are to make any progress at all we must agree on a working basis of co-operation between our three Governments, at least to carry us over the period until we know the outcome of the work of the United Nations Atomic Energy Commission. I have therefore sent the immediately following telegram to President Truman urging that the Combined Policy Committee should make a further attempt to work out a satisfactory basis of co-operation and suggesting that, as a last resort, the matter should be dealt with by the heads of the three Governments each issuing instructions for the exchange of technical information. I am sure that you will appreciate how important it is that the deadlock which seems to have developed in the Combined Policy Committee should be broken and I hope that I may count on your support in this matter.'

Truman's reply was received four days later. It failed to meet satisfactorily any of Attlee's points. Instead, after declaring that under the war-time Quebec Agreement the United States was clearly 'not obligated to furnish to the United Kingdom in the post-war period the designs and assistance in construction and operation of plants necessary to the building of a plant', President Truman went on to argue that the reference to 'full and effective co-operation' in the memorandum signed by Attlee, Mackenzie King and himself was 'very general', and that he could not therefore agree that it altered the Quebec Agreement or made it obligatory on the United States to furnish engineering and operating assistance in the construction of another atomic energy plant. In conclusion he argued that in any event the building of such a plant would be 'unwise from the standpoint of the United Kingdom as well as the United States,' and that if it were said that on the morning after their joint declaration on the need for international control they had entered into a new agreement to enable the United Kingdom to construct another atomic energy plant it would have a bad effect at the United Nations.

To this Attlee replied at length in a telegram tracing the whole history of Anglo-American co-operation in atomic development and pointing out that the American attitude was utterly inconsistent with this:

'Prime Minister to President Truman. 6.6.46

'Your telegram of the 20th April about the exchange of information on atomic energy.

'I have held back my reply until I had been able to discuss the matter with Halifax and with Mackenzie King.

'I should like first to go back a little over past history. In the early years of the war, in 1940 and 1941, our scientists were amongst the first to become convinced of the enormous military possibilities of the atomic energy project, and it will not, I think, be denied that both then and later, if we had been willing to face the diversion of industrial effort that would have been needed, we had the resources and the scientific and technical skill that would have enabled us to embark on the development of the project in this country. But to do that we should have had to reduce our efforts in other directions in which we were already heavily engaged, both in comparatively new but highly important fields of development such as radar and jet propulsion, and in the more established forms of war production. To do so at that time would not have been opportune, particularly so long as the threat of invasion lasted and while our principal centres of production were subject to air attack. Nevertheless, if we had continued to stand alone, I do not believe that we could have afforded to neglect so revolutionary a development and to gamble on the chance that the war would end without our enemies succeeding in developing it. At whatever cost we should have been bound to make the attempt to develop it in this country. Whether or not we should have succeeded before the war ended, we should certainly have gained much knowledge and experience.

'Fortunately, however, it was not necessary to make the choice. President Roosevelt had become interested in the idea of an atomic weapon and had decided to engage upon it all the vast resources of the United States. In October 1941 he wrote to Mr Churchill and proposed that any extended efforts in this field should be co-ordinated or even jointly conducted. It was thus possible for us to decide that we would concentrate on assisting to the best of our ability the developing of the enterprise in the United States. It is not for me to try to assess what that assistance was worth, but we gave it in the confident belief that the experience and knowledge gained in America would be made freely available to us, just as we made freely available to you the results of research in other fields such as radar and jet propulsion, on which, as a result of this decision, we were able to concentrate. It was part of that wise division of effort and pooling of resources which was made possible by the system of reciprocal aid which, without attempting to compare and measure the aggregate contribution on each side, enabled both countries to concentrate their efforts on those fields where they seemed likely to be most productive. I must repeat that, but for that system, we should have been forced to adopt a different distribution of our resources in this country, which would not have been so advantageous to the common interest.

'As I said, we entered on these arrangements in a spirit of partnership and in the belief that both countries would pool the experience which they gained. It was, in fact, later expressly provided in the Quebec Agreement that there should be complete interchange of ideas and information on all sections of the project between members of the Policy Committee and their immediate technical advisers, and, at the lower level, interchange of information in the field of design and construction of large-scale plants was not ruled out but was made subject to *ad hoc* arrangements to be approved by the Combined Policy Committee. At the same time it was left to the President of the United States to specify the terms on which any post-war advantages of an industrial or a commercial character should be dealt with as between the United States and Great Britain.

'In the latter days of the war, we considered more than once whether, under the existing arrangements, we were making the best use of our resources and whether the time had not come when we ought to undertake a policy of more active development in this country if we were not to fall too far behind in a field of development in which we had, but a short time before, been in the forefront. But, on each occasion, after full deliberation, we came back to the principle of the Quebec Agreement – that the earliest possible realisation of the project must come first and before any separate national advantage, and that, while our scientists could still contribute anything to the work in the United States, they should not be withdrawn. We felt that we could rely on the provisions of the Agreement to ensure that we should not suffer, that we should be given full access at the highest level to the knowledge of all sections of the project, and that the dissemination of such information to lower levels would be limited only by considerations of security.

'This situation continued until the goal had been reached and the first bomb dropped. At that point, we considered, we might reasonably prepare to undertake a more active programme of development in this country and might expect to be able to make use of the experience which had been gained up to that point in the joint enterprise.

'Almost immediately the war came to an end, and we were told that until new arrangements could be concluded the supply of information must be stopped. When I visited Washington, therefore, in November, it was an important part of my purpose to secure that, as President Roosevelt had promised Mr Churchill at Hyde Park in September 1944, the co-operation which had existed during the war should be continued and that it should be full and effective. I was very much reassured, therefore, when you agreed that this should be so and that the Combined Policy Committee should be asked to recommend arrangements to that end. It seemed a natural and a logical continuation of the previous agreement that the arrangements for peace-time collaboration would cover at least the same ground as before and would take account of the fact that this country was now free to devote a substantial industrial effort to the atomic energy project. The matter was discussed, in the first instance, at a conference held in Judge Patterson's room at the War Department and afterwards in greater detail by Sir John Anderson with General Groves and Mr George Harrison, and together they drew up the memorandum to which you refer. I can find no support in the paragraph of that document which you quote for the view that there was no obligation to exchange information about the construction of large-scale plants. It is indeed clearly laid down that, while the principle was not in doubt, the best means of giving effect to it should be considered further by the Combined Policy Committee.

'Such discussions did, in fact, take place and lasted many weeks. Finally a unanimous report was submitted to the Combined Policy Committee by a sub-committee on which your Government was represented by General Groves. The draft agreement which the sub-committee drew up provided that there was to be full and effective co-operation in the exchange of information required for the development programmes of the two countries. We made it clear in the discussions that our own programme would include the construction of large-scale plants in this country.

'When the sub-committee's report was considered by the Combined Policy Committee, it came as a surprise to us to find that your Government was not prepared to enter into any agreement, nor to proceed on the basis of the agreements previously reached between us, nor yet to agree that co-operation should, in fact, continue by administrative action. The clause of our Agreement, signed in November, by which the Combined Policy Committee was to recommend the arrangements required for continued co-operation has thus remained a dead letter.

'I cannot agree with the argument that to continue such co-operation would be inconsistent with the public declaration on the control of atomic energy which you and Mackenzie King and I issued in November. That our three Governments stand in a special relationship to one another in this field is a matter of record and was, in fact, the reason why we took the initiative in issuing the declaration. It is surely not inconsistent with its purpose that the co-operation begun during the war should continue during the peace unless and until it can be replaced by a wider system. And until recently, at any rate, I think it is fair to say that it was generally assumed in both our countries that this co-operation was continuing. And, indeed, in one important part of the field it is: I am referring to our joint control of raw materials. We have not thought it necessary to abandon that – in my opinion, quite rightly. Why then should we abandon all further pooling of information?

'You evidently feel that it would be inconsistent with the declaration issued at Washington that another atomic energy plant should be constructed and that the United States should assist in its construction. The purpose of the Washington Declaration was to promote the development of atomic energy for peaceful ends and to ensure that it should not be used as a means of destruction. It was certainly not intended to stifle all further development in other countries, any more than it was suggested that the development which has already taken place in the United States should be abandoned. We have made no secret of the fact that we intend to produce fissile material, though naturally the use which we shall make of it will be much affected by the deliberations of the Atomic Energy Commission.

'In the meantime, I can see nothing in the Washington Declaration, or in the Assembly Resolution, which requires us to dissolve our partnership, either in the exchange of information or in the control of raw materials, until it can be merged in a wider partnership. I should be sorry to think that you did not agree with this view.

'I have set out the position fully and frankly as I am sure you would have wished me to do. I realise that an additional complication may arise from the fact that the McMahon Bill containing stringent provisions about the disclosure of information has within the last few days been passed by the Senate.

'I would nevertheless most strongly urge that for the reasons I have given our continuing co-operation over raw materials shall be balanced by an exchange of information which will give us, with all proper precautions in regard to security, that full information to which we believe that we are entitled, both by the documents and by the history of our common efforts in the past.'

To this long and forceful exposition Truman made no reply. He has since declared in his memoirs that he took the view that it had become impossible for him to make any statement of policy to Britain until Congress acted, especially as it was already clear that, whatever the outcome of the Congress debates, co-operation with Britain in the atomic field would be seriously hampered and restricted in the future.

When the McMahon Bill was finally passed and received the Presidential signature in August all hope of co-operation on production had to be abandoned. Britain at once, therefore, began her own development programme – although without any of the information and assistance she had had a right to expect from America.

Attlee: I don't blame Truman. He showed himself very aware of the need for co-operation in our Washington talks and we did in fact fix up what looked like a pretty good agreement. The trouble was they couldn't get it through the Senate. The Senate wanted to have everything for America. Once Congress proceeded to pass the McMahon Bill we had to go ahead on our own. And although we were involved in a very much bigger expenditure than if we'd had the help and information due to us from America, we actually got ahead of them.

Williams: In what way?

Attlee: In technical work generally at that time. A considerable achievement by our scientists.

Williams: Do you feel the Fuchs case set back co-operation with America even more?

Attlee: To a certain extent, although a short time afterwards they were gunning for Oppenheimer and their own people instead. But I don't think you can put their attitude down to Fuchs. They were extremely cagey long before that.

Williams: A good deal of argument was based on development for industrial purposes, which wasn't properly considered at Quebec. But you did also decide to manufacture a British bomb. Why?

Attlee: It had become essential. We had to hold up our position *vis-à-vis* the Americans. We couldn't allow ourselves to be wholly in their hands, and their position wasn't awfully clear always.

Williams: In what way?

Attlee: Well, at that time we had to bear in mind that there was always the possibility of their withdrawing and becoming isolationist once again. The manufacture of a British atom bomb was therefore at that stage essential to our defence.

You must remember this was all prior to NATO. NATO has altered things. But at that time although we were doing our best to make the Americans understand the realities of the European situation – the world situation – we couldn't be sure we'd succeed. In the end we did. But we couldn't take risks with British security in the meantime. We had worked from the start for international control of the bomb. We wanted it completely under the United Nations. That was the best way. But it was obviously going to take a long time. Meanwhile we had to face the world as it was. We had to look to our defence – and to our industrial future. We could not agree that only America should have atomic energy.

9

Loan from the U.S.

The extent to which Britain had been ready to throw her resources of men, knowledge and material into the joint war effort, often without requiring any safeguards for her own post-war interests, since to require such safeguards seemed to the War Cabinet altogether inappropriate in the circumstances of total war, brought problems in other fields besides those of atomic energy.

One such problem, fortunately happily and quickly solved, came early, when Attlee found that the return of British servicemen from overseas was being delayed by American insistence on getting 'American boys' home first. The dispute came to a head over the use of shipping, and particularly over the disposal of the *Queen Elizabeth*, the *Queen Mary* and the *Aquitania*. These great ships had been converted into troop transports and made available for American troops as soon as the United States came into the war. They had brought many thousands of American servicemen safely across the seas and were put completely at American disposal after victory in Europe for the specific purpose of transferring American troops as rapidly as possible from Europe to the Far East.

Early in November 1945, however, Attlee was informed that, despite the fact that the Japanese war was over, not only were the American Chiefs of Staff insisting on their right to hold on to the ships for the transport of American troops back home quickly but they had refused to make any equivalent American-controlled transport available for British servicemen. They insisted that the demobilisation of their own troops came first, although great numbers of British soldiers had been overseas far longer than had any of the Americans.

This seemed to Attlee intolerable. He at once sent a strongly worded telegram of protest to President Truman:

'Prime Minister to President Truman. 3.10.45

'The British Cabinet have recently given the most urgent and earnest consideration to the need to speed up the return of British servicemen from overseas in the period before Christmas of this year. Many of these men have been on active service and away from their homes for five or more years, and the demand by the people of this country for their early return now that hostilities are over has become loud and insistent.

'Even after eliminating or deferring movements which would normally command a high priority, we cannot with our present allocation of personnel shipping achieve the minimum repatriation programme at which we have hitherto aimed, let alone achieve any acceleration.

'In these circumstances, I have no alternative but to remind you that the arrangement to loan you the two *Queens* and the *Aquitania* until the end of 1945 was conditioned solely by the urgency of redeploying American forces for the war against Japan. With the unexpectedly early termination of the Japanese war, these conditions have for some time now ceased to exist.

'It is our desire that the two *Queens* and *Aquitania* should continue in your service for a period, and we fully realise the desire on the part of the United States to welcome back their soldiers and airmen who have been fighting in Europe. Our own urgent necessities, however, have compelled us to request that you should loan us in return for the *Queens* and *Aquitania* an equivalent personnel lift in American-controlled troopships with a view to their being used on the main British trooping routes, i.e. from India and Australia to the United Kingdom. It will be understood that help on the North Atlantic route would not solve our problem.

'Our Combined Chiefs of Staff have discussed this question

between them but have failed to reach agreement. Your Chiefs of Staff "Regret that the necessity to return U.S. forces from Europe as expeditiously as possible requires all lifts scheduled under present agreements to December 1945," and that therefore they are unable to provide assistance in U.S.-controlled troop shipping before the end of 1945. Your Chiefs of Staff go on to say that "Action on certain of the captured German passenger ships will, in part, fulfil the need for additional troop lift as expressed by the British Chiefs of Staff." This latter statement may be true for some time in early 1946, but the captured German passenger ships will not alleviate the position in the all-important period before the end of this year.

'Your Chiefs of Staff seem to think that this question, which is absolutely vital to us, can await discussion at an overall personnel shipping review to be held some time this month, the results of which could not possibly take effect till very nearly the end of the year.

'I shall speak with the utmost frankness. While so many of our troops overseas are awaiting repatriation after nearly six years of war and of separation from their families, I cannot continue to justify to the British public the use of our three biggest ships in the American service. I am reluctant to suggest the return of the *Queens* and *Aquitania*. I must, however, ask you most earnestly, Mr President, to provide us in the immediate future with an equivalent lift for these three ships.'

This telegram brought an immediate response. Truman was under the heaviest pressure from his own public opinion to bring American troops home in time for Christmas. Letters and telegrams were pouring into the White House from parents and from innumerable organisations up and down the country, every Congressman was being bombarded with appeals from individual voters and powerful organisations in their constituencies, most of which they passed on to the White House. Despite all this, Truman at once agreed that Attlee was manifestly right and countermanded the orders of his generals. His telegraphed reply to Attlee was unequivocal: 'I have directed the Joint Chiefs of Staff to return to you the two *Queens* and the *Aquitania* or to provide equivalent personnel lift.'

Although this eased the position it could not resolve one of the most difficult aspects of the man-power problem. This was how to combine the urgent need on both moral and material grounds to press forward with demobilisation at the greatest possible speed with the requirement to maintain British forces in Europe at the strength the international situation demanded, particularly in view of the rapid withdrawal of American troops and the consequent development of a power vacuum in Europe which, in Stalin's post-war mood, the Soviet might quickly seek to turn to her own advantage.

In the debate on the Address immediately on his return from Potsdam, Attlee had warned the House that the call-up of young men must continue and that for the time being there was no option but to retain the age limit at thirty. But the demands of industry for man-power were urgent. In a broadcast early in September Attlee himself had put the number of men needed to restore employment in civilian and export industries to the pre-war level as at least five million above the figure to which it had fallen by the end of the war. This, however, was only part of the problem. It was essential to expand the export trade greatly beyond pre-war level. In addition, workers were urgently needed to carry out the housing and reconstruction programme and to catch up on the immense arrears of production in all directions that had accumulated during the war. In the Cabinet the Ministers directly concerned were pressing for more men for the building and development programme, while at the same time industries were pleading that they should not be denuded by the continued peace-time operation of the call-up of workers engaged in essential work in production and agriculture.

And naturally enough both in Parliament and among the trade unions there were constant demands for a speed-up of the demobilisation plans drawn up by Bevin as Minister of Labour while the War Cabinet was still in existence, and which had then been generally approved. News of the extent of American demobilisation – subsequently sadly described by President Truman as 'frenzied' – when compared with the British, increased the spate of criticism, not only from the Opposition but from the Government's own supporters.

This criticism took an unexpectedly sharp turn at the Annual Conference of the T.U.C. in September. Here the General Secretary of the Municipal and General Workers' Union, second only to Bevin's Transport Workers in size, moved a resolution demanding reconsideration of the demobilisation plans. With considerable force he pointed out that by June of the following year Britain would have demobilised only 1,400,000 men and women while the United States would have released 8,200,000 in the same period. It was also, he went on to argue, completely wrong that while the United States should be keeping only two and a quarter million men under arms Britain should be keeping three and a half million. And he urged, as many M.P.s were doing, that where those nearer home could be released more quickly than those in the Far East, considerations of equality of treatment as laid down in Bevin's original plan ought not to be allowed to stand in the way of their early release. The resolution was carried with acclamation.

In the middle of this storm, to which Winston Churchill added further fire in a wide-ranging vote of censure, Attlee remained firm in the belief that, although the rate of demobilisation could be accelerated as a result of the Japanese surrender, they must adhere to the general principles of Bevin's scheme. He was certain that the moral case for equity between those serving in distant theatres of war and those nearer home must be defended. The men in Burma and elsewhere could not, and must not, be put at the end of the queue. Moreover he was determined that in the interests of world security British armed forces must not be allowed to run below the level imperative for European stability, until such time as America could be brought to realise the dangers inherent in too large and too rapid withdrawal from Europe.

As he returned from his Washington talks on atomic energy

the man-power crisis took a new turn and one that threatened serious disunity within the Cabinet itself. Awaiting him there was a personal letter from Ernest Bevin.

Bevin had taken on the chairmanship of the Manpower Committee in addition to his work as Foreign Secretary. He now wrote to say that the constant pressures of a number of Ministers were becoming impossible and hinted at resignation from the Government unless the policy to which he regarded himself as morally bound by earlier pledges was given renewed backing by Attlee.

'Foreign Office, S.W.1. 15th November 1945

'Dear Clem, I am very concerned about the attitude that is being adopted at the Manpower Committee by certain Ministers who are seeking to force us to break our undertaking to the troops that we would call up men between the ages of 18 and 30 in order to allow the other men who have been in the war so long to be demobilised. I am being pressed to blanket these men in agriculture, in the provision of housing equipment, and in a number of other categories. The result will be that the forces cannot be maintained, as you require, without retaining the men who have been through the war. This question has now become very acute and I had to make it quite clear last night that if there is any violation of the pledge which both you and I, as well as other Ministers, gave during the election, and on the strength of which the soldiers have voted for us, then I could not accept any responsibility. Indeed, I should have great difficulty in being associated with an administration that would go back on its word to these men who have done so much for us. But the pressure is very heavy. I said that the matter would have to go to the Cabinet but I desire to make my own position quite clear. I gave that undertaking with the approval of everybody. When I called men up during those five terrible years I made the promise to them solemnly. I placed it on records which were played over to the troops in all the theatres of war. There were, I believe, nineteen officials of the Ministry of Labour who were sent out to explain the scheme and this was one of the solemn pledges they were told to make, so that I now feel very disturbed at the attitude adopted and the demands that are being made.

'As to manpower generally, I am also disturbed at the approach to it. The fact of the matter is that, while we have to maintain our forces as at present and until the international situation clears, we are short of men. And the curious thing is that we have approximately the same shortage now as we had all through the war years. You will remember that during that period, when I had to face a deficit of about a million to one and a half million people all the time and yet manipulate manpower to keep the whole of the munitions factories and the forces going, I managed it by having before me the actual industrial requirements as set forth in contracts and I was able to put before the country from time to time, and before the trade unions, where the most urgent need existed. I cannot see that being done at all now on the production side. The assumption is that all that the Minister of Labour has to do now is to find the men, and the departments then rather take the view that it is for them to manipulate them afterwards. But when the Minister of Labour is so short of men, surely he must have some order of priority.

'Neither am I happy about the housing equipment problem. I cannot believe that so many highly skilled men are necessary. If the Minister of Health has given the orders and the Minister of Supply in turn acts with vigour, as was necessary during the war, then I believe this necessary production can be carried out with less people. It may involve alternative methods but, in any case, the houses are not up yet and there is time to move in this equipment business ready for output as the houses go up.

'Therefore, with the very inadequate facts before me as chairman of the Manpower Committee I cannot really do the job. I do not know what to determine when claims are made as between one industry and another, and although the Minister of Labour is going to have a shot at producing a manpower budget, I cannot see how he can work it out. I know you take a very keen interest in this difficulty and I do not feel competent under the present arrangement to do the job.

'There is one other matter. The manufacturers of the country are assuming that they are going to be spoonfed with a flow of labour, as they were during the war and as they got accustomed to before the war with unemployment. But that is not going to happen. We shall never get the industries of this country going in order to maintain our home and export trade unless the employers and managements generally are frankly told that they have got to give us the output under the present conditions and with a good deal of improvisation. And I think the unions must be told this as well.

'I look with grave concern at the present position. I have only sent you this letter so that you and I may discuss it when you return before dealing with the matter in the Cabinet. I thought you ought to know my anxieties in the matter. Yours very sincerely, Ernest Bevin.'

There was, on Attlee's part, no tendency to disagree with Bevin's analysis. He was as firm as Bevin that the pledges given to the Services must be kept and he came down heavily on his side.

It was against this grim post-war background of shortage of man-power, as well as of raw materials and industrial power and equipment, and of the constant necessity to allocate inadequate resources in the most effective way possible, that all his own economic thinking and that of his Cabinet had to be determined and that compelled them to continue many war-time controls and restrictions that he would have liked to end overnight. These difficulties were added to by an unexpected blow – the ending of Lend Lease.

The news came less than three weeks after Attlee's return from Potsdam. When the telegram announcing it reached him it seemed all the more incredible because at that very moment Mr W. Clayton, the U.S. Assistant Secretary of State, and M. E. G. Collado of the U.S. Treasury, who had been in London for a meeting of the Council of U.N.R.R.A., were, on the President's own instructions, taking part in informal discussions with the British Government on post-war economic arrangements. There had been a joint meeting between them and British finance and trade exports under Sir Stafford Cripps at the Board of Trade and this had been followed by further conversations with Treasury and other officials headed by Maynard Keynes, whom Hugh Dalton had asked to stay on as one of his principal advisers at the Treasury.

Neither of these two eminent Americans knew anything of what was coming. They had had no prior notice of the President's decision and had been able to pass on no warning to their British friends. Indeed the first Collado heard of it was in a Cambridge teashop at the end of a long day's sightseeing when a waitress casually switched on the wireless for the news bulletin. Clayton heard the news in a similar fashion at a friend's house in the country where he was staying for the week-end. Both immediately dashed up to London and telephoned to Washington from the American Embassy to try to discover what had gone wrong.

Lord Halifax, our Ambassador in Washington, was also in London for consultations. He also knew nothing. It was a bolt from a clear sky.

That the whole position of Lend Lease would have to be reconsidered following the capitulation of Japan had been known. But no one had expected it to be cut off in this sharp and drastic way. It happened as a result of a series of accidents.

President Truman had only recently arrived back in Washington after nearly a month at Potsdam and was pre-occupied with events following the dropping of the atomic bomb and the Japanese surrender when he was formally notified by Mr Crowley, Director of the Foreign Economic Administration, that since Lend Lease, the major part of which was going to Britain, had been introduced as a war-time measure the legal authority for its operation terminated with the end of hostilities. That this would be the situation was, of course, known to those concerned. In readiness for it both the State Department and the U.S.

Treasury had prepared memoranda setting out proposals to keep essential goods flowing to allies whose economies were out of balance because of the agreed policy on division of war effort.

Unfortunately neither of these reports had reached the President and they therefore formed no part of the background of his decision when Mr Crowley brought the legal position to his attention during a Cabinet meeting. Nor was he himself acquainted in any detail with the Lend Lease position, which had not come before him as Vice-President. Unfortunately, it also happened that Mr Dean Acheson, the new Secretary of State, who had been directly concerned with Lend Lease in his previous office of Assistant Secretary, had not formally taken up his new appointment when the matter was raised by Mr Crowley. He was not therefore at the Cabinet meeting but was taking a week's holiday in Canada in the interval between his two offices. Mr Clayton, his successor as Assistant Secretary of State, was, as already mentioned, in London, to which he had gone straight from the Potsdam Conference. To add to this chapter of accidents, there had also been a change at the Treasury, where Mr Vinson had succeeded Morgenthau as Secretary of the Treasury. Vinson was present at the Cabinet, but he was not fully briefed on the matter and although he argued in favour of some postponement was unable to do so effectively without the facts given in the Treasury memoranda.

The formal decision was thus taken without any of the careful consideration anticipated by those most concerned on the American side, and without any opportunity being given to the British Government to suggest alternative arrangements or, if these proved impossible, to prepare against the cutting off of supplies.

Attlee comments: 'It was a great shock. The tap was turned off at a moment's notice. All we had was what was in the pipe line and even that looked like being in jeopardy when the news first came. We had not had a chance to reorganise ourselves on a peace-time basis. The Americans, I suppose, didn't realise what it meant. It was done by Harry Truman on official advice. Apparently, from what we were told later, he didn't realise in the slightest bit what it involved. He thought it was an ordinary routine thing. If the facts had been fully put before him he might possibly have got Congress to carry on. But they went by the letter of the law. It made quite an impossible situation. That's why we had to go and ask for an American loan right away.'

Meanwhile the two American negotiators, Clayton and Collado, who had been angrily telephoning Washington, managed to secure some slight, although only slight, alleviation of the first shock. They got Washington to agree that payment for goods in the pipe line at least should be regarded as still open to negotiation.

With this news they called upon Bevin and Dalton. They were, however, able to hold out no hope that the decision to stop Lend Lease as a whole was capable of being altered. This decision had been published. It could not be reversed. Mr R. H. Brand, who had been Keynes's deputy in Washington during negotiations on Lend Lease arrangements to cover the period of war against Japan after victory in Europe (made abortive by the early Japanese surrender), and who was in a position to advise on the attitude of the Administration, was therefore asked to return to London at once.

When he arrived Keynes, Halifax and he were summoned by Attlee to a meeting of Ministers at 10 Downing Street at eleven o'clock that same night. It was a sombre meeting. As Attlee informed the House of Commons the following day, Lend Lease had been one of the major factors enabling Britain to mobilise her man-power for war to a degree unsurpassed by any other country and to undertake vast military expenditure over a wide area without having to produce exports to meet the cost and cover import of food and raw material. This system had been accepted by both countries as necessary to the most efficient and complete division of effort between them for a common purpose. Because this division had been the right one and had been carried to the furthest limit possible the sudden cessation of support was bound to have the gravest consequences.

As a result of the Washington decision Britain was, in fact, now faced with a gap between overseas expenditure and income of the order of at least £1,200,000,000 a year, for even after excluding all purchases of munitions our total overseas outgoings on the eve of the defeat of Japan were equivalent to expenditure at the rate of £2,000,000,000 a year, the bulk of it covered by Lend Lease. Without Lend Lease we had, to set against this, exports of only £350,000,000 a year, plus receipts, in large part temporary, of another £450,000,000 from various sources, such as reimbursement for war expenditure made by us on their behalf by Commonwealth countries, and payments from U.S. forces in Britain.

Mr Brand, straight from the Washington scene, was not hopeful. He told the meeting of Ministers that the American mood was now such that even if the Administration were prepared to give assistance it would be very difficult, perhaps impossible, to get Congress to agree. Keynes however had by now swung over to optimism. The more he had thought about it during the tense hours following the shock of the Washington announcement the more it seemed to him, he said, that Britain had an overwhelming case, for her economic difficulties were entirely due to her war effort, which had been as much in America's interests as her own.

Apart from her current balance of payments position she had in the course of that effort sold overseas investments to a total of £1,118,000,000 and incurred overseas debts (to some extent to neutrals, but in large measure to allies to provide them with the means to fight a war in which they were partners with her and with the United States) of another £3,355,000,000. Even when sterling balances outstanding when the war began were taken into account the net total of the external cost of the war shouldered by Britain was at least £4,000,000,000 and probably more. Keynes could not believe that the American statesmen and officials whom he had found so helpful and reasonable in his war-time discussions would, in the light of all these facts, be less so now or fail in their readiness to recommend that, both on grounds of equity and practical economic necessity, America should agree to share the burden.

He proposed that Britain should ask for £1,500,000,000 as a free gift or, failing that, an interest-free loan. This was, after all, small in comparison with the total of Britain's overseas expenditure for war purposes and seemed to him wholly reasonable. He could not believe that the Americans would not also regard it as so, if the full facts were presented to them. His optimism was infectious, for indeed the case was good. 'When I listen to Keynes,' said Bevin, 'I can hear the money jingling in my pocket.' But he added shrewdly, 'I'm not sure it's really there.'

The Cabinet decided that Keynes, Halifax and Brand should return to Washington and that President Truman should be asked to agree to full-scale consultations between them and American Ministers and officials on the whole economic and monetary position following the end of the war. Keynes was authorised to lay his cards completely on the table and to make available to the Americans every relevant detail regarding Britain's financial and economic position.

However, when they arrived the position was found to be very different from that anticipated by Keynes. The leading officials at the State Department and the Treasury were sympathetic. But American public opinion was pre-occupied with its own post-war problems and it did not want to be reminded that per head of population the British had made a much larger contribution to victory than the United States. Moreover it was suspicious of anything that seemed likely to bring too large or too permanent an entanglement in European affairs. And even in high places the post-war belief that America and Russia could get along together if Britain did not interfere was still strong. Warnings that the Soviet might exploit European weakness for her own purposes were taken as examples of ingrained British suspicion and 'colonialism'. The American people wanted to get on with their own affairs and return to 'normality' as soon as they could. The understanding of the world situation that two years later was to make possible the Marshall Plan was still a long way away.

Even those officials most aware of the strength of the British case had to warn Keynes that any question of a free gift or interest-free loan was out of the question and that even an interest-carrying loan of an amount such as he contemplated was likely to be possible only if Britain gave firm guarantees on freedom of trade and an early return to sterling convertibility. Moreover Keynes had to report back that the Americans had refused to take seriously his figures on the British balance of payments position and were convinced that the situation was much exaggerated. They challenged also the British figures of gold and dollar holdings. What it had been anticipated would be a sympathetic exploration of difficulties turned out to be a matter of hard bargaining spread over several months and leading at the end to a loan agreement that plunged the British Government into acute controversy at home.

The Government accepted the terms of loan agreement only with extreme reluctance, finding it had to believe that some of the conditions, particularly those concerning convertibility within a year which was later to cause much trouble, had become inevitable if any sort of a loan was to get through Congress.

So difficult indeed did Attlee and his principal colleagues find it to believe that this could be America's final word that he dispatched Sir Edward Bridges, Permanent Head of the Treasury and Secretary of the Cabinet, to Washington to check on Keynes's judgment.

Bridges fared no better than Keynes: indeed he found the American negotiators even more adamant against him because they considered his arrival a slight on Keynes and the other British negotiators with whom they had, after so much difficulty, hammered out agreement. He was forced to telegraph back that it was either these terms or none at all, and after another long meeting the Cabinet reluctantly accepted them. Attlee remains convinced that they had no alternative but to do so.

Attlee: I think we had to. We weren't in a position to bargain. We knew the convertibility clause was quite impossible and would create great difficulty later on and we told the Americans so. But they wouldn't see it and we were forced to accept the fact that without the convertibility clause there would be no loan.

We had to have the loan. Without it it would have been impossible to exist, certainly without hardships on a scale no one had a right to ask of the British people at the end of a long war. The Americans thought we'd overstated the case. We hadn't. Even while Lend Lease was working, the outlook was black and everyone in the war-time Coalition knew it. When the end of the war brought the end of Lend Lease it was made as black as it could possibly be. We'd used up all our resources. We'd allowed the Americans to have all kinds of export trades that we used to have. We'd emptied the till of our foreign investments even before the Americans came in. We'd had to sell out practically everything and now we had to switch over. We had to get on our feet. We had to get our exports going. When they cut off Lend Lease we were given a body blow.

Williams: The loan was linked with the attempt to get an international trade organisation going that would increase the flow of world trade and do away with tariffs. Why wasn't it more successful?

Attlee: Partly because there was an insurgent nationalism all over the world. Countries were determined to protect their own markets. And although they were all for free trade in theory the Americans themselves were not prepared to do much for it in practice; they're awfully keen on it for the rest of the world but not for themselves. They don't like letting other people into their markets. You can criticise the loan and the arrangements surrounding it – and we fought inch by inch throughout the negotiations – but the fact remains that we couldn't do without it. The critics could shout. We had to run things.

10

Defence against Famine

Although Britain's own problems were severe and were bound to compel the continuance of controls and restrictions that everyone had hoped to see quickly ended with the end of the war, Attlee dared not look at them in isolation. The war had left behind such devastation and disorganisation in Europe and over much of Asia that there was the gravest possible danger of widespread famine and the breakdown of ordered government unless quick relief was provided.

With eyes fully open to the possible political consequence at home he had to accept the fact that such help could only be given by asking the British people to accept heavy sacrifices in their own standards of living, some of them greater even than those required in the worst days of the war. He did not hesitate as to where his duty lay.

Attlee: It quite early became clear to me that the situation was enormously serious. In spite of the sacrifices it would mean asking of our own people at a time when they had every right to hope for better days, we dared not stand aside. Germany was down to her last potato almost. Many of the countries that had been occupied were facing imminent famine. And it wasn't only Europe. India was very badly off and could not be left to look to herself. The Burma rice on which they depended had been interrupted. We had to decide, as a deliberate act of policy, that Britain would have to go without in order to help. Our own food supplies, particularly of wheat and fats, were right down. We'd been carrying on during the war on the minimum of stocks.

About thirteen days of supplies was regarded as the danger limit, but towards the end we went down to five. But if we didn't help there was the certainty of famine and chaos in Europe. It would have been impossible for settled government to carry on. You would have Communist revolutions, with all that might follow, and large numbers of people would probably have died from starvation.

Williams: Did you realise how long a business it was going to be to get Europe back on its feet?

Attlee: Oh yes, we realised that. We knew what we were up against. We had to help quickly. And we had to get America to help.

By the beginning of 1946 the situation was menacing in the extreme. Over Europe as a whole, food production was twenty-five per cent below normal – for the world the figure was twelve per cent below pre-war. More than 125 million Europeans were down to a subsistence diet of 2,000 calories a day, a large number to no more than 1,000, compared with an average of 3,300 per day per person in the United States. Although there was a record wheat crop in North America and a near record production of foodstuffs generally, the severe drought in many other parts of the world on top of the dislocation of war seemed certain to bring the worst food crisis in modern history. In Europe and North Africa the wheat crop, which it had been estimated would be low, turned out to be worse than the most pessimistic forecasts.

In many parts of Asia the situation was no less critical. The rice crop, normally accounting for ninety-five per cent of total world production, was fifteen per cent below normal. This meant that in the first half of the year, when available world wheat supplies were likely to be nearly 7,000,000 tons below the amount the importing countries had already asked for, between 1,000,000 and 2,000,000 tons of wheat would also have to be diverted to India and the Far East to make good the rice shortage if large numbers of people at or near starvation level were not to be driven below it.

In this situation Attlee telegraphed to Truman asking for his personal interest in measures to meet the world-wide emergency.

'Prime Minister to President Truman. 3.1.46

'My colleagues and I have been considering carefully world wheat supplies in relation to the demands which are likely to arise in the immediate future, and the outlook appears to us to be of the utmost gravity. Ben Smith,[1] whom you know, is now on his way to Washington to discuss with members of your Administration the problems of world wheat supply and demand and also similar problems with regard to rice. May I invoke your personal interest, for without it and the full co-operation of your agricultural, transport and shipping experts, I am sure that we shall not solve these problems.

'2. The position as we see it is that in the first half of 1946 there will probably be a deficit of nearly 7 million tons between available supplies and the quantities that the different importing countries have asked for. Claims of course must be rigidly pruned to the greatest extent practicable, but after every reasonable economy the gap that remains will be formidable. In addition, large quantities of wheat may also be necessary to make good a shortage of rice now estimated at between 1 and 2 million tons.

'3. As I understand it, the crux of the wheat problem lies not so much in the actual quantity of wheat which exists in the producing countries as in its collection from farms, its transport to the ports and its shipment from there. It is our view that unless the maximum quantities that can be spared are exported from all producing countries, there is a grave danger of wide famine in Europe and in Asia during the next few months. I need not emphasise to you that the effects of this would spread far beyond the national boundaries of the countries concerned and would undoubtedly make infinitely more difficult the work to which we shall be setting our hand when the U.N.O. meets.

1. Sir Ben Smith, Minister of Food and formerly Minister for Supply in Washington during the latter part of the war.

'4. For these reasons, I have ventured to plead for your personal and active interest.'

Truman at once replied that he was instructing Cabinet officers to investigate the situation urgently in conjunction with the British experts and that Attlee could be sure of his continued personal concern.

As the Washington discussions got under way Attlee cabled Mr Chifley, the Prime Minister of Australia, whom he knew well, asking for Australian co-operation in increasing wheat exports.

'Personal for Mr Chifley from Mr Attlee. 15th Jan. 1946

'1. My colleagues and I are gravely concerned about the prospective world shortage of wheat. You know, I think, that Sir Ben Smith, the Minister of Food, has been in Washington recently to discuss the situation with the United States Administration and with the President.

'2. Very briefly, world import requirements exceed by at least 5½ million tons the amount of wheat which we can at present rely upon from the four main exporting countries during the period from 1st January to 30th June, 1946. In order to bridge the gap it will be necessary to make severe cuts in the amounts asked for by importing countries. Some of these demands could probably have been scaled down a little without causing undue hardship; but the drastic cuts that will be necessary to close this gap will cause real suffering in many countries. Our own requirements here will not be met in full, and we shall find it hard to make the economies needed.

'3. The consequences of famine either in Europe or in Asia during the next few months will be very grave. In Europe I am specially concerned about Germany. The ration there is already very low and substantial further cuts will bring starvation and unrest, which, apart altogether from humanitarian considerations, will increase our military commitments and retard Europe's economic recovery by reducing the export of essential supplies from Germany, particularly the coal which is so urgently needed. In Asia, I need hardly emphasise the political dangers of famine in India at the present time. In these circumstances it is obviously of vital importance to ensure that maximum quantities are exported from all producing countries.

'4. In the calculations that have just been made in Washington covering exports and imports during the six months to the end of June, Australia is being counted upon to export wheat and flour amounting in terms of wheat equivalent to a total of 1,100,000 tons. I believe this is based upon a recent estimate given to the Cereals Committee in Washington by Mr McCarthy. It would mean the export by Australia of an unusually high proportion of her supplies during this part of the year and the physical collection and movement of this quantity will, I know, present considerable difficulty under present conditions. But the world's need is so urgent that I am sure that the Australian Government will make a supreme effort to achieve this export figure. May I appcal to you to give this matter your personal attention and to let me know whether, as I earnestly hope, we may count upon Australia for this quantity?'

The Washington conversations brought encouraging evidence of American readiness to co-operate, but by the time Sir Ben Smith arrived back and reported it had become clear that the situation was likely to be even worse than had originally been anticipated.

Attlee at once telegraphed to President Truman informing him of the sacrifices he proposed to ask of the British people and requesting that the American people should accept comparable burdens.

'Prime Minister to President Truman. 4.2.46

'1. The Minister of Food has reported to me and the Cabinet the results of his recent discussions in Washington with you and your Secretary of Agriculture on the serious world shortage of wheat and rice. I am most grateful to you for the help which you gave in those discussions and for the directions which you have issued since.

'2. We recognise that heavy sacrifices must be made to help the less fortunate peoples of the world. We ourselves accept the reduction of nearly a quarter of a million tons in U.K. wheat imports for the first half of 1946, although the consequences for us will be very serious. We shall have to reduce our stocks far below the safety level, and run the risk of interference with internal distribution of flour and bread if there is any irregularity in the arrival of imports. We shall have to increase the extraction rate of flour from 80 per cent to 85 per cent and return to the darker bread which we accepted as a war-time necessity but hoped we had discarded with the end of hostilities. We shall also have to reduce our fat ration from 8 oz. to 7 oz. a week, which is lower than at any time during the war. This is a direct consequence of the wheat shortage, since as a result of drought and other disasters in Madras, Mysore, Bombay and Punjab, India fears a recurrence of famine worse than the Bengal famine of 1943 and is unable to rely on the imports of wheat and rice which she needs. Consequently she will have to use for food in India groundnuts which she would otherwise have exported to us for fats manufacture.

'3. The decision to increase our flour extraction rate, coupled with the decision taken at Washington to divert coarse grains from animal to human use, will substantially reduce our supplies of meat, bacon and eggs. Our plans for re-establishing our livestock herds will suffer a heavy setback and a considerable slaughter of pigs and poultry will be inevitable. Finally, we shall have to launch a vigorous publicity campaign to economise to the utmost all food, particularly bread, and to encourage increased sowings this spring of crops to be harvested during the coming summer.

'4. Sir Ben Smith will broadcast this grim story to the British public on Tuesday evening. The further sacrifices for which he must call will be a severe strain on our people, who have been looking forward to some relaxation of the standards of austerity which they have cheerfully accepted throughout the war.

'5. Even when we look further ahead the outlook is little

better. Even after the next harvest, European production will be far below pre-war figures and the demand from Far Eastern countries will not be reduced. And world stocks will have been exhausted by our efforts to meet the crisis in 1946.

'6. I am sending a personal cable to the Prime Ministers of Canada and Australia urging them to take all possible measures to increase the export of wheat by raising the extraction rate, curtailing the use of wheat for feeding animals and preventing all waste. I am also asking them to increase their wheat acreage for the next harvest.

'7. The people of this country will be strengthened in their determination to face the new hardships demanded of them by the knowledge that other countries are making similar exertions. And I am sure that the Governments of Canada and Australia will also be greatly influenced by your decision to increase wheat exports from the United States. We greatly value the steps which you have already taken; but, knowing your deep concern in this problem which is bound to affect all our post-war settlements, I venture to ask you to consider whether you can make still further contributions on the following lines.

'8. If it were possible for you to increase your flour extraction rate, this would not only provide a major increase in the supplies of wheat available for export, but would also give a most valuable lead to other exporting countries. Our extraction rate, as I have said, will have to be raised to 85 per cent and as a result of the allocations proposed in the Washington discussions it is clear that all countries in Europe will have to adopt a figure of at least 80 per cent and in many cases higher.

'9. Secondly, to meet the continuing shortage next year, I hope that you will do everything possible to increase your wheat acreage, especially as carry-over stocks will be so small.

'10. Thirdly, since Sir Ben Smith's return from Washington, there has been a serious deterioration in the food situation in Asia, especially in India, and we are facing a grave world shortage of rice. We have decided to continue our policy of not issuing rice for the civil population in this country and we are urging

European countries to do the same. If your country could provide some contribution from its own rice resources, it would be of great assistance in stemming the flood of famine in the East and would materially assist in reducing demands for wheat.

'11. The world will pass through a period of great strain and hardship before we see the next harvest. I fear that thousands may die of starvation and many more thousands may suffer severely from hunger.

'It is for these reasons, Mr President, that I make this earnest appeal for your continued help in mitigating the disasters which threaten the world.'

On the same day he sent long personal telegrams to Mackenzie King and Chifley in similar terms asking them to do everything in their power both to increase wheat acreage and reduce their own domestic consumption.

In his telegram to Chifley he added that although in the new circumstances the British people would be more than ever dependent on Australia for supplies of bacon and eggs and would much regret any reduction in them, so long as human beings were exposed to famine and starvation as a result of the wheat shortage human needs must have priority over animal feeding. If therefore in order to increase exports of wheat to the maximum, supplies of feeding stuff for poultry and pigs had to be cut and the output of eggs and pig products reduced, 'we shall quite understand the reason.'

What President Truman subsequently described as Attlee's 'vivid picture of the measure of hardship the British people would have to undergo' made an immediate and deep impression on him and two days later he announced a nine-point emergency programme which included control over all wheat and flour exports, the diversion of supplies from livestock feeding to human consumption, and an increase in the American wheat flour extraction rate (the quantity of flour produced from each bushel of wheat with a consequent reduction in quality), although not to the level Attlee had asked the British people to accept. Canada and Australia also responded with measures to increase wheat exports.

Prime Minister Chifley of Australia, however, declared himself unwilling to alter the wheat extraction rate unless it was absolutely unavoidable and Attlee cabled him again:

'Prime Minister to Prime Minister. 25th Feb. 1946

'I much appreciate the consideration you have given to my suggestions for increasing the amount of wheat and flour for human consumption during the coming months to meet the grave situation with which many countries will be faced. I fully understand your attitude towards the suggested increase in the extraction rate of flour, as we had to face some of the same considerations when we decided to put up our rate from 80 per cent to 85 per cent.

'I realise that during the next few months your problem will probably be one of internal transport. This is the same problem that confronted the United States. Clearly an increase in the extraction rate will not result in increased exports of wheat and flour if transport is already working to capacity.

'But taking a longer view, an increase in the extraction rate does mean that a larger proportion of the wheat crop will be available for human consumption. We are very much afraid that the present wheat shortage will last for at least another 18 months. According to our calculations the quantity of wheat available for export in the four principal exporting countries during the year July, 1946, to June, 1947, will be 15 million tons as compared with 23 million tons for the year July, 1945, to June, 1946. These figures are based upon the latest available estimates of 1946–47 acreages and assuming average yields. The very great drop in available supplies in 1946–47 as compared with 1945–46 arises from the fact that during 1945–46 the world has been drawing on stocks, whereas next year little will be available for distribution from that source.

'An increase in your extraction rate would, therefore, mean that more wheat would be available for export during the next 18 months than would be the case were the extraction rate not raised, even if exports could not be stepped up during the next few months. There would be a larger quantity in stock to be carried forward into the next season when, as the above figures indicate, there will still be a grave shortage.

'I recognise that an increase in the extraction rate, by reducing the amount of bran and pollard available for livestock, must have adverse effects on the pig and egg industries. This has happened here and, as the result of increasing our extraction rate and the general shortage of feeding-stuffs, we shall be able to provide only one-sixth of the feed for pigs and poultry which they enjoyed before the war. This will result in a reduction in our livestock herds and, in due course, a drop in our production of bacon and eggs.

'Similar consequences will follow in your own country and I can only repeat what I said in my telegram no. 28 that, so long as human beings are exposed to famine and starvation as a result of the present wheat shortage, human needs must have priority. If, therefore, in order to increase your exports of wheat to the maximum you have to take steps which will affect the output of pigs and pig products, we shall quite understand the reason, though we naturally hope the reduction will be as small as possible.

'This view is reinforced by the situation in India, which grows graver daily. The more wheat you have available for export, the more assistance it will be possible to give to India. The Indian Delegation which is here at present has represented to me how grave is the position that faces them and we are most anxious to do everything we can to remedy the situation so far as possible. This situation is likely to last well into 1947.

'May I also reinforce the appeal I made to you in my previous telegram to do everything possible to increase your wheat acreage for the next harvest? The figures I quoted above regarding exportable supplies of the four principal producing countries are based, as I said, upon existing extimates of acreage. Every additional acre which can be put under wheat during next season will make some contribution to meet the problem – particularly in those Empire countries like India, Ceylon and Malaya where shortage conditions are bound to last for some considerable period and where every assistance we can give will not only save human lives, but may have far-reaching political effects on maintaining the stability of the Empire.'

But the international situation continued to get worse and, on 25 February, Attlee sent Truman a further long cable:

'Prime Minister to President Truman. 25.2.46

'Since I telegraphed you on 4th February the cereal situation has, I fear, become even worse as the result of later estimates of both supply and demand. In particular, we have now fresh and most clamant demands from India, owing to a disastrous failure of the monsoon. The Viceroy estimates that he will need imports of over 4 million tons of wheat or rice this year to maintain even a very inadequate minimum ration. It is doubly unfortunate that there should be a food crisis in India at this moment, as it is bound to have repercussions in the political field there. As you will have seen, three members of the Cabinet are due to go to India next month to try and reach a settlement of the constitutional problem. Their task is difficult enough already: it will be made much more difficult if India is in the grip of famine.

'I have recently seen the members of an Indian delegation which is proceeding to Washington to lay India's case before the Combined Food Boards. I have assured them of our deep anxiety and that I would bring this matter to your attention. I earnestly trust that you will be able to help.

'A meeting of the London Food Council has been held this week to review the requirements of the countries within the L.F.C. area. On the basis of that review we shall be submitting a new appreciation of requirements to the Combined Food Board. That appreciation will relate to the immediate problem of the first half of 1946.

'I am, however, even more anxious about the position at the

end of that period. According to a provisional estimate which has just been given me, the quantity of wheat available for export from the four principal exporting countries during the twelve months July, 1946, to June, 1947, will be under 15 million tons. This is based on target acreage as known at present and on long-term average yields. In the twelve months July, 1945, to June, 1946, the comparable figure will, we hope, be over 25 million tons. The difference is almost entirely due to the fall in stocks. We are able to draw on these to meet immediate needs, but they will not be there for us to rely on next year.

'My experts cannot at this stage give us any precise figure for next year's demand, but I think it is a safe guess that it will be very considerably more than 15 million tons (it is nearly 19 million tons *for the current six months*). At the best there will clearly be no margin of safety.

'I suggest, therefore, that it is incumbent on us to make a very big effort to see that the maximum acreage is sown to wheat for the 1946 harvest. In this country we are doing all we can to encourage spring sowing and we shall also bring pressure to bear on European countries. But it is late for these efforts to have much effect, since the main wheat-sowing season both in this country and in Europe is in the autumn. In the United States, on the other hand, I believe that a substantial proportion of your wheat crop is spring-sown and if you were able to take steps to increase the United States acreage it would, I am sure, make an immense difference to the world's welfare in the next fifteen months. There seems to be no likelihood that farmers will find themselves left with an unsaleable surplus and we in this country are extending our ploughing-up grant and urging the maximum autumn sowings for the 1947 harvest also.

'I am also very much concerned at the rice situation. To India's increased needs must be added increased demands from many other countries. I believe import requirements for 1946 now exceed 6 million tons and it will be hard to find more than 3 million tons to meet them.

'Disappointingly small quantities are at present coming out of

Burma, Siam and French Indo-China. One of the first tasks of Lord Killearn, one of our most experienced ambassadors, who is just going out as a Special Commissioner in South-East Asia, will be to co-ordinate all efforts to increase the procurement of rice throughout the area.

'But however successful he is, the gap between supply and demand will still remain large and it will be necessary to take special measures to meet the emergency. May I also invoke your assistance over this? I have in mind three points in particular.

'First, I hope you will join with us in ensuring that demands from importing countries throughout the world are kept to the minimum that is really essential.

'Secondly, it is most important to stimulate planting of rice for the next harvest. The prospect for next year seems to me almost as bleak for rice as it is for wheat. However hard we try, I think it unlikely that it will be possible to step up production in Asiatic countries of anything like pre-war levels. As in the case of wheat, there will again be no stocks to fall back on and again there seems to be virtually no danger of over-supply. If you agree with this view, anything you can do to secure increased plantings in the United States and in the many areas of United States influence throughout the world would be most valuable.

'Thirdly, it would help materially if you could find means of reducing the consumption of rice in the United States itself and Cuba.

'I am sorry to burden you with this long telegram but the prospect for the next few months causes me the gravest anxiety and that must be my excuse.

'I am also taking up the question of increased acreage with Mackenzie King and Chifley.'

Again Truman generously responded. 'In the light,' as he said, of Attlee's appeal he called together a Famine Emergency Committee and asked Ex-President Hoover, famous for his international relief work after the First World War, to head it and to make a 30,000 mile round-the-world trip to investigate the food needs of twenty-two famine-ridden countries and report back with proposals for American action.

By these and other measures in the U.S. and in Australia and Canada and other wheat-exporting countries, and by strict self-denial on the part of importing countries, the worst consequences of what had at one time seemed almost inevitable post-war famine and social breakdown over a large area of the world were avoided – in large part as a result of British energy and initiative.

As part of Britain's own contribution, which included the sending of no less than 400,000 tons of foodstuffs badly needed at home to her former enemies in the British Zone of Germany, Attlee was compelled in July to introduce bread rationing – a measure that had been avoided even in the worst period of the war. It was politically a dangerous and highly unpopular decision. But Attlee believed that it was morally right and that Britain's duty to the world required it and he was confident, as always, that if the British people were told the facts they would respond. He did not believe that popularity should ever be allowed precedence over duty and he was satisfied that despite the sacrifices it entailed Britain could not have done other than she had.

11

Holding the Line against Russia

In the main Attlee left foreign affairs to Ernest Bevin, intervening only in moments of particular crisis or when Bevin asked him to. He believed that 'foreign affairs are the province of the Foreign Secretary. It is in my view a mistake for a Prime Minister to intervene personally except in exceptional circumstances.' He took the view that the constant participation by Heads of State in matters which depend upon skilled and patient negotiation and in which there are few short cuts to success was often more likely to promote than avoid crisis and that one should appoint a strong Foreign Secretary and leave the handling of affairs to him. The fashion of Summit Conferences in peace-time with all their attendant publicity seemed to him to have, more often than not, more risk than advantage – 'There's a lot in the proverb: "If you've got a good dog you don't bark yourself." '

The two men were very close; closer than any others in the Cabinet. They understood each other and trusted each other wholly, there were never any reservations between them, and Bevin, who preferred speech to memoranda, made a habit of privately talking over problems which troubled him with Attlee, not so much on a Foreign Secretary-Prime Minister basis as for the purpose of thinking aloud and drawing upon Attlee's sharp, detached judgment as a corrective to his own exuberant vision; their minds were in many ways complementary. No record was kept of these conversations and they did not, of course, in any way replace Cabinet discussions on foreign policy. But they played an important part in formulating both men's views, as did also the personal letters which Bevin often wrote to Attlee from abroad.

Attlee has described his feeling for Bevin in this judgment:

'My relationship with Ernest Bevin was the deepest of my political life. I was very fond of him and I understand that he was very fond of me . . .

'Like Stafford Cripps he was a tremendous egotist – Ernest having the egotism of the artist, Stafford the egotism of the altruist, and Stafford thought well enough of Ernest to suggest to him that he would make a better Prime Minister than I would in 1947. Ernest did not reciprocate this compliment.

'We understood each other very well. I was not a working man but I had lived and worked among the workers in Limehouse. It was my view that the purpose of a Labour Prime Minister was to work for the common man – not the little man but the man that is in all of us – irrespective of class and income. Ernest came to see that because a man had been to a public school it did not mean that he was on the other side of the hill. As the years went by he saw more and more of the foolishness that trade unionists can sometimes display and more of the loyalty of Labour supporters among the professional middle classes. He certainly knew that I would give up being leader at any time this seemed in the interest of the party and I think this appealed to him. I also think he liked the fact that I didn't talk too much. . . .

'Because of his own genius for organisation and his confidence in his own strength, he did not fear – he embraced – power. Lord Acton's famous dictum on power probably never occurred to him. And if he agreed that power corrupts he would have said that it corrupted only the men who were not big enough to use it. Power was given to him. He attracted it as a natural leader. It did not corrupt him . . .'

There was at all times close understanding between them. Bevin always kept Attlee fully informed as to what was in his mind and regularly sought his judgment, so that foreign policy was in a very real sense a joint affair, and there were never any serious differences between them. Attlee therefore kept clear of most of the regular business of diplomacy and international negotiation, knowing that Bevin would always turn to him if the need for his intervention arose.

One such occasion came early during the first Foreign Ministers' Conference in London when, adopting a method that was to become only too well-known later on, Russia suddenly faced the Conference with a procedural crisis.

When Bevin informed him of what had happened, Attlee at once telegraphed to Stalin, sending a copy to President Truman on the same day.

'Prime Minister to Marshal Stalin. 23.9.45

'A difference of opinion arose yesterday over the composition of the Council of Foreign Ministers for the purpose of its work on the preparation of peace treaties. Discussion centred round the interpretation of the Berlin Protocol.

'Mr Bevin maintained that the overriding provision was the decision to establish the Council composed of the Foreign Ministers of the U.K., U.S.S.R., China, France and the U.S.A. to do the necessary preparatory work for the peace settlements (paras A and A (i) of Part 1 of the Protocol of the Berlin Conference), and that the Council as a whole is thus responsible for discharging all the tasks remitted to it. He therefore maintained that the following decision reached by the Council on September 11 is correct:—

> "It was agreed that all five members of the Council should have the right to attend all meetings and take part in all discussions, but that in matters concerning peace settlements members whose Governments had not been signatories to the relevant terms of surrender should not be entitled to vote."

'I also share this view. I have spoken to Mr Eden, who tells me that his understanding at the Potsdam Conference was that the Council was free to arrange its own procedure and that it was not bound within the limits of the exact terms of the Potsdam Agreement.

'M. Molotov considers that the decision of the Council on September 11 was a violation of the Potsdam Agreement, that it should be rescinded and that in future the Council, for the work on the peace treaties, should be composed only of the Foreign Ministers of the States signatory to the Armistices and that, whilst the U.S.A. would be added in the case of Finland, China would be excluded altogether and France from all the treaties except the Italian. This does not accord with my understanding of the spirit and intention of the decision arrived at in Potsdam.

'The decision of the Council on September 11 was agreed to by the five Ministers present, including M. Molotov, and it accords with the understanding held in good faith by the U.S. and British Foreign Secretaries. It seems to be beyond question that the Council was entitled to adopt the above resolution (see paragraph A(4) (ii) Part 1 of the Berlin Protocol). Moreover, it cannot be held to depart in any way from the Potsdam decision, as the restriction of vote means in effect that the Council will be composed for taking decisions as proposed. Since this question has been referred to me I should like to touch on a broader aspect of the matter. The decision of September 11 was adopted unanimously after discussion and I should view with grave misgiving the institution of a precedent for calling in question decisions so taken and seeking to reverse them and therefore rejecting the conclusion arrived at by the British Foreign Minister acting in faithful concert with the other Foreign Ministers. That, I should fear, would change altogether in an adverse sense the nature and indeed the value of the Council of Foreign Ministers and introduce an element of confusion into their proceedings. Indeed I doubt whether it would be possible to gain unanimous consent of the Council to a reversal of its earlier decision and any attempt to do so would clearly cause grave offence to France and China and be completely misunderstood here by the public and Parliament, to whom we reported in good faith that the Council would act as a Council of

Five, a statement which was received with a sense of relief in this country. M. Molotov argues that under his proposals the work of the Council would be greatly accelerated. Even if this were so, which is by no means proved by the course of the discussions, it would certainly not counterbalance the damage to harmonious collaboration caused by the offence given. To my mind the success of the present conference and indeed the whole future of the Council and confidence in a just peace is at stake. Therefore I earnestly hope that you will agree to authorise your delegation to adhere to the decision taken on September 11. After all it is peace we are endeavouring to establish, which is more important than procedure.'

This telegram had some result. When, having reached deadlock in London, the Foreign Ministers met for a second time in Paris, Molotov, acting as always on the instructions of his master – for it soon became clear to all the others that he was allowed no power of independent judgment – abandoned his demands without further argument or explanation.

But the final sentence of Attlee's letter awakened no response in Stalin's mind.

Instead it became clear as the months passed and the Foreign Ministers moved from capital city to capital city that Russia and the Western Powers were fundamentally opposed in their attitudes towards a German peace treaty. Nor was Stalin interested in lessening tension and bridging the differences between East and West. The Soviet tactics were directed to securing piecemeal agreements on reparations and kindred matters in which they were particularly interested while blocking any wider approach. Bevin with Attlee's backing sought an overall agreement and refused to compromise on detail, convinced that whatever was done must be done as part of a total pattern. Nor was he ready to secure a peace treaty at the cost of allowing Russia to take from Germany immense reparations which would in practice have to be met by the Western occupying Powers.

'I am not prepared,' he told Molotov, 'to face Parliament after leaving this room with the implication that I have bought the peace conference from the Soviet Union for one hundred million dollars.'

His growing irritation with tactics which were to continue throughout his period of office – and that still continue to bedevil hope of agreement – was later expressed in a long personal letter, sketching in sharp and pessimistic phrases the atmosphere of these seemingly endless talks, which he wrote to Attlee from Moscow when the Foreign Ministers met there in the course of their interminable perambulations:

United Kingdom Delegation to the Council of Foreign Ministers, Moscow. 16th April, 1947

'Dear Clem,

'I have been waiting to give you a reply on the question you raised as to the atmosphere of the Conference, but it was very difficult to determine at that moment whether there would be a good outcome or not. And I agree with you that it is very difficult to get the sense of things from the telegrams.

'The time has now come, however, to give you a picture of the whole situation here as I see it. At the opening of the Conference, as you realise, Marshall, from the United States, was new to it and largely in the hands of his delegation, and he seemed to be groping his way to get a grip of the essential problems. I therefore had to take the lead for several weeks and decided, in order to try and focus attention on the issue as a whole which would have to come before the Conference, that after a reasonable exchange of views I would table what we have called our New Potsdam, which is a constructive piece of work and which is in line with the Cabinet decisions. The method I adopted was at each discussion to make my statement and then table a section and finally put in a paper as a whole.

'But the real issue of the Conference has not been faced and I am afraid we are going to break down because the Russians will not face it, and that is the fundamental question of economic unity in Germany and the type of political principles that must be adopted if we are to get a democratic Germany, that is, democracy as we understand it, and the carrying out of the organisation of Germany to the next stage towards the final evolution of a German state and government. The Russians clearly in this field want to create a situation in which everyone will forget what they have done in their Zone and we shall be forced to ignore the hundreds of millions we have had to put into our Zone, and the Americans into their Zone, and that they shall be able to come in, disregarding all this, force the British and American taxpayer to stand it, rehabilitate their own Zone at our expense and then on top of that get reparations from current production.

'The discussions on these items have been very cold, frank but firm. The result is that it is impossible to reconcile the instructions given to me by the Cabinet with the desires and determination of Russia to loot Germany at our expense. It is true that they have accepted some of the principles, but certain other vital ones they will not accept.

'The strategy I employed was to avoid the mistake made at Yalta and Potsdam of dealing with things separately and getting committed on one point, only to find that the Russians would not budge on the next item. Therefore I stipulated that I would not be committed until I had seen the problem as a whole and could ascertain whether any decision would involve additional cost for Great Britain, whether it would provide repayment for what we had put into Germany, and whether over reparations we should be treated quite fairly.

'Another very serious situation has developed and that is this. At Yalta the Russians talked about 20 billion dollars' reparations for the Allies. At Potsdam I understood, and I thought you did, that the decisions taken there settled reparations from the Western Zones; also there was the fact that, with the territory that had been taken away from Germany and other obligations imposed upon her, there was a tremendous population in a circumscribed area. Taking this and the cutting down of her industrial potential under the Potsdam Agreement into account,

I cannot see how current reparations can be paid unless they are provided from America and Great Britain.

'We have had this tussle over again on the question of Ruhr coal. The Russians refuse to put their coal into the pool and we cease to allocate through the Control Council. The Russians and the French have therefore been pressing that we should have a special régime for the Ruhr. I have stuck to Cabinet policy that I would not have any four-Power control of the Ruhr unless it applied to Germany as a whole. It is quite clear what the Russians are after, namely, to get into the Ruhr, to make our Zone impossible to work and to create a disturbance so as to get a grip on that great area. In this the United States stood with me, but France first of all stood for the detachment of the Ruhr altogether from Germany. She has withdrawn from that position and is now pressing for a four-Power régime, whereas no one more than France prevented the Central Agencies, agreed at Potsdam, from being put into operation. Again therefore I have had to say that when I get Potsdam as a whole I will honour it as a whole, but it is not permissible to pick out little bits which suit this or that country and ignore the obligations and then try to impose it upon the British. In all this I have had a very difficult task, but I regard it as imperative that it should be maintained.

'On the political principles the Russians and ourselves came very near together. The Americans and the French wanted the Central Government appointed from the Laender, that is to say, you would elect people to the local government and from that local government you would select so many people to form the national government. Whereas in the principles that I submitted, I put forward that all powers should be retained in the Laender that were not specifically reserved to the Central Government, but that the Central Government should be elected by Germany as a whole. Since the discussion I have had another talk with the Americans and I find there has been some misunderstanding. They do not appear to object to the Government being elected as a whole but what they are anxious about is that the control of the electoral machinery should be in the hands of the Laender. On that I am prepared to meet them. I think that is right and never intended anything else. It would be the same as our own constituencies controlling the elections in the localities. The other great difficulty is that the Russians want proportional representation, which applies practically throughout the Continent. I have reserved my position on this until we have had a chance to consult the Germans. In the end I am afraid I should be compelled to give way to proportional representation because of its universality, but I have put it straight to the Russians that I could be no party to enabling them to get a one-party Government in Germany.

'The other great issue we have had to face is the question of the Austrian Treaty. Discussion in detail will be reached to-day. But the trouble there in the main is the question of German assets in Austria. We have made two attempts to resolve this and have referred it back to the Deputies, but the disagreement seems worse than ever now and I do not know what the outcome of this discussion will be today. On the one hand I am told that it is better for Austria to have the Treaty even if we have to yield on this question of German assets, while on the other I get messages conveyed to me from other parties in Austria that it would be fatal if I did it. It is a difficult thing to decide. It all comes out of Potsdam because we failed to give a definition of German assets and we have taken the line that the Soviets ought not to profit by the rascality of Hitler. We have made proposals as to debts and also as to machinery for determining the definition of the German assets so as to exclude those taken by Hitler under force and duress during the period of the Anschluss.

'You will have seen from the papers to-day that the talks on the Four-Power Treaty have virtually broken down. It would have been farcical were it not so tragic. I admit that the Americans put this forward in Paris without very much thought, but it did offer to France, Great Britain and Russia a chance to build a bridge on the one issue of demilitarisation and the prevention of aggression. I felt that, if it had been received in the manner it ought to have been by Russia, the bridge between East and West would really have been built and the antagonism which is growing so fast in the United States would have been checked. Instead of that the Russians wanted to put in economics, demilitarisation, limitation of industrial potential, agrarian reform, which we have already agreed should be part of the German Treaty, and a whole host of things which made it quite clear that they did not want the Four-Power Treaty at all. Marshall reacted very coolly but very strongly. In fact, it was the first time in the Conference in which he was quite clearly speaking as the Secretary of State and not as the spokesman of the delegation. Bound up with this discussion yesterday was the future fate of Europe and of the world and it was very sickening and saddening to see such a great opportunity thrown away. The best description I can give of Molotov's statement was that it was a product of an irascible mind and very, very much like the old discussion that used to go on in the old International pre-1914, where they argued for days about words and theories of the most unpractical kind. I took the line, when the proposal was made, that this thing should go to a special committee with all these additions of the Russians; that we had been here five weeks; that we had been discussing every item proposed but had failed to settle even the short-term aspect, and that if he now passed it on to a committee with no decision it was really playing with the whole situation. For myself I think Russia has made a great mistake – as bad as she made just before the outbreak of war when she lined up with Hitler.

'For us as Britishers in between the two of them, our task is very difficult. I have caused the discussion to be started in connexion with our treaty and the Russians have put up counter-proposals, but I feel we dare not go an inch beyond the French Treaty. We run too great a risk if we do. I am waiting for the replies from the Chiefs of Staff on the points which we sent, and after that I will write to the Soviet Government, but I feel that whatever happens we must content ourselves with a treaty on those lines.

'I have tried to keep in touch with the other three delegations here as far as one humanly can.

'Finally, returning to the atmosphere here, it looks to me as if we are getting perilously near a position in which a line-up is taking place. I had hoped that when I came to Moscow it could all have been avoided, and I think a little more salutary attitude on the part of the Russians and better methods of handling their problems would have succeeded. I do not of course know what happened last night. Marshall saw Stalin and whether the outcome of that talk will make it better or worse I have not yet heard a word and cannot judge. We shall see to-day.

'There is courtesy, there are no high words being used, no tempers, but all of it is cool, calculated and between the two big boys looks to me to be pretty determined.

'I trust you are well and will get through the Budget difficulties all right. I can assure you that I shall be glad to leave Moscow. I am fed up with this long stay here. There are such little or no results.

Yours sincerely,
ERNEST BEVIN'

In their approach to foreign policy, circumstances, it seemed to both Attlee and Bevin, compelled them to give most weight to three main considerations.

There was in the first place the need, if it could by any means be managed, to make the United Nations a powerful and effective international instrument. This was not only because that it should become so was to both of them a matter of moral principle – especially so in an atomic age when a new pattern of international relations seemed to offer the only real hope of the survival of civilisation – but also because they saw in it the best means by which responsibilities that Britain's resources no longer enabled her to carry could be transferred in such a way as to help unify and not divide the world.

British interests were historically opposed to the domination of Europe by one Great Power. They required that the complex of world communications linking the Commonwealth should be kept open and secure and that political and economic means should be found to make possible the rapid, peaceable development of new nations in Asia and Africa, as old colonial relationships inevitably came to an end. And they called for peaceful and stable advance in the Middle East, which might otherwise become a new cockpit of power politics.

If the United Nations could be made into a reality all these issues would take on a different and more amenable form. Problems of security directly affecting British and Commonwealth interests would become more soluble. The risk of a dangerous power vacuum developing if Britain was compelled by economic and other circumstances to reduce her commitments would appreciably diminish.

For all these reasons both were anxious to avoid the kind of power line-up to which Bevin referred in his long private letter to Attlee, since any such line-up, by placing the United States and Soviet Russia – 'the big boys' – firmly on opposite sides, would make co-operation within the United Nations more difficult, if not impossible.

But the development of international confidence to such a level as to make the United Nations a fully effective and practical instrument was, even on the most optimistic view, bound to take considerable time. While it developed it was essential to avoid reducing British commitments in such a way as to create power vacuums out of which might come new conflicts. To leave nothingness behind might tempt the Soviet to strike out for domination over the whole of Europe and the Middle East and thus divide the world beyond hope of repair.

Attlee and Bevin were thus compelled throughout the whole of the post-war period to play for time. They had to fight a holding operation. It was one which Britain's limited resources and pressing economic and defence problems made it virtually impossible for her to win without American help, only obtainable if the United States could be brought to realise that her own interests, no less than those of Britain and Europe, required her to oppose the expansion of Soviet power in Europe and the Middle East.

From Potsdam onwards it was plain that Stalin was determined, if he could, to block any peace treaty that would facilitate the emergence of democratically elected Governments in liberated Europe and thus reduce the likelihood of Communist domination. It was plain also that Britain's material weakness was a potent factor in Soviet calculations. Russia herself was, at this time, in no position to risk a major conflict. But if Britain could be forced to contract her dangerously extended commitments before America was ready to take over, she might be able to move in without one.

To an extent that is often forgotten in the light of later events Britain therefore became during this period the primary, and, indeed, for long periods at a time almost the sole, target of Soviet diplomatic and propaganda attacks in Turkey, the Dardanelles, Persia, Greece, the Middle East and elsewhere.

While trying to prevent so absolute and frozen an alignment of Big Power groupings as to destroy any real hope of the ultimate development of an effective United Nations organisation, Attlee and Bevin were for this reason compelled to face up to the reality of Soviet ambitions much earlier than the preoccupations of American domestic politics allowed the United States administration to do so. American public opinion was slow to move from the belief that a satisfactory division of interests between Russia and America was possible, or to shake itself free of a traditional suspicion of what were regarded as British imperialist motives. To this was added in some important official quarters a considerable contempt for British weakness.

Admiral Leahy, President Truman's Chief of Staff, was known to have canvassed at Potsdam the opinion[1] that Britain was 'prostrate economically' and 'relatively impotent militarily' and that the Soviet Union must be accepted as 'the unquestioned, all-powerful influence in Europe.' And Harry Hopkins, whom Truman had sent on a mission to Moscow immediately after the end of the war in Europe, had reported back that in his opinion no

1. Subsequently repeated in his memoirs, *I Was There*, published in 1950, based on his diaries and notes.

major source of conflict between Russia and American interests existed in any part of the world. It was, therefore, he advised, of vital importance that the United States should not be manœuvred into a position where they were lined up in a bloc against Russia to implement Britain's European policy.

These may seem strange views in the light of future American policy, but they were important at the time. Although not shared in the same measure by Truman himself, they coloured American thinking. Above all at this stage American public opinion was unwilling to support any policy that seemed to be pulling British chestnuts out of the fire or entangling the United States in a British alliance. Attlee and Bevin had to play for time – although time was running out – and be very careful not to frighten America into a new isolationism by precipitate action.

It was in this delicate situation that Winston Churchill delivered his famous Fulton speech. The immediate reaction of the Foreign Office was one of consternation, not so much because of the content of the speech as because of its possible effect in America. This anxiety was increased when the first telegrams from Washington reported that the speech had been widely misinterpreted as an expression of British official opinion and that the reference to 'fraternal association' contained in it had been seized on by a good deal of public opinion as the beginning of an attempt to manœuvre America into an unwanted alliance. This was the more troublesome in that it came at the very moment when the American loan to Britain was before Congress.

However, while Attlee and Bevin were considering the implications of these reports a personal telegram from Churchill arrived containing important news.

Dated 7 March 1946 and marked 'Personal from Churchill for the Prime Minister and Foreign Secretary', it reported that although Churchill had not, of course, consulted any members of the American Government on the exact text of his speech, President Truman had read a mimeographed copy of the final draft on the train to Fulton some hours before it was delivered: 'He told me that he thought it was admirable and would do nothing but good though it would make a stir.' The President, Mr Churchill's telegram continued, had 'seemed equally pleased before and after.' A copy of the speech had also been shown in advance to Mr Byrnes, the Secretary of State, who was excited by it and suggested no alterations, and to Admiral Leahy, who was enthusiastic. Mr Churchill added that, although, of course, he took personal responsibility for what he had said, and had altered nothing as a result of his contacts with these high American authorities, he thought Attlee and Bevin ought to know their reaction.

His telegram also contained advance news of a significant development in American policy towards the Near East which was to prove of considerable importance in paving the way for the 'Truman Doctrine' of a year later that security in the eastern Mediterranean was an American interest.

The Turkish Ambassador had died in Washington and Churchill telegraphed that on the train to Fulton President Truman had told him that he had decided to send the body back to Turkey in the American battleship *Missouri*. This was the ship on which the Japanese surrender had been signed and was probably the strongest battleship afloat. The *Missouri* would be accompanied by a strong task force which would remain in the Sea of Marmora for an unspecified period. Mr Churchill commented: 'This strikes me as a very important act of State and one calculated to make Russia understand that she must come to reasonable terms of discussion with the Western democracies.' He added that from the British point of view he felt sure that the arrival and stay of such a powerful American fleet in the Straits must be entirely beneficial. It would reassure Turkey and Greece and it would place 'a demurrer on what Bevin called cutting our line through the Mediterranean by the establishment of a Russian naval base at Tripoli.'

Finally Mr Churchill wrote that after spending nearly three days in intimate friendly contact with President Truman and his immediate circle and after having a long talk with Mr Byrnes he had no doubt that the American leaders were deeply distressed at the way they were being treated by Russia and did not intend to put up with treaty breaches in Persia or encroachments in Manchuria and Korea or pressure for Russian expansion at the expense of Turkey or Greece in the Mediterranean. 'I am convinced,' he concluded, 'that some show of strength and resistance is necessary to a good settlement with Russia. I predict that this will be the prevailing opinion in the United States in the near future.' This was good news indeed.

Churchill's attitude on the American loan while he was in the States was also encouraging.

A personal telegram from Sir Ben Smith, the Minister of Food, who was in Washington, reported:

'Minister of Food to Prime Minister. 12th March, 1946

'Yesterday I attended a lunch which the National Press Club gave to to Winston Churchill. He answered questions for the best part of an hour. He was cross-examined particularly on the British loan.

'After admitting that there were a number of points about it which he did not like, he developed a strong case in support of the loan's passage by Congress and said it would be "a disaster" if it were turned down. He also vigorously repudiated the suggestion that the loan would merely be a subsidy to Socialism and stressed the fundamental solidarity of the British people. He added that if the loan were not granted we should still get through somehow because the British people would never be beaten.

'Altogether he gave us helpful support and his statements should go a good way to offset the effect here of the attitude of the Opposition to the loan agreement.'

Attlee telegraphed his thanks to Churchill:

'Prime Minister to Mr Churchill. 13 March, 1946

'I have just heard from Ben Smith of the very helpful remarks which you made at the National Press Club luncheon about the

American loan, and I should like to send you my warm thanks and appreciation for the friendly line you took.

'Thank you also for the long and interesting telegram which you sent Bevin and me on March 7 – I hope we may have a talk on your return. I have shown the telegram to Eden.

'I trust that the remainder of your stay will be pleasant, and that you are keeping well. Best wishes to Mrs Churchill and yourself.'

However, although Truman's decision to send a task force to the eastern Mediterranean represented an important step in American involvement in European affairs – and a plain warning to the Soviet that the United States would not stand aside if Russia translated aggressive diplomacy into aggressive action – it did little at this stage to reduce the financial and defence burdens which Britain was finding it increasingly difficult to carry in view of her own grave economic problems. At the Treasury Hugh Dalton continually pressed for a reduction of financial commitments overseas. They were not easy to achieve.

From Paris, on 13 August 1946, Bevin wrote to Attlee in the course of a letter on proposed Cabinet changes, 'I am not making the headway I would like in making it possible to reduce our commitments so as to help Hugh; the Russians are very difficult.'

On the same day two other letters arrived on Attlee's desk from Bevin. One expressed Bevin's anxiety lest too much was being given away about British methods in the Defence White Paper on the setting up of a Ministry of Defence:

Paris

'Dear Clem, 13 August 1946

'I was very concerned when I read your scheme for Minister of Defence and Defence Organization was to be published as a White Paper. Why must we reveal this to the world? It is the result of years of experience and effort. We have not promised. Cannot we get the Bill through without revealing every detail as this does? The intelligence, planning and execution is opposite to the German and, I think, the Russian systems. If the Germans had used this system they might have won. Why must we weaken ourselves? See paragraph 30. It may justify our Chiefs of Staff system, but I cannot see that the paper has much to do with a Minister of Defence except as a piece of internal organization.

'Please look into it again. Yours sincerely,

ERNEST BEVIN'

The other, on reorganisation at the Foreign Office as part of a Ministerial reshuffle regarding which Attlee had written to him, revealed his growing sense of the strain of continual conferences:

Paris

'Dear Clem, 13th August 1946

'I am answering your note under separate headings,

'1. *Foreign Office.*

I have long been considering the reorganization of the Foreign Office. I agree with you about N.B.[1] I think he will do well and his knowledge of my Policy will be useful in shaping defence, and he did well at War Transport. This will relieve me of having anyone on a functional basis.

'I have refrained from asking you to appoint another Parliamentary Secretary because of the difficulty of fitting one in, but it is no use disguising the fact that I cannot stand the strain of the last six years. Further, I am satisfied that I must make arrangements for the posts abroad to be visited, reorganized and brought up-to-date, and I must be able to have more contacts with other States. At the same time, if we are to do the job properly these young men must be trained. Therefore what I would like, if you can give it to me, is as follows:—

'Hector McNeil as Minister of State, and he would be my chief substitute in my absence for Defence Committee, conference

1. Mr Philip Noel-Baker, Minister of State, who was promoted to be Secretary of State for Air. Subsequently Secretary of State for Commonwealth Relations.

work, helping me with peace conferences, i.e., Germany and Japan (I am writing you separately on Control of Germany) and certain branches of U.N.O.

'I would like Mayhew, the present Parliamentary Private Secretary to Morrison, as a Parliamentary Secretary. I like him; he has a good economic sense and would be able to help me in the economic field and handle the House well. I have had my eye on him. It would also help the Party in East Anglia.

'Then Gordon Walker as the second Parliamentary Secretary. He is good and reliable and would help me with the British Council, Public Relations and the B.B.C., and he is a good negotiator.

'I should then have a good set-up.

'I hope you can see your way to do this.

Yours sincerely,
ERNEST BEVIN'

But although Bevin sometimes felt that the pressure of work was growing almost unbearable, this did not prevent him from adding to his responsibilities.

Next day yet another letter for Attlee arrived, this time proposing that the Foreign Office should be given a much larger control of German and Austrian affairs:

United Kingdom Delegation
Paris
14th August 1946

'Dear Clem,

'The question of the Control Office for Germany and Austria has been giving me great concern. I have to face all the political implications, at home, at meetings of the Council of Foreign Ministers, and in our relations with France.

'I had thought of putting up to you the proposal contained in the draft minute which I attach. The effect of it is to give me and the Foreign Office a more effective part in the political side and to confine the Control Office to the purely administrative problems.

'I am in a real difficulty about this because while on the one hand I do not want Hynd to be displaced or reduced, as I think he is capable and promising, I am advised that in practice division between political and administrative questions may not be possible. Sargent had a private talk with Jenkins, the Permanent Secretary at the Control Office, and Jenkins's view was that the only satisfactory arrangement would be the drastic course of reducing the Control Office to a department of the Foreign Office reporting direct to me.

'Would you have a look at my draft paper and let me know what you think? Perhaps we could discuss it when I return.

Yours sincerely,

ERNEST BEVIN'

Detailed suggestions for bringing directly under Bevin himself all major German and Austrian issues, including directions to the Commander-in-Chief in Germany on all political matters, followed.

Such preoccupations at no time prevented Bevin from taking an interest in many other things nor from corresponding regularly with Attlee when he was away on any matter on which he thought his friend the Prime Minister might like to have his views. Thus from Paris the same day that he sent his memorandum on Germany he also wrote Attlee a note urging him to 'keep a pretty close control of it [defence] yourself' when a Defence Minister was appointed. Another suggested that 'Shawcross needs to be spoken to. His actions and speeches in Poland outside of his sphere were not too helpful.' A third came down strongly against a suggestion that a former Labour Member who had refrained from fighting at the 1945 Election should be given a seat in the Lords: 'A man who plays for safety as he has done and then to be taken into office or put up to represent the Party in the Lords is a bad decision and will cause misgiving. Is there no defeated candidate who made at least a good fight?'

The complications of a diplomacy in which Britain had little power of manoeuvre and in which Attlee and Bevin were forced increasingly to recognise the real nature of Stalin's aggressive ambitions, not only by Russia's public acts but by Molotov's attitude in the face of every effort to reach agreement at the Foreign Ministers' Conference, were sometimes made worse by the public utterances of prominent members of the Labour Party whose opinions were given more weight abroad than they really had. Almost inevitably Harold Laski often appeared in this role, much to Attlee's and Bevin's irritation. One such utterance by Laski quite early on brought the following letter from Attlee:

'My dear Harold, 20 August 1945

'Your letter has just reached me and I hope you will make useful contacts in the Scandinavian countries. I thank you also for your kindly reference in your *Reynolds*' article. I am however bound to point out to you that the constant flow of speeches from and interviews with you are embarrassing.

'As Chairman of the Labour Party Executive, you hold an important office in the Party and the position is not well understood abroad. Your utterances are taken to express the views of the Government.

'You have no right whatever to speak on behalf of the Government. Foreign Affairs are in the capable hands of Ernest Bevin. His task is quite sufficiently difficult without the embarrassment of irresponsible statements of the kind which you are making.

'I had hoped to have seen you but you were away in Paris. I can assure you there is widespread resentment in the Party at your activities and a period of silence on your part would be welcome.

Yours ever,

CLEM'

Divisions within the Parliamentary Labour Party on major issues of policy were of more consequence. To Bevin, schooled in the trade union tradition of loyalty, some of the attacks launched against him by the 'left wing' at a time when he was in the middle of negotiations in which any suggestion of British weakness or disunity could in his view prove fatal were quite intolerable. He could not accustom himself to what he considered 'the irresponsibilities' of the political life. In Attlee's words, 'he was a majorities man and was impatient with minorities, in which respect he ran counter to one of the most important traditions in the Labour Party. There was no place for rebels in his idea of organisation.' Critics to him were mischievous and malevolent and quite unwilling to find out what he was really trying to do.

Although he had early reached the view, as had Attlee also, that the best, indeed perhaps the only, hope for European security lay in American assistance, he still, in fact, refused to abandon hope of Soviet co-operation. He was anxious to bargain – but to bargain from a position of strength, not weakness. Attacks by members of his own party suggesting that he had 'sold-out' to the Americans infuriated him. He did his best to come to terms with the Soviet. In Moscow at a personal meeting with Stalin he offered to extend the war-time Anglo-Russian Treaty into a fifty-year alliance, and when Stalin replied, 'I should need to amend it', responded, 'Let me know what would suit you.' This he meant sincerely – trying over many weary months without success to get from Stalin exactly what amendments he wanted. 'Our interests are bound to meet in some places,' he said. 'The thing for you and me to do is to keep the ball bearings greased so that there won't be friction when we do meet. I'm ready to do that.' Nor did he think Stalin wanted war. What he feared, as he said in reply to a question from Field-Marshal Smuts at a meeting of Commonwealth Prime Ministers, was that 'the Soviet Policy of expansion has engendered its own dynamic which may prove too strong for him in spite of all his shrewdness and power. I don't think he's planning for war, but he may be unable to control the forces he's started. We've always got to be prepared for that.' It seemed to him that the critics who were always so ready to 'stab him in the back' were wilfully blind.

Attlee, trained in the Parliamentary tradition, was more

tolerant of the left wing, although no less convinced that they did not understand what Britain was up against.

Attlee: There is always a tendency on the part of some people in the Labour Party to over-simplify foreign affairs. It's partly due to a certain woolly idealism; seeing everything black and white when in fact there are all sorts of shades of grey. They mean well but they don't like looking at unpleasant facts. Some of them thought we ought to concentrate all our efforts on building up a Third Force in Europe. Very nice, no doubt. But there wasn't either a material or a spiritual basis for it at that time. What remained of Europe wasn't strong enough to stand up to Russia by itself. You had to have a world force because you were up against a world force.

Williams: And you don't think you sacrificed too much independence to get America in?

Attlee: Of course not. Without the stopping power of the Americans the Russians might easily have tried sweeping right forward. I don't know whether they would, but it wasn't a possibility you could just ignore. It's no good thinking that moral sentiments have any sway with the Russians, there's a good deal of old-fashioned imperialism in their make-up, you know. Their foreign policy has been carried on in much the same way from the days of Queen Catherine the Great. Some of our friends wouldn't see that.

It was the same later on over the American air bases. We had to face this possible danger of the Russians sweeping right across Europe and we had to have something to hold them. One way was air power, where the West was superior to the Russians because of the atom bomb. But the American planes had to be based somewhere – they couldn't fly from across the Atlantic. So we based them here. Obviously it added a certain amount of danger to our own position, but we couldn't have asked other countries, Continental countries, to put themselves in a dangerous position while keeping ourselves out. It was a case where one had to take unpleasant decisions – realistic decisions.

Williams: What would you put as the turning point as far as American policy was concerned?

Attlee: The Berlin air-lift. I think that was the decisive thing. Of course they'd begun to realise earlier that they couldn't just stand out – when we'd had to make it plain to them that we couldn't go on holding the front in Greece, which rather upset them at first. We had to stay in Greece after the war because, if we hadn't, the Communists would have taken over everything and there wouldn't have been any hope of a peaceful Government. But as soon as that danger was out of the way it was high time for us to get out. We were holding the line in far too many places and the Americans in far too few. Germany we had to hold, of course. There was no suggestion, to my mind, that we could afford to withdraw troops from Germany. But Greece was a different matter.

By giving America notice at the right moment that we couldn't afford to stay and intended to pull out we made the Americans face up to the facts in the eastern Mediterranean. As a result we got the Truman Doctrine, a big step. But the Administration was ahead of the people, Harry Truman learnt fast. And although Greece and the Soviet *coup* in Czechoslavakia opened the eyes of Congress quite a lot, it wasn't, I think, until the Berlin air-lift that American public opinion really wakened up to the facts of life. Their own troops were involved in that, you see. Before that there'd been a lot of wishful thinking. In spite of everything I don't think they really appreciated Communist tactics until Berlin.

Williams: Why?

Attlee: Inexperience. I don't think little Jimmy Byrnes had a very clear understanding when he was Secretary of State. Took rather a lawyer's view of things. Marshall had a much bigger grasp, as he showed in the Marshall Plan, and that helped in educating the public.

Williams: Did you have any prior warning of the Marshall Plan?

Attlee: No, I knew nothing of it until he made his speech at

Harvard. Ernie Bevin came round to see me as soon as we got the first reports and we talked it over. We both saw what it could lead to. Ernie took it up very quickly. Without him, in fact, it mightn't have come to anything. It was in very general terms and there were quite a lot of the Americans who didn't want to go anything like so far. They'd have been glad to see it die. But Ernie got on to the French and the others right away and gave it life, and that encouraged America to go ahead.

Even the iron curtain countries wanted to come in at first. The Russians missed a big chance there, they should have agreed and come in themselves. We hoped they would. The satellites were keen and even Molotov's first response wasn't too bad. But Stalin stamped on it. I suppose he thought: 'This is a danger to our ideology. Everyone must depend on us. We are the only people.' A great pity.

Williams: When the stand was made over Berlin did you think there was a real danger that it might bring a response from Russia that would lead to war?

Attlee: It was quite a danger. But it was a risk that had to be taken. I don't, as a matter of fact, believe that Russia was in a position to attack at that time, although one couldn't be sure. They hadn't really begun to rebuild their economy and I didn't think they were ready for a showdown. However, one couldn't depend on it.

I flew out to Berlin when it was on. First time I'd been there since Potsdam. It was mid-winter, bitterly cold, heavy snow on the ground. My plane was interpolated between streams of arriving planes. I saw something of the Berliners. They had a very good Burgomaster – Herr Reuther, a very stout fellow. The spirit of the Berliners was admirable. We saw them at the unloading points, working mighty hard. I think it was a real turning point for them. The spirit of our own and the American troops and air people was very good. They counted it as a great adventure and worked extremely well together. Our troops were mostly young boys, you know. They were in very good fettle, but it could have been very nasty.

With the lifting of the Berlin blockade by the Russians in April 1949 and the signing in Washington in the same month of the North Atlantic Treaty, towards which, at first in the face of many American doubts, Attlee and Bevin had been working patiently for more than a year, there seemed a hope that international relations would improve. Once again these hopes proved false. On 29 September, as the Foreign Ministers' Conference dragged on and on, Bevin wrote to Attlee from New York to say that although he had urged the State Department to be conciliatory on a number of small issues he found the Americans stiff and adamant even on quite unimportant points. 'The atom bomb and the general feeling regarding Russia all combine to make a settlement appear very difficult.'

As for Russia: 'One detects here,' he wrote, 'the feeling that Russia is reverting to the attitude they adopted before the lifting of the blockade. You will find evidence of this in Berlin and Austria, and they particularly resent the United Nations taking up the question of China.

'I mention this because I feel that mischief is brewing again. What form it will take, I cannot tell. It may be a recrudescence of Communist activities in Malaya, or violence in Hong Kong, or industrial upsets at home. I have no doubt that they are closely watching the nervous tension that has developed in France . . .'

As so often now, he concluded: 'I am longing to be home again and I shall be glad when this and the Canadian visit are over.'

12

Danger for the Middle East

While the long, frustrating attempt to reach a settlement in Europe carried the Foreign Ministers from capital city to capital city in an almost unbroken series of conferences, and Attlee and Bevin patiently pursued their policy of persuading the United States to take over some of the strategic and economic burdens Britain could no longer carry, they had constantly to consider equally intransigent problems in another area of the world – the Middle East.

Attlee: Europe came first. In the order of priority in world strategy that was Number One. From our point of view the Middle East was Number Two, although from the American point of view, and probably also that of Australia and New Zealand, the Far East was. But for us the Middle East was the critical area after Europe. It still is in many ways.

We wanted to help the Arab States to independence – the old state of things couldn't continue. But we couldn't just withdraw and leave a vacuum. The trouble was that not many of the people in control were much good. A poor lot. Farouk was still on top in Egypt – a paltry representative for any country. And, of course, his dignity had been upset by the action of our people in Cairo during the war, which may or may not have been justified, when they gave him his marching orders, until he caved in at the last minute. That didn't make him any easier. Monckton drew up the instrument of abdication, I remember: he'd had practice.

There were, of course, one or two people who were quite good while they lasted, like Abdulla in Jordan, an admirable man. But there weren't many, and they tended to be out of touch with the people. There was quite a good little fellow in the Shah of Persia, too, but he got in the hands of corrupt, awkward gangs like so many of them did. Over the whole of the Middle East I had every sympathy with the peasants but I must say I had a very poor view of the governing classes.

Because we had interests there – spheres of influence and so on – some people seemed to think we could say what sort of Governments they must have. The Americans thought so, they were full of suspicions because they assumed we could just order people about. But you can't do that. The American oil interests didn't make things any easier either. They were playing their own hands most of the time.

Williams: Do you think there is a justifiable criticism that you didn't give enough support to new movements of nationalism in the Arab countries?

Attlee: I don't think so. Nationalism is a thing that attracts the best and the worst and there was a good deal of corruption everywhere. The Russians were active and we always had to watch them, because many of these patriots were quite as ready to sell out to the Communists as to try to do anything genuine for their people. And one has to take into account the constant conflict between the Arabs themselves. There was a long-standing feud between the Saudi Arabians and the Hashimites, and although there was an Arab League it didn't work very easily, and didn't speak with one voice. When it did it was generally rather mischievous.

One of Bevin's earliest acts at the Foreign Office was to circulate a memorandum on the theme of peasants not pashas, directing his officials' attention to the need to look at the problems of the Middle East from a new standpoint. Both Attlee and he saw that the need was for economic developments to raise the standards of living of the mass of the people and put them in a position to take a more direct part in the government of their countries. But Britain lacked the economic resources to give such aid herself and the time had long since gone when she could force reforms on reactionary Governments against their will. We had to deal with those in possession, hoping by a process of influence and persuasion to make them more liberal within a framework of treaties which would regularise Britain's relations with the Arab countries while ending the old and increasingly distasteful system of British suzerainty. But it did not prove easy.

A treaty of independence was negotiated with Abdulla in Transjordan, but in Iraq the tide of nationalist feeling was running so strongly that the signing of a treaty withdrawing British troops led to popular disturbances and the overthrow of the Government because airfields at Habbaniya and Shaiba were still reserved for the R.A.F. under it. And in Egypt repeated efforts to reach agreement broke down owing to the inability of Egyptian Ministers to get popular ratification for the terms they themselves accepted and owing to the Egyptian demand for control of the Sudan.

Attlee: We had to consider the real interests of the Sudanese people. We were not prepared to hand them over to the ruling classes in Egypt. We went a long way towards getting a sensible Anglo-Egyptian treaty. We withdrew our troops from the citadel of Cairo, we reduced our numbers in the Canal Zone.

The perfect plague of my life was to get those numbers down. One was constantly up against the military capacity for delay. We'd accumulated an immense mass of stores which we were told were enormously valuable: we had to guard them. But apparently no one knew what they were. Some bright boy during the war had failed to put any marks on the cases. We couldn't tell whether the stuff was really wanted or whether it was obsolete. There was an idea that in the general world situation it was useful to have a collection of arms in Egypt handy for any trouble, but no one could tell me if those were the sort of arms that were needed, although it was an immense trouble guarding them, involving a large number of troops. I used to have fortnightly or weekly reports about how the numbers of troops were going down, but I could never get them down very far because I was always told, 'Ah, but there are these stores, we can't leave them unguarded'. I sent out a general to get the thing straight but even then I could never get a real report on them. Wonderful capacity to play for time some of the military had.

There was also a tendency to cling to Egypt, because it was a pleasant place to live in. 'Probably get shoved out to Aden or some other God-forsaken place if we go from here.' We did make an effort to try and shift our base to Kenya, even made provision for stores over there, but events rather overtook that.

Most of the military were inclined to put too much weight on the Middle East as a base. They overlooked the political issues and the facts of Arab nationalism and insisted that we must hang on to it as a vital main support area. Monty did when he was C.I.G.S. He still had a hangover from the days when the Middle East was the essential link between our two great places of arms, Britain and India. But India had ceased to be a British Imperial place of arms and the Suez Canal had never been a particularly good waterway in war-time and the idea of the Mediterranean as a kind of covered passage for Britain had also been exploded. Monty over-emphasised the importance of the Middle East from the strategic point of view.

Williams: Was he a good C.I.G.S.?

Attlee: Fairly good. But it wasn't really his job. His strong point was fighting and winning battles and raising the morale of troops, not overall strategy. As C.I.G.S. he wasn't as good as Alanbrooke or Slim.

Of course it wasn't only the Military who found it difficult to adapt to changed conditions in the Middle East. Some of our business people out there were slow to realise what was happening. The Anglo-Persian oil people – Anglo-Iranian as it was afterwards – were very difficult. They'd been a kind of imperial power, and they couldn't get out of the habit. Ernie Bevin tried hard to get them to change and they did make some improvements, but they never made an attempt, as they might well have done, really to adjust themselves to new conditions. They ought to have got the Persians working with them, but they didn't, they clung on, wouldn't relax their hold and move with the times. They brought a lot of trouble on themselves and us as a result.

It was quite the opposite in Burma. Burmese independence created a difficult position for our people, but the Burma Oil people went right in and got the Burmese into their show and made it not just a British enterprise but one in which local people were interested. Very good effort.

Some of our financial people were not awfully awake to changing circumstances in the Middle East either. They could have done a good deal to help with investment on a proper basis. Most of all, of course, we needed to change gracefully, little things as well as big ones were important, sometimes, indeed, they loomed larger than big ones on the spot. But far too many of our people just couldn't accept the inevitable pleasantly.

Policy in the Middle East occasionally produced controversy in the Cabinet as well as elsewhere, as the following tart reference in a letter from Bevin to Attlee shows. Shinwell, then Minister of Fuel and Power, had put in a statement criticising some aspects of policy both in the Middle East and towards Germany:

United Kingdom Delegation to the Council of Foreign Ministers.

27 November 1946

'Dear Clem,

'I have your letter with enclosure of November 22nd and will of course keep it very private . . .

'With regard to frequent discussions on foreign policy I have been to the Cabinet every week when I have been home and reported, and every step I have taken has been known to you.

'I am naturally very perturbed about the record of statement by the Minister of Fuel and Power. I was not aware, and you have never told me, that any member of the Cabinet had the slightest doubt about my policy in the Middle East. I have reported over and over again. As you know, the key to that policy was Egypt, and all I remember from the Minister of Fuel and Power was a most chauvinistic attitude regarding our oil supplies in Persia. If I had pursued his suggestions at the only meeting at which I remember him referring to the matter it might have led to tremendous conflict with Russia and possibly with the United States.

With regard to his references to Germany, as you know, his criticisms were mainly in connection with the administration, but I have never heard the slightest criticism of my foreign policy towards Germany. I have submitted papers on the Ruhr, and before I came away I submitted a voluminous document on its future organisation. I therefore felt that when the matter came before the Council of Foreign Ministers I had the backing of the Cabinet. But if there are doubts in the Cabinet about it, it ought not to be left until I get home: I should be told now. Not only did I submit papers to the Cabinet but I made a public statement on the basis of that paper in the debate in the House of Commons, and I took into account both the Minister's paper and everything that had been said. As you are aware, I am now negotiating with the United States Government to try and get out of the morass for which I am not responsible so far as finance and production is concerned.

'Needless to say the views expressed by a colleague, which he is quite entitled to hold, are very disturbing to one who is trying to carry the burden here, especially as no details are given and only doubts created.

'With regard to discussions of foreign policy in the Cabinet, I am entirely in your hands.

Yours very sincerely,

ERNEST BEVIN

It is against this background of the anxious and at times highly controversial search for greater stability in the Middle

East that British policy in Palestine has to be viewed.

Palestine led to sharper disagreements between Attlee and President Truman than did any other issue.

Williams: How difficult was it to make the Americans see the British point of view?

Attlee: Very difficult. There's no Arab vote in America, but there's a very heavy Jewish vote and the Americans are always having elections. There was naturally a great deal of sentiment and very powerful lobbies, and, of course, immense sympathy, which we shared, for the Jews who'd been ousted from Europe. The Americans thought we should introduce a hundred thousand Jews into Palestine right away without the slightest consideration for the effect on the Arabs. They had no obligations there. We had.

The President went completely against the advice of his own State Department and his own military people. The State Department would tell us one thing and then the President would come out with the exact opposite. The State Department's view was very close to ours, they had to think internationally, but most of the politicians were influenced by voting considerations. There were crucial elections coming up at the time, and several big Jewish firms had contributed to Democratic Party funds. Domestic issues of that kind often affected American international thinking, one used to see it on Italian matters as well: their attitude was very much influenced by the Italian vote. They'd been remote from foreign affairs for the greater part of their history and the effect on domestic issues always bulked much bigger with them than with us. And some of the American Jews were very extreme and quite uninterested in any reasonable solution. Unlike Weizmann, who was a big man, not an extremist. But the pressure was enormous.

Williams: Did you ever think it possible to get a solution in Palestine without the violence that actually resulted?

Attlee: I think it was extremely difficult. We set up an Anglo-American Committee of Investigation, but a good many of them ran away from the real problem. They had a sort of conception that you could get both sides to live in peace with the other. You couldn't.

Williams: There was a good deal of criticism, and still is in Israel itself, about the way we finally ended the Mandate and left.

Attlee: We'd held the Mandate and we couldn't get any agreement, and it was no good our holding the baby any longer with everybody gunning for us. The only thing was to pass the problem to the U.N. and agree to do what they said. It was one of those impossible situations for which there is no really good solution. One just had to cut the knot.

We'd started something in the Jewish National Home after World War One without perceiving the consequences; it was done in a very thoughtless way with people of a different outlook on civilisation suddenly imported into Palestine – a wild experiment that was bound to cause trouble. True, at that time no one anticipated the driving out of the Jews in Central Europe, it was Russia that had the problems then, but the original idea wasn't so much the building of a regular State as giving the Jewish people a point on which they could rest; it was only later that the Jews came in large numbers. And you have to remember that even when the idea of a State got hold there were a large number of anti-Zionists among the Jews themselves who believed that the Jews should fit into whatever nation they were in.

The interests of Arab and Jew in Palestine were quite irreconcilable. It's true the Arabs had a lot of land and not much development and you might think that an Arab struggling to keep alive on a bare strip of sand would jump at the chance of going to Iraq or somewhere else where there was more opportunity for a better life. But oh no. One patch of desert doesn't look very different from another patch of desert but that was the one they wanted – their own traditional piece. Even the Bedouins circle in the same area. They have this attachment to one place and nothing else will do.

Whether there's any hope of ending the hostility between Arab and Jew I don't know. Israel has an open door for all Jews and you can understand the Arabs being afraid it will burst at the seams. It is such a tiny narrow State that there is bound to be great danger unless one can get a genuine settlement. However, they're extremely clever, hardworking people, and they've got some useful mineral resources, so that if anyone can make a nation that size prosperous, they will.

Attlee found a memorandum from President Truman on Jewish immigration waiting for him the day he became Prime Minister. It had been addressed to Mr Churchill two days before the result of the Election was known. It read:

To: The Prime Minister. The White House,
From: The President. Washington.
July 24, 1945.

'There is great interest in America in the Palestine problem. The drastic restrictions imposed on Jewish immigration by the British White Paper of May, 1939, continue to provoke passionate protest from Americans most interested in Palestine and in the Jewish problem. They fervently urge the lifting of these restrictions which deny to Jews, who have been so cruelly uprooted by ruthless Nazi persecutions, entrance into the land which represents for so many of them their only hope of survival.

Knowing your deep and sympathetic interest in Jewish settlement in Palestine I venture to express to you the hope that the British Government may find it possible without delay to take steps to lift the restrictions of the White Paper on Jewish immigration into Palestine.

'While I realise the difficulties of reaching a definite and satisfactory settlement of the Palestine problem, and that we cannot expect to discuss these difficulties at any length at our present meeting, I have some doubt whether these difficulties will be lessened by prolonged delay. I hope, therefore, that you can arrange at your early convenience to let me have your ideas on the settlement of the Palestine problem, so that we can at a later but not too distant date discuss the problem in concrete terms.'

At this stage Attlee replied only briefly:

Berlin
31st July 1945

Memorandum to the President from the Prime Minister.

'I have read your memorandum of July 24 about Palestine. You will, I am sure, understand that I cannot give you any statement on policy until we have had time to consider the matter, and this is simply to inform you that we will give early and careful consideration to your memorandum.'

By this time the breach between the President and the State Department on the Palestine issue had already begun to manifest itself. Within a few days of Truman's assuming office the then Secretary of State, Mr Edward R. Stettinius Jr had approached the President to warn him that Zionist leaders were likely to try to secure his support for unlimited Jewish immigration into Palestine and the establishment of a Jewish State, and to urge him to avoid any such commitment in view of the continual tension in the Middle East. Subsequently Mr Joseph C. Grew, Acting Secretary of State while Stettinius was at the San Francisco Conference, forwarded a memorandum to the President pointing out that President Roosevelt had 'on a number of occasions within the past few years authorised the Department to assure the heads of the different Near Eastern Governments on his behalf that in the view of this Government there should be no decision altering the basic situation in Palestine without full consultation with both Arabs and Jews', and that at his meeting with King Ibn Saud earlier that year 'Mr Roosevelt promised the King as regards Palestine he would make no move hostile to the Arab people and would not assist the Jews as against the Arabs.' The State Department memorandum concluded by declaring that, as recently as 3 March, President Roosevelt had reaffirmed this policy for the guidance of the State Department and had 'told an officer of the Department that in his opinion a Jewish State in Palestine (the ultimate Zionist aim) could be established and maintained only by military force.'

This was followed by a further State Department memorandum in September stressing the difficulties which inevitably faced Britain as the Mandatory Power for Palestine during the interim period while a search for a viable long-term policy was being made: 'No Government', it concluded, 'should advocate a policy of mass immigration unless it is prepared to assist in making available the necessary security forces, shipping, housing, unemployment guarantees. In view of the foregoing the United States should refrain from supporting a policy of large-scale immigration into Palestine during the interim period.'

The State Department view referred to in President Truman's memoirs, from which these quotations are taken, had been known to the Foreign Office for some time. It accorded with their own. Much of the bitterness that subsequently developed can be accounted for by the fact that those primarily concerned on the British side felt that this considered opinion, on which they had believed they could rely in trying to secure a reasonable Arab-Jewish settlement, had been set aside purely as a result of domestic political pressure.

The same view was taken by many within the U.S. Administration itself – a fact that, as it became known, did nothing to reduce British resentment.

Thus according to the published diaries of Mr James Forrestal, U.S. Secretary of Defence, he, Byrnes, who had succeeded Stettinius as Secretary of State, Judge Robert P. Patterson, Under-Secretary of War, and John Snyder, Director of War Mobilisation and later Secretary of the Treasury, met on 26 July 1946, to discuss the situation arising from the fact that 'Jews are injecting vigorous and active propaganda to force the President's hand with reference to the immediate immigration of Jews into Palestine.'

Five weeks later he recorded that Robert E. Hannegan, the U.S. Postmaster General and one of the chief organisers of the Democratic Party machine, had raised at a Cabinet lunch the question of the President making an early statement demanding the entrance of 150,000 Jews into Palestine. This, Hannegan said, 'would have a very great influence and great effect on the raising of funds for the Democratic National Committee.' He added that 'very large sums were obtained a year ago from Jewish contributors and they would be influenced in either giving or withholding by what the President did on Palestine.' To this Forrestal himself replied that an earlier statement by the President 'prompted by Rabbi Silver of Cleveland' had not had the influence expected on the New York election but had had the net effect of making the British 'exceedingly angry, particularly when it was coupled with the rejection of the Grady Committee Report which amounted to a denunciation of the work of his (the President's) own appointee', and of making 'Secretary of State Byrnes wash his hands of the whole Palestine matter, which meant that it was allowed to drift without action and practically without American policy'.

Shortly after this Byrnes added his own testimony when he told Forrestal that he had dissociated himself from the President's policy because he considered his decision 'to criticise the British for their conduct of Palestine affairs had placed Bevin and Attlee in a most difficult position' and had been taken only because David K. Niles, the Administrative Assistant to the President, and Judge Samuel Rosenman 'had both told Truman that Dewey was about to come out with a statement favouring the Zionist position in Palestine and had insisted that unless the President anticipated this move New York State would be lost to the Democrats.'

Two months later, after Hannegan had again raised the issue at a Cabinet lunch and said that those who had contributed to the Democratic Campaign funds were pressing hard for assurance, and after Forrestal had been warned by Senator McGrath, the Democratic National Chairman, that 'Jewish sources were responsible for a substantial part of the contributions to the Democratic National Committee' and that these contributions were made with 'a distinct idea' that their views on the Palestine issue would be 'seriously considered', Forrestal himself saw Senator Vandenberg and Governor Dewey, the Republican leaders. He was hoping to get a non-partisan policy on Palestine by enlisting Republican support. However, he met with an unpromising response. 'There was', said Senator Vandenberg, 'a feeling among most Republicans that the Democratic Party had used the Palestine question politically and the Republicans felt they were entitled to make similar use of the issue.' Governor Dewey was equally uncompromising. He agreed in principle, he said, but the Republicans could do nothing because they knew 'the Democratic Party would not be willing to relinquish the advantages of the Jewish vote.'

It is against this background, and the British feeling that policies which both the Foreign Office and the State Department agreed were necessary to hold an equitable balance between Jewish and Arab claims were again and again repudiated because of domestic American pressures, that the exchanges between Attlee and Truman which follow must be read. It was one of the few occasions when the mutual understanding and sympathy between them which played so important a part in the development of Anglo-American relations in this period were put under heavy – although fortunately not lasting – strain.

President Truman's proposal that 100,000 Jews should immediately be allowed into Palestine, which bedevilled both Anglo-American relations and the attempt to reach a settlement acceptable to the Arabs from the start, was first made in a letter to Attlee from the White House on 31 August 1945 addressed 'My dear Mr Prime Minister'.

With this letter the President forwarded a report he had received from Mr Earl G. Harrison, Dean of the University of Pennsylvania Law School and U.S. Representative on the Intergovernmental Committee on Refugees, whom he had sent on a mission to Europe to investigate the condition of Jewish refugees among displaced persons. After referring at some length to Mr Harrison's qualifications and to the scope of his inquiry among displaced persons in the American and British zones of Germany, President Truman continued: 'In view of our conversations at Potsdam I am sure that you will find certain portions of the report interesting. I am, therefore, sending you a copy.

'I should like to call your attention to the conclusions and recommendations – especially the references to Palestine. It appears that the available certificates for immigration to Palestine will be exhausted in the near future. It is suggested that the granting of an additional one hundred thousand of such certificates would contribute greatly to a sound solution for the future of Jews still in Germany and Austria, and for other Jewish refugees who do not wish to remain where they are or who for understandable reasons do not desire to return to their countries of origin.

'On the basis of this and other information which has come to me, I concur in the belief that no other single matter is so important for those who have known the horrors of concentration camps for over a decade as is the future of immigration possibilities into Palestine. The number of such persons who wish immigration to Palestine or who would qualify for admission there is, unfortunately, no longer as large as it was before the Nazis began their extermination programme. As I said to you in Potsdam, the American people, as a whole, firmly believe that immigration into Palestine should not be closed, and that a reasonable number of Europe's persecuted Jews should, in accordance with their wishes, be permitted to resettle there.

'I know you are in agreement on the proposition that future peace in Europe depends in large measure upon our finding sound solutions of problems confronting the displaced and formerly persecuted groups of people. No claim is more meritorious than that of the groups who for so many years have known persecution and enslavement.

'The main solution appears to lie in the quick evacuation of as many as possible of the non-repatriable Jews, who wish it, to Palestine. If it is to be effective, such action should not be long delayed.

Very sincerely yours, HARRY TRUMAN'

To this Attlee telegraphed an acknowledgment, pointing out that immigration certificates available had not in fact been taken up and promising a fuller reply. A fortnight later he telegraphed at length:

'Prime Minister to President Truman. 16.9.45

'I am now in a position to give you a considered reply, which I am telegraphing in order to save time, to your letter of August 31 enclosing a copy of Mr Harrison's report.

'I am sure you will appreciate the very grave difficulties that have confronted our representatives on the Control Commission, and from my own investigation of the matter it is quite clear that they have endeavoured to avoid treating people on a racial basis. Had they done this, then there would have been violent reactions on the part of other people who had been confined to these concentration camps. One must remember that within these camps were people from almost every race in Europe and there appears to have been very little difference in the amount of torture and treatment they had to undergo. Now, if our officers had placed the Jews in a special racial category at the head of the queue, my strong view is that the effect of this would have been disastrous for the Jews and therefore their attempt to treat them alike was a right one. After all, the situation in Central Europe is appalling. The number of displaced persons, refugees from concentration camps, the violent driving of people from one territory to another, is one of the most horrible events in human history. So concerned are we about the starvation generally in that area that we have been taking steps to try and prevent epidemics arising and spreading to other countries. On this matter we shall be communicating with the State Department as soon as possible.

'With reference to immediate relief there is a camp at Philippeville, North Africa, capable of taking 30,000 and another one at Felada with a capacity of 5,000. I suggest that, in order to relieve immediate suffering, these two places be used. I understand that UNRRA have it under their control. It would of course involve our Commanders in the task of sorting them out. This, however, should relieve the situation.

'In the case of Palestine we have the Arabs to consider as well as the Jews, and there have been solemn undertakings, I understand, given by your predecessor, yourself and by Mr Churchill, that before we come to a final decision and operate it, there would be consultation with the Arabs. It would be very unwise to break these solemn pledges and so set aflame the whole Middle East. I know you realise that, as things are, the responsibility of preserving order with all the consequences involved rests entirely on this country.

'As I mentioned in my earlier telegram, the Jews are not now using the numbers of certificates available and up to the present have not taken up the 1,500 available for this month which were offered them. Apparently they are insisting upon the complete repudiation of the White Paper and the immediate granting of 100,000 certificates quite regardless of the effect on the situation in the Middle East which this would have.

'In addition to this problem we are engaged upon another related one and that is India. The fact that there are ninety million Moslems, who are easily inflamed, in that country compels us to consider the problem from this aspect also. Therefore, while sympathising with the views of Mr Harrison and weighing them very carefully, we believe that the suggestion which he has made raises very far-reaching implications, which would have to be most carefully balanced against the considerations which I have set out above. We have got the matter under urgent examination, with a view to the formulation of a long-term policy which we propose to refer to the World Organisation as soon as practicable. Meanwhile we are considering how to deal with the immigration problem in the interval and I shall be happy to let you know as soon as I can what our intentions are in this matter.'

On 25 October he followed this with a further short telegram advising Truman that the Cabinet had the problems of Palestine and of helping the Jews in Europe urgently before it, but pointing out that these two problems were not necessarily the same. He added that he hoped very shortly to be in a position to put a proposal to the President. This came three weeks later in a formal memorandum to the U.S. Government proposing an Anglo-American Committee of Investigation.

In line with the opinions Attlee had already expressed to Truman, the memorandum made it plain that the British Government could not accept the view that Jews in the European areas under British and American administration were living under worse conditions than other victims of Nazi persecution, or that a major solution could be found by immigration into Palestine, which could, it was stated, be considered only as one among several possible 'countries of disposal'.

In Palestine itself, the memorandum argued, the main cause of the trouble in the past twenty-six years had been due to the dual obligation under the Mandate to facilitate Jewish immigration and settlement while ensuring that the rights and position of other sections of the community were not prejudiced as a result.

The document then continued, 'Every effort has been made by the Mandatory to devise some arrangement which would enable Arabs and Jews to live together in peace and to co-operate for the welfare of the country, but all such efforts have been unavailing. Any arrangement acceptable to one party has been rejected as unacceptable to the other. The whole history of Palestine since the Mandate was granted has been one of continual friction between the two races, culminating at intervals in serious disturbances.

'The fact has to be faced that there is no common ground been the Arabs and the Jews. They differ in religion and in language; their cultural and social life, their ways of thought and conduct, are as difficult to reconcile as are their national aspirations. These last are the greatest bar to peace. Both communities lay claim to Palestine; the one on the ground of a millennium of occupation, the other on the ground of historic association and of an undertaking given to it during the First World War. The antithesis is thus complete.

'The repercussions of the conflict have spread far beyond the small land in which it has arisen. The Zionist cause has strong supporters in the United States, in Great Britain, in the Dominions and elsewhere; civilisation has been appalled by the sufferings which have been inflicted in recent years on the persecuted Jews of Europe. On the other side of the picture, the cause of the Palestinian Arabs has been espoused by the whole Arab world and more lately has become a matter of keen interest to their ninety million co-religionists in India. In Palestine itself, there is always serious risk of disturbances on the part of one community or the other, and such disturbances are bound to find their reflection in a much wider field. Considerations not only of equity and of humanity but also of international amity and world peace are thus involved in any search for a solution.'

Finally, after promising to consult with the Arabs to try to avoid an interruption of Jewish immigration and to explore with both Jews and Arabs the possibility of other temporary arrangements pending the submission of a final plan to the United Nations, the memorandum concluded with a categorical statement that immigration could only be allowed for the time being at the current rate and with a sharp reminder of previous American assurances to the Arabs:

'In regard to the immediate future, His Majesty's Government have decided that the only practicable course is to maintain the present arrangement for immigration. The Government of the United States will realise that His Majesty's Government have inherited, in Palestine, a most difficult legacy and their task is greatly complicated by undertakings, given at various times to various parties, which they feel themselves bound to honour. Any violent departure decided upon in the face of Arab opposition, would not only afford ground for a charge of breach of faith against His Majesty's Government but would probably cause serious disturbances throughout the Middle East, involving a large military commitment, and would arouse widespread anxiety in India. Further, the Arabs have not forgotten the assurances given by the late President Roosevelt and by President Truman, to the heads of Arab States, of their desire that no decision should be taken in respect to the basic situation in Palestine without full consultation with both Arabs and Jews. It can hardly be contended that a decision to depart from the present policy in respect of immigration would not constitute a decision in respect to the basic situation in that country.'

To this, Truman, who as soon as the idea of an Anglo-American Committee became known had received a telegram from American Zionist leaders urging him to reject it out of hand and insist on 100,000 immigrants at once, responded by saying that he would agree to American participation only if Palestine were made the focus of the inquiry instead of being considered as one among other potential places of settlement for European Jews. Attlee and Bevin at first resisted. However, at his Washington meeting with the President for the Atomic Energy discussions in November, Attlee finally agreed, as the only means of getting American participation, and the Anglo-American Commission set to work.

Its report, when it came, served only to deepen the division between Truman and Attlee. 'It 'expressly disapproved' that Palestine had in some way been ceded or granted as their State to the Jews of the world, laid down the principle that 'Jew shall not dominate Arab and Arab shall not dominate Jew in Palestine' and that Palestine should be 'neither a Jewish State nor an Arab State', ruled out as impracticable any early attempt to establish an independent State or States in Palestine and called on the Jewish Agency to co-operate in suppressing terrorism and illegal immigration. But it did recommend the early issue of 100,000 Jewish immigration certificates and it was on this point that Truman concentrated to the exclusion of most of the rest of the report. Although prepared to accept the need for consultations with both Jews and Arabs before the two Governments determined their attitude, he proposed that both Jews and Arabs should be required to transmit their views within a fortnight.

Attlee at once sent an interim reply pointing out that the report had military and financial implications which required study and suggesting that this should be done as a matter of urgency by expert officials of both Governments. He followed this with a longer telegram in which he also drew attention to the British need not to upset negotiation with Egypt at this stage:

'For President from Prime Minister. May 10, 1946.

'I have now been able to consult the Foreign Secretary and the Cabinet on your message of 8th May concerning Palestine. We agree that the consultations with the Jews and Arabs, to which both our Governments are committed, should be initiated as quickly as possible. I hope, however, that in view of the delicate negotiations which we are at present conducting in Egypt, you will feel able to postpone any approach to the parties concerned until 29th May at the earliest.

'We also think that the suggested period of two weeks is too short for the Arab Government and Jewish Organisations to prepare and submit their views on the Anglo-American Committee's recommendations, and that it would be preferable to allow them one month.

'As I said in my previous telegram, we think it important that there should also be some provision for the study by expert officials of our two Governments of the implications of the Committee's Report, with particular reference to the military and financial liabilities which would be involved in its adoption. We would prefer these official discussions between experts to precede the consultations with Jews and Arabs, but if this suggestion does not meet with your approval they can be conducted either simultaneously with or after those consultations.

'It also seems to us most desirable that, as a final stage in the consultations which we are contemplating, every effort should be made to convene a conference at which Arab and Jewish representatives would meet with representatives of our two Governments to consider the whole question of the basis of the Committee's Report and of the results of the preliminary consultations both between Arabs and Jews and between our own experts.

'Our two Governments would then be in a position to make known their decisions on the issues dealt with by the Committee of Enquiry, having had the fullest opportunity of bringing their own views into harmony and of promoting the largest possible measure of agreement between the other interested parties.'

At this stage relations were further strained when the President publicly endorsed the 100,000 figure without any prior notification to the British Government that he intended to do so. Attlee decided that the time had come to make two things plain. The first was that before taking any action on the Report we would ask the U.S. Government to share the additional military and financial responsibilities that would arise. The second was that large-scale immigration into Palestine would not in any event be resumed until illegal Jewish armed units were eliminated. This he did in a Parliamentary statement.

This British reaction Truman found 'unsympathetic.' Although anxious for large-scale Jewish immigration he had no intention of accepting military responsibility for what might follow from it. He was well aware, as he said later, that 'while there was much clamour in the United States that something should be done the country was neither disposed nor prepared to assume risks and obligations that might require us to use military force.' Moreover he had already received a report from his Joint Chiefs of Staff recommending that no U.S. armed forces should be involved in carrying out the Committee's findings and urging that the guiding principle should be that no action should be taken which might cause repercussions in Palestine beyond the capabilities of British troops to control.

Attlee, however, was by now determined that if the Americans wanted to press Zionist claims and lecture Britain on what she should do they must be made to realise that it was up to them to help foot the bill, both financially and militarily. He therefore again cabled Truman, on 26 May, this time setting out no less than forty-five points which he considered it necessary for the experts of both Governments to consider before any decision on the Report was reached. These included the cost of transporting, housing and maintaining 100,000 immigrants, the measures needed to bridge the gap between Jewish and Arab standards of living, the steps needed to suppress terrorism and liquidate private armies, the repercussion in the Middle East generally of the adoption of a Palestine policy based on the Report, the additional military commitments that might follow, and the sources from which these commitments would be met.

Somewhat reluctantly the President agreed that their experts should meet. However, he continued to press for early action on the 100,000 immigrants, to which Attlee replied in a telegram of 10 June that this could only be considered during the general discussion on the Anglo-American Report. On 24 June he cabled to the President again, advising him of the composition of the British expert team. He added, 'I should like, however, to draw your attention again to the decision of H.M. Government, to which I referred in my telegram of June 10th, that we cannot determine our policy on any one of the Committee's recommendations until we have examined the results of the official consultations on the Report as a whole. More particularly, we cannot contemplate accepting the proposal to admit large numbers of Jews to Palestine without very careful consideration of the effects which such a decision, when announced, would have in the light of the other proposals we were making at the same time. Tension is mounting in Palestine and we are satisfied that precipitate action on the immigration question alone would provoke widespread violence. I am sure you will appreciate that H.M. Government cannot take this risk.'

When at last the experts were ready to meet it was against a background of mounting Zionist terrorism and violence in Palestine – much of it, in the British view, aided, inspired and financed by Zionist groups in America. On 29 June, therefore, Attlee sent a telegram to Truman informing him that the British Government could no longer refrain from drastic action.

'Prime Minister to the President. 29th June 1946

'In view of the continuance of terrorist activity in Palestine culminating in the recent kidnapping of six British officers, His Majesty's Government have come to the conclusion that drastic action can no longer be postponed. The High Commissioner has accordingly been authorised to take such steps as he thinks necessary to break up the illegal organisations, including the arrest of any individuals against whom there is clear evidence that they are responsible for the present campaign of violence. The authority does not extend to any comprehensive disarming of the whole of the civil population at this stage.

'I understand that the High Commissioner intends to take action early on the morning of Saturday 29th June. It is proposed to raid the Jewish Agency and to occupy it for a period necessary to search for incriminating documents. At the same time members of the Agency considered implicated directly or indirectly in Haganah outrages will be arrested. Similar action will be taken in the case of headquarters of the illegal organisations.

'I regret that such action should have become necessary while we are engaged in discussing the Report of the Anglo-American Committee; but we could not resist the conclusion that we could no longer, without abdication of our responsibility as the Mandatory Government, tolerate such open defiance and that, while the discussions regarding the future of Palestine are proceeding, law and order must be maintained. We shall make it clear that our action is not merely made necessary by recent outrages by the Jews, but is also a first step towards restoring those conditions of order without which no progress can be made towards a solution of the long-term problem. Our action will be directed, not only against the maintenance of existing private armies or similar illegal organisations, but also against their future creation by either community.

'You will remember that the Anglo-American Committee called upon the Jewish Agency to resume active co-operation with the Mandatory Government in suppressing these illegalities. I need not add how much we should welcome any statement you may feel able to make indicating your support of our determination to bring to an end violence and terrorism in the Holy Land.'

It was in this critical situation that the British and American experts met, with Sir Norman Brook (now Secretary to the Cabinet) as the British chairman and Mr Henry F. Grady as the American chairman. They worked quickly under constant pressure from both Attlee and Truman as tension mounted and in Palestine itself Jewish terrorism reached a new peak with the blowing up of the King David Hotel in Jerusalem. Their report when it came proved to be very close to the British view which Attlee had constantly put before Truman.

Representing not only the State Department and Foreign Office but also the Treasuries and Defence Departments of both countries, the experts unanimously agreed that the admission of another 100,000 Jews could only be peaceably carried through with the agreement of the Arabs and must be conditional on it. As a longer-term solution a federal system of two autonomous states, one Jewish, one Arab, was proposed, with a strong central Government which would retain control of the cities of Jerusalem and Bethlehem in view of their importance as religious shrines and would also have reserved to it control over immigration and various other matters.

To Attlee and Bevin this plan seemed to offer a hope, however faint in view of the bitterness that had developed, of a solution that might ultimately enable Jews and Arabs to live in harmony together and help to promote what had been their greatest desire throughout, a situation in which the skill and intelligence of Jewish communities could play an active and constructive part in social and economic development throughout the Middle East. When set against the background of suspicion and hostility that existed it was a small chance only, and even this ended when, on 24 August, Truman decided to throw over his own expert advisers. On that date, as the British Government completed arrangements for a conference with Jews and Arabs to consider the British-American expert proposals, he telegraphed to Attlee informing him that he was not prepared 'to give formal support to the plan in its present form as a joint Anglo-American plan.' The opposition in the United States to the plan had, he declared, 'become so intense that it is now clear that it would be impossible to rally in favour of it sufficient public opinion to enable this Government to give it effective support.'

At the same time he instructed the American Ambassador in London to press upon the British Government an alternative plan put up to him by the Jewish Agency.

Attlee telegraphed back:

'Prime Minister to President Truman. 18.8.46

'It is, of course, a great disappointment to us that you should feel yourself unable to give support to the plan recommended by the Anglo-American Expert Delegations. The discussion of the summary of this plan which we recently presented to Parliament will form the first item on the agenda at the coming conference. We earnestly hope that, as a result of the conference, some solution will emerge which, even if not fully accepted by either Arabs or Jews, may be possible of implementation without too gravely endangering the peace of Palestine or of the Middle East as a whole. But you will appreciate that any such solution must, as matters stand, be one which we can put into effect with our resources alone.

'As regards the plan of partition submitted by the Jewish

Agency, it is, as I have said, our intention to place the outlines of the provincial autonomy plan before the conference. On various matters, and in particular as regards the boundaries of the provinces and the degree of self-government to be conceded to them, we designedly refrained from committing ourselves in any way when presenting the plan to Parliament. While we are adopting the plan as the initial basis for discussion, we do not propose to take up an immovable position in regard either to the plan itself or to its constituent features in advance of the conference.

'It is accordingly open to the Jews or to the Arabs, if they accept our invitation to attend the conference, to propose alterations in the outline plan as announced, to make recommendations as to its details or to submit counter-proposals. All such proposals and recommendations will be given due consideration.'

In fact, however, the conference was doomed. Conscious that they could rely upon American support however intransigent their attitude, the Zionists announced through their official organisation, the Jewish Agency, that they would not even sit down with the British to discuss their proposals. In reply the Arab States insisted that Palestine was and must always remain an Arab State. Bevin did his best to remain hopeful. There were separate meetings with Jews and Arabs. They were followed by private meetings between Bevin and leaders of British Jewry which seemed for a time to offer some prospects of success. But when proposals emerged from these discussions which seemed to Bevin to open the way to a possible settlement, they were at once repudiated by the American Zionists. And the American Zionists were in control. No voices but theirs counted.

It was in these circumstances and after the final collapse of the round-table talks that Attlee and Bevin recommended to the Cabinet that the problem should be passed to the United Nations and that, come what may, Britain should give up the Mandate and withdraw completely and finally from Palestine at midnight on 15 May 1948. They knew that this decision would arouse the most bitter controversy. They knew that it would almost inevitably mean war between Jew and Arab. But if that came it was for the United Nations to act. The future of Palestine was an international responsibility. They were not prepared to sacrifice any more British lives in maintaining unaided what had been made an impossible situation.

13

Independence for India

On 17 July 1947 Attlee received a letter from an old friend and political opponent that much pleased him. It came from the Rt. Hon. L. S. Amery, Secretary of State for India in the war-time Government and in the Caretaker Conservative Government that followed. It read:

112 Eaton Square, S.W.
'My dear Clem, 17th July 1947

'Just a line, which needs no answer, of sincere congratulations on the passage of the Indian Independence Act. It is a great personal triumph for you which I am sure none of your political opponents will grudge you, and least of all one who, like myself, has long worked with you on the Indian problem.

Yours ever,
LEO AMERY'

Whatever differences of opinion may still exist regarding many of the major domestic and international policies of Attlee's Administration – and it is inevitable that a Government which carried through so many and such sweeping changes and was compelled by the conditions of the time to confront so many grave problems of international policy should be a subject of controversy for many years – there are few who would not now subscribe to Amery's tribute or deny that Attlee's decision on India proved to be one of the great acts of his career.

Yet at the time it was taken it was fraught with danger and surrounded by controversies almost more bitter than any Attlee had to meet in the course of his career; it was, declared Winston Churchill, an act that meant 'the clattering down of the British Empire with all its glories'.

Attlee was more directly and personally involved in the policy which culminated in the birth of three Asian members of the Commonwealth – India, Pakistan and Ceylon – and the formation of the independent republic of Burma than almost any other issue throughout the course of his whole administration. One of his first acts after his return from Potsdam was to call the then Viceroy, Lord Wavell, to London for urgent consultations. Thereafter he was actively engaged at every stage of difficult and often dangerously critical negotiations on the future of India, and the major decisions were his.

He had been in India eighteen years before as a member of the Simon Commission. The experience he then gained, reinforced by much study and consideration of the Indian situation subsequently, played an important part in the decisions he made as Prime Minister. Indeed one of the first letters he received after the passing of the Indian Independence Act (it arrived on his desk the day following Amery's) was from a Conservative who had been a member of the Simon Commission with him, Sir Edward Cadogan, who wrote from the Carlton Club to say: 'As a former colleague of yours on the Simon Commission you must allow me to offer a tribute of congratulations to yourself on the distinguished and successful part you have taken in negotiating one of the most difficult problems that has ever faced British statesmen – the Indian Constitution. No better solution could have been found. . . . It is satisfactory to the surviving members of the Indian Statutory Commission that so much of the credit goes to yourself.'

Attlee: You have to see the place and smell it and talk with people of every kind before you realise the strength the Indians have on the one hand and the extraordinary amount of minority opinion that exists in that country on the other. On the Simon Commission everywhere we went the minority always claimed they would be oppressed unless they had special representation. By the time you had added up all the special representation they wanted, the majority ended up with about five per cent. As a matter of fact the unity of India was really due to Britain. They talked of some semi-mythical king hundreds of years ago but it was British rule that united India. Of course, when one went round as we did on the Simon Commission – especially as we were boycotted by the Congress Party – we heard more of minority views than one would otherwise have done. But we found exactly the same complaint made by Hindus in the Punjab as by the Moslems in Madras.

Williams: Although the Simon Commission was very valuable to you as a background, had it ever had any hope of success?

Attlee: Looking back, we didn't do a bad job on the Commission. We went about as far as was possible at that time with the proposal for a fuller development of provincial self-government and, in particular, with the handing over of law and order to Indians. But our trouble at the centre was this: that if you wanted to form a united India you had first of all to get over the problem of ninety million people who were under their native rulers. There was not a big popular movement at that time. A great many were utterly devoted to their own rulers and we were bound by all kinds of treaties and obligations to support those rulers. We'd asserted a certain amount of suzerainty but it was a very indirect form of rule.

That was the first big stumbling-block. The second was that India was protected by an Indian Army – Indians officered by British in all the higher ranks – and by British units. It was absolutely essential in the conditions of the world at that time that we should have a certain number of British forces there and Indianisation of the officers could only be done very slowly. Earlier there had only been Viceroy-commissioned Indian officers – almost glorified sergeant-majors – and although there were some young ones coming on there wasn't at the time, I think, a single officer of field rank. But it is axiomatic in the British Commonwealth that British troops can only be employed under the orders of the British Government at Westminster. You can't hand over British troops as mercenaries to the will of a Prime Minister of another part of the Commonwealth. We couldn't put our people in the position of fighting on the decision of another Government.

Those were the two biggest stumbling blocks and what we recommended was a steady progress of Indianisation and a federal system to provide an opportunity for Indian princes to come in as units of the Federation. But that, of course, disappointed the Congress Party, who wanted all or nothing right away. Nor did it please a good deal of Labour opinion at home. But it was realistic and India was, in fact, governed on the basis of the Simon Commission plan from 1935 onwards. The India Bill which Sam Hoare piloted through the Commons was practically, although he didn't say so, an implementation of the Simon Report. An immense amount of careful work was done on the Bill. I was on the Committee for looking at it in detail, and it forms the basis of a good deal of the administration today.

But it took a very long time to get through and a great deal of harm was done during the debates by Winston and his die-hards. Halifax, who was Viceroy, believed that there was a good chance that we might have got it accepted and had an all-Indian Government but for Churchill and his die-hards. That is one of the things one has to chalk down against the old boy. Then came the war and the Chamberlain Government declared India to be at war without asking any advice or opinion, or seeking support anywhere. That was a grave mistake. It promoted the general feeling that it wasn't India's war, so that when Japan came in there was a good deal of Asianism and a certain amount of wanting to go in with the Japs. It didn't extend very far, but it went some distance.

Williams: Do you think you helped things by ordering the arrest of Gandhi and Nehru – a decision that you yourself actually took, as I remember, when Churchill was away and you were in charge?

Attlee: Yes. It was necessary.

Williams: Why was it necessary? Surely it was a risky thing to do, considering its possible effect on Indian opinion.

Attlee: I don't think so. If they chose to set themselves against the Government in war they had to answer for it.

Williams: Did you consider there to be a substantial danger of a Japanese invasion of India?

Attlee: Yes. Very much so. If it hadn't been for the successful defence in Burma they might have been right in.

Williams: Then wasn't it very desirable to have the civilian population on your side?

Attlee: We had to, yes.

Williams: Then wasn't it a risk to arrest their leaders? Mightn't it have made them more pro-Japanese?

Attlee: I don't think so.

Williams: Why?

Attlee: Because I think at the bottom of their minds they knew perfectly well that the Japanese were not really going to fight for the liberation of India. Nor did they want to come in under Japan. We had to make the arrests to stop a dangerous drift. But after that we got to work to try to improve things. We had a strong committee – a special Committee on India, with John Anderson, who'd been Governor of Bengal, P. J. Grigg, who'd been Finance Member of the Government of India at one time, Leo Amery, Cripps and myself. We did a lot of planning and we arranged for the Cripps Mission to go out to try and get on terms with the Indian leaders. It was greatly to the credit of Winston that he accepted that, when he didn't like the idea of any change in India really.

The idea was to set up a great constitution-making body immediately after the war with a firm promise of Dominion status. The plan we put up was very much on the lines we'd discussed with them before the war, when they seemed attracted by it, and the Cripps Mission got very near to success. Cripps did as good a job as any man could possible have done and there seemed a real chance that Nehru would co-operate. But Gandhi turned difficult.

Williams: What was your judgment of Gandhi?

Attlee: A combination of saint and astute politician – Gladstone must have been a bit like him – but with ideas difficult to reconcile with modern views of progress, difficult for the West to appreciate anyway. But a tremendous force.

Williams: Which did you find uppermost – politician or saint?

Attlee: On the whole the saint, I think. It didn't make it any easier. Saints don't fit in awfully well with a democracy any more than do sinners. And the dictatorial saint can be quite as bad as the dictatorial sinner, you know, especially if he thinks you're a sinner. Anyway in spite of all Cripps's efforts – and he had a liking for saints himself of course; a bit of the same mixture – he couldn't get Gandhi to agree, nor in the end Jinnah. So we were back where we started.

It was against this long background of breakdown and frustration, now further aggravated by serious food shortage and famine in many areas and complicated by bitter dissensions between Hindu and Moslem and by mounting violence, that Attlee set to work to try to solve the Indian problem. The last effort of the war-time Government to reach some foothold for future progress had been the calling of a Viceroy's Conference at Simla to establish a more widely representative Executive Council. A fortnight before Attlee took office this Conference broke down, mainly because of difficulties raised by Jinnah and the Moslem League.

He at once called Wavell, who had succeeded Lord Linlithgow as Viceroy in June 1943, to London for further consultations. Two weeks later he and Wavell broadcast simultaneously from Downing Street and New Delhi announcing that elections to the Central and Provincial Legislatures, which had been postponed throughout the war, would be held as soon as the cold weather season began, and a constitution-making body convened thereafter. At the same time a goodwill party of M.P.s of all parties was sent to India. None of these measures, however, produced any improvement in the situation. In yet another effort to get both Hindu and Moslem support for an All-India Constitution-making Convention, Attlee dispatched a Cabinet Mission to India to negotiate with political leaders and representatives of the Indian States.

Attlee: I sent out three Ministers to negotiate – Cripps, Pethick-Lawrence and A. V. Alexander. They laboured very, very hard. However, by this time the Moslem objection to Hindus, which was always rather strong, had grown to breaking point. One reason was that in the interim period there had been Congress Ministries established under the old régime and they had managed to put off the Moslems pretty effectively. The mission broke down on the absolute refusal of the Moslems to come in. The three of them came back and reported. The Viceroy came and reported. Then the question was what was the next thing to be done.

Wavell had been a very good Viceroy in many ways but he was not quite the man to deal with politicians, particularly Indian politicians. He was a soldier and a singularly silent soldier. A great man in many ways, you know, but a curious silent bird, and I don't think silent people get on very well with Indians, who are very loquacious. His mind wasn't supple enough. Moreover I'd come to the conclusion from my own experience of Indians that there was a great deal of happiness for them in asking for everything, and putting down everything that was wrong in India to British rule, and then sitting pretty. I thought that most of them were not really keen on responsibility. They would talk and talk and talk, and as long as they could put the responsibility on us they would continue to quarrel among themselves. Therefore I concluded the thing to do was to bring them right up against it and make them see they'd got to face the situation themselves.

I decided that the only thing to do was to set a time-limit and say: 'Whatever happens, our rule is ending on that date.' It was, of course, a somewhat dangerous venture. But one had also to remember that inevitably the machine of administration in

India was running down. It couldn't go on much longer. The process of Indianisation had gone a good way. We had got over the problem of the Army I mentioned earlier, which had been a serious factor at the time of the Simon Commission. There were now plenty of well trained Indian officers available to take over. But this Indianisation had also resulted in a very heavy reduction in the British cadre in administration. More than half the British in the Indian Civil Service had gone. The I.C.S. Indians worked extremely loyally, but it was idle to suppose that they weren't just as patriotic as everybody else and just as enthusiastic for Indian nationalism. There'd been no recruitment during the war and it was extremely difficult, if not impossible, to get people of the high qualities needed when the whole thing might soon come to an end. Therefore the machine was running down, and the longer it went on, the worse would administration be and the more difficult it would become for whomever we handed over to in the end.

So we decided on a time-limit. The Indians were to be told, 'We are going out at a certain date.' Then I had to consider who could do it.

Wavell was frankly pretty defeatist by then. He produced a plan worked out by his I.C.S. advisers for the evacuation of India with everybody moving from where they were by stages right up through the Ganges valley till eventually, apparently, they would be collected at Karachi and Bombay and sail away. Well, I thought that was what Winston would certainly quite properly describe as an ignoble and sordid scuttle and I wouldn't look at it. I came to the conclusion that Wavell had shot his bolt, and that I must find somebody else. I thought very hard on that and looked all round. And suddenly I had what I now think was an inspiration. I thought of Mountbatten.

Now Mountbatten was an extremely lively, exciting personality. He had an extraordinary faculty for getting on with all kinds of people, as he'd shown when he was Supremo in South-East Asia. He was also blessed with a very unusual wife. So I put it to him. Bit of a shock for him, you know, because one of Dickie's great hopes was that he would one day succeed to the position of First Sea Lord, from which his father had been most disgracefully thrown out in the anti-German cry at the beginning of World War One. He didn't want to drop his naval career. But I talked to him and he very patriotically agreed to take on the job. I told him I would talk to the Lords of the Admiralty with regard to his sea service and see to it his naval career wasn't jeopardised by taking a shore job. I saw the King and rather unexpectedly he warmly approved of the idea right away – not everyone would let a member of the Royal Family go and take a risky job, hit or miss, in India as he did.

I told him, as I'd told Mountbatten too, that I thought the odds were about six to four against success, but they both agreed Mountbatten should take on the job. He went out under conditions on which we were both entirely agreed – that he was going out not to continue the British Raj but to end it. He made an extremely wise selection of assistants in Ismay, who at great personal sacrifice took on the job as his Chief of Staff, and Sir Eric Miéville, and he was extraordinarily successful from the start. He got on the right side of Nehru and he managed to get a joint Government going for the time being with Jinnah and Nehru and the rest. He got on the right side of Gandhi, too, and soon he had all these people talking constantly. And always prominently on his desk to remind them was a card with the date when we going.

It took a lot of work and a lot of negotiation. But he won, and eventually the day came when we passed the Independence of India Act in the House of Commons.

At the bitter end of course Winston was very strongly opposed and several Indian authorities like Anderson and Butler also thought we were being precipitate. The argument always is of course: 'Go slow and things will get better.' But there are occasions when if you hesitate and go slow things get not better but worse. I was quite sure this was one of the instances where the dictate 'Go slow' could not be applied and we must go ahead and fix the date early. And it came off.

There followed, as you know, terrible massacres, but they were not just the result of handing over, or of any feebleness by the Government. They'd been brewing for a long time. They started with one lot killing the other in Bengal. Then they did the same in Bihar and on up to the U.P. and so on eventually up to the Punjab, where there were a very sticky lot of people, not only a good many Moslems and Hindus but also the Sikhs, very undependable and rather a rough people: they were the biggest cause of the trouble. Whether we could have stopped it then if we'd still been in control I don't know – it's very doubtful. But there it was. I can only say that the death roll would have been far higher if we hadn't come out – if we'd tried to hold India.

We were very lucky in having Nehru to deal with and that he and Mountbatten got on so well. At first both sides wanted to have Mountbatten carrying on as Governor-General of both Dominions, although eventually, of course, Jinnah decided to be Governor-General of Pakistan himself. But it was a very high tribute to Mountbatten, because it's very rare that a nationalist Government doesn't want to sweep away everything. The Indians wanted Mountbatten to carry on for a limited time as the first Governor-General and they did the same in continuing Archie Nye as Governor of Madras, again a very high tribute.

What we had to agree to, unfortunately – it wasn't our wish at all – was the division of India. We'd argued on every possible safeguard for the Moslems but they wouldn't do it. By this time they'd become absolutely fixed on a separate Moslem State – Pakistan – and we had to agree to it. We sent out Lord Radcliffe to fix the boundaries. We couldn't have had anyone better, but, of course, anybody who attempts to fix boundaries anywhere offends everybody: a thankless task. Jinnah was not a man I ever thought very highly of. I'd known him since 1927, and he'd destroyed one of the most promising experiments in joint government in the Punjab. But fortunately he had good people around him and a first-class man in Liaquat Ali Khan as his Prime Minister.

We would have preferred a United India. We couldn't get it,

though we tried hard. But broadly speaking the thing went off well, I think. That was because we handed over power in India on a definite announced date and they knew they had to take it. That was absolutely essential. And of course our own people in India played up remarkably well. When Halifax, who was the most sympathetic Viceroy there'd ever been, I think, left India he had a letter from the younger members of the commercial community in India thanking him for what he'd done and saying they would always be prepared to work towards the success of his ideas. A very fine thing. When we came to hand over, a lot of people said we must have safeguards for British trade and industry. But the British business people there said: 'No. We don't ask for anything. We are perfectly content to rest on goodwill.' They were abundantly justified. There are more British business people in India than ever before and they're treated absolutely fairly. The same goes for the Civil Servants. Of course a good many retired, but those who did stay worked admirably and helped in all sorts of ways in setting up these new states. This was important in the case of Pakistan because the Moslems hadn't been very strongly represented in the Indian administrative services and without the British administrators they wouldn't have been able to carry on.

It was the same with British officers. Unfortunately the Indian Army had to be split, but the old traditions remained. There were a number of very able generals who hadn't, on the whole, ever played politics in India and who stayed on to help. It was a remarkable demonstration altogether. It was because of this sort of co-operation that the experiment came off and that when we came out of India we left behind so much goodwill.

Williams: What about Burma?

Attlee: We had to deal with the parallel problem of what to do there. I'd had a look at Burma when I was on the Simon Commission. Its conquest had been mounted from India and it had been treated for years as an Indian province administered very largely by Indians who tended to regard the Burmese as rather inferior – in fact, they were slightly imperialist over it. During the war, of course, Burma was overrun and a lot of Burmans co-operated with the Japanese.

However in the course of the war they found out what the Japanese were like and then the young Burmans began to start negotiations with us. That was one of the points that inclined me to Mountbatten. As Supremo in South-East Asia he had not hesitated to enter into negotiations with the young Burmans and as a result some of them took part in the closing stages of the campaign on our side. Naturally they wanted independence in the same way as the Indians did. There was a Government in exile in India with the Governor, Sir Reginald Dorman-Smith, but they were very elderly sort of people quite out of touch with the nationalist movement that had grown up.

The country was in such a bad state that there had to be a period of military government after the war. This was quite good from the point of view of pulling the country together again but naturally brought a lot of resistance from those who wanted to press on to independence. Inevitably there was disturbance and a good deal of banditry, which used to be one of the national sports in Burma, and when I became P.M. I didn't at all like the reports that were coming in. We urgently needed Burmese rice for India and other places, but there was complete confusion and breakdown, with White Flag Communists and Red Flag Communists and all kinds of other people. A previous decision to hand over to civilian control as soon as possible didn't help things because it came prematurely. I kept getting conflicting reports about the new young leaders in the Anti-Fascist People's Freedom League, as they called themselves. At one time we were told they wanted to co-operate. Then the next report that would come along was that it was necessary to clap them all in quod.

So eventually I sent for them. Very nice lot of lads I found them when they came. They were nervous and shy at first, thought we were all tyrants and imperialists and were very surprised at the way they were treated. They asked for Burma's self-government. I said, 'Certainly; how are we going to do it?' and gradually we won them over. I had considerable admiration for their leader, U Aung San. He was a man of courage and capacity, a stout fellow. So were several of the others, like Thakin Nu, and we agreed pretty well with them. The question whether they should stay in the Commonwealth was at that time still open. They had committed themselves heavily to being a republic, but I think if their leaders had lived they might well have remained in the Commonwealth.

However, among those who came over was a nasty fellow, U Saw. I'd met him before the war – a smiling fellow whom I didn't trust. He'd been a co-operator with the Japanese, then he came over to this country and we found him trying to make contact with the German Embassy in Lisbon one day and had to intern him.

We had very useful talks with Aung San and the others. I think they began to see that you could be free and still be in the Commonwealth and were moving from their first position. But when they got back to Burma, U Saw murdered the lot of them. He sent men with sten guns to a meeting of the Executive Council and shot them as they sat round the table.

Fortunately, we had a very able Governor in Sir Hubert Rance. I was indebted to Mountbatten for him. I wanted someone who would manage Burma and I asked him to help me. We found Rance. He'd done civil affairs under Mountbatten and he acted very promptly when this murder took place. It was largely due to him that they got hold of U Saw and his supporters and that Thakin Nu was able, with great courage, to take over – by great good fortune he'd just gone out of the room when the gunmen arrived.

We left it entirely open to the Burmese to decide regarding the Commonwealth – whether they would stay in or go out. They decided to go out, but it hasn't worked badly although they took a long time to get rid of Communist opposition – armed opposition, which faded quite easily at the end, and I think they might have been wiser to have held on to more English personnel. Rance did a first-class job in the interim period. When Mountbatten first suggested him to me he was a colonel in the Signals. The War Office was shocked when I told them I proposed to make him Governor of Burma. They pointed out that there were several more senior officers sitting in corners waiting for something to turn up who ought to be given precedence over a mere colonel. They didn't seem to realise that one might prefer special qualifications in a man. Rance did extremely well. He was the effective midwife of Burma.

On the day of the declaration of Indian independence and the transfer of power Mountbatten wrote personally to Attlee to describe the pro-British scenes. They were, he declared, so remarkable that he had asked his former Private Secretary, Sir George Abell, to seek an interview on his arrival in London to describe them in more detail.

'The man who made it possible,' he concluded, 'was you yourself. Without your original guidance and your unwavering support nothing could have been accomplished out here.' It was a considered and generous tribute by one whose own personal contribution to the success of the Cabinet's policy had been of unique importance.

Prior to Attlee's decision to replace Wavell by Mountbatten and give a definite date for British withdrawal the situation had seemed almost hopeless: any possibility that it could be resolved in such a way as to leave behind a firm basis of friendship appeared out of the question.

Indeed even those most friendly to India saw almost no possibility of a happy outcome. 'No one seems to expect us to succeed in getting the parties to come to agreement among themselves. Most Indians seem to assume that it will be the English who will settle the matter for them, and then no doubt they will combine to make an Aunt Sally of us.' So Pethick-Lawrence had written to Attlee during the Cabinet mission, describing 'our latest effort in this Alice in Wonderland croquet party'. This was the general opinion.

It was the decision to announce a time-limit and Mountbatten's constant reminder to the Indian leaders that it was running out, combined with the remarkable degree of personal friendship and understanding he succeeded in establishing with them, and particularly with Nehru, that made it possible for Attlee to carry his Indian policy to success.

Mountbatten had from the first been wholly charged with the need both for a strict time-limit and for making it abundantly clear that there was no intention of perpetuating the Viceregal system. His first hope indeed was that it would be possible for him, as he wrote to Attlee on 20 December 1946 following their first talk, 'to go out at the open invitation of the Indian parties in a capacity which they would themselves define.' 'I know', he wrote in this same letter, 'you would not wish me to accept your offer unless I felt I had a reasonable chance of succeeding in these tasks and I do not feel I could tackle this job with confidence if the manner of my appointment suggested to the Indians that we wished to perpetuate the Viceregal system or intended to exercise the right to impose our nominees to arbitrate in their affairs. I feel, at this late stage, such an impression would constitute a disadvantage which neither Wavell nor the Cabinet Mission had to face.'

With this view Attlee agreed entirely. Although it was, as he explained to Mountbatten, impossible for many reasons to secure an open invitation from the Indian parties, he was firm in his view that the announcement of the appointment of the new Viceroy must include a declaration terminating the British Raj on a definite and specified date or earlier (as in fact happened) if the Indian parties could agree on a constitution and form a Government.

Sir Stafford Cripps, who had had long personal associations with Gandhi, Nehru and other Congress leaders apart from his two official visits to India, was equally convinced of the necessity. So anxious, indeed, was he to help that he went so far as make a suggestion which proved somewhat embarrassing. This was that he should himself accompany the new Viceroy to India and give him any help his knowledge of the country and its leading personalities might permit.

Very wisely Mountbatten, while declaring himself honoured and touched, refused to accept the offer. 'I felt', he wrote to Attlee on 3 January 1947, 'that the presence of a man of his prestige and experience could not fail to reduce me to a mere figurehead in the eyes of the people we would be negotiating with; and that this was not the impression that either he or you would wish the appointment of a new Viceroy to create.' Instead he suggested that, so that he could have full advantage of Sir Stafford's unrivalled knowledge, the Prime Minister might be prepared to consider his becoming Secretary of State. This, however, Attlee did not think necessary or advisable.

Mountbatten also discussed with Attlee his desire to meet not only the Indian leaders but ordinary Indian people on much less formal terms than had been the case with previous Viceroys. 'Although it would,' he wrote in this same letter, 'be our intention to observe the protocol necessary to uphold the position of Viceroy and Vicereine, my wife and I would wish to visit Indian leaders and representative British and Indian people in their own homes and unaccompanied by staff; and to make ourselves easier of access than the existing protocol appears to have made possible.'

It was a course of which Attlee thoroughly approved and which played a large part in the successful outcome of the negotiations.

When the final agreements on partition were taken, there remained the problem that the Congress Party was committed to a republican State. Could this be made compatible with membership of the Commonwealth?

The King, who had taken a close and enlightened interest in the Indian negotiations, concurred wholeheartedly with Attlee that it was very desirable to find some way in which the republican status of the new State could be reconciled with Commonwealth membership. Attlee then saw Mr Churchill and other Conservative Leaders to obtain their views before meeting Commonwealth Prime Ministers. He reported to the King:

10 Downing Street
Whitehall

'Sir, 2nd March 1949

'With my humble duty, I venture to think that Your Majesty may be interested to receive an early account of my meeting this afternoon with Mr Churchill and his colleagues on the subject of India's relation to the Commonwealth. I shall give a report on this discussion to the Cabinet tomorrow.

'I saw Mr Churchill, Mr Stanley, Lord Swinton, Mr Butler and Sir David Maxwell Fyfe. I explained very fully the position which had arisen with regard to India's membership of the Commonwealth and the steps which were being taken to inform the Governments in the other Commonwealth countries of the factors to be considered in coming to a decision. I informed them of the intention to hold a Prime Ministers' Conference and handed them copies of the paper, "India's Future Relations with the Commonwealth".

'Mr Churchill said that he would consider this with his friends. In the course of a short discussion which followed Mr Churchill gave it as his own opinion that it was most important to keep India in the Commonwealth While fully agreeing with the importance of not weakening the link of the allegiance to the Crown, he thought that it should be possible to retain a republican India in the Commonwealth.

'Mr Churchill made the same suggestion which Your Majesty made yesterday, as to the possibility of Your Majesty being the President of India. I felt that the other members were in general agreement with the broad line which Mr Churchill had taken. I was gratified with the general attitude. I hope to see the Liberal leaders tomorrow.

'I remain, with my humble duty, Your Majesty's most faithful and devoted servant,

C. R. Attlee'

A meeting of Commonwealth Prime Ministers followed.

Attlee comments: 'They were extremely useful because they could explain to Nehru, as Peter Fraser of New Zealand did, that the Commonwealth was not independence minus but independence plus. Greatly to the credit of his statesmanship, Nehru decided to come in. I went over the Indian insistence on republican status very carefully with the Commonwealth Prime Ministers because one of the links in the Commonwealth had always been union in allegiance to the Throne, and it was therefore a very interesting proposition. But they agreed that the right thing was to accept India as a republic and we all went together to see the King – the first time, I think, a King had ever had the collective advice of all his Prime Ministers. We told him what we advised, and he agreed.

'There was then the question of a new title. The old G.R.I. had gone, because the King was no longer Emperor. We proposed that for this should be substituted "Head of the Commonwealth", which appealed not only to the Indians but to everybody else because it had a wider application for the future than the first suggestion, President of India, could possibly have had. Thereby we put a new title to the Crown. George VI made not the slightest objection to removing the Imperial Crown from his head – the chief jewel of the British Empire. That is a remarkable fact. It shows the great advantage of having a King who was never static but who moved forward with the times.'

14

Political Crisis at Home

It is one of the ironies of the political life, which abounds in changes of fortune and fluctuations of reputation, that 1947 should have been not only a year of personal triumph for Attlee in the Indian Independence Act but also one of crisis, culminating in an attempt led by almost his closest associate in the Indian settlement, Stafford Cripps, to replace him as Prime Minister by Ernest Bevin.

The year opened disastrously at home with the fuel crisis, which temporarily brought all industry to a stop as the country was gripped in the hardest winter since 1880. Attlee still believes that but for the ill-luck of the weather it would have been just possible to get through without a breakdown, although even while the War Coalition was in office there had been expert warnings of industrial crisis in the immediate post-war period as a consequence of the running down of the coal industry and the suspension of capital investment in new power stations and rolling stock and other essential plant during the war.

Several Ministers, however, felt that both the country and the Cabinet had been misled by the Minister of Fuel and Power, Emanuel Shinwell, and there was heavy criticism of him. Dalton, who as Chancellor of the Exchequer was inevitably brought into very close association with Shinwell in the effort to overcome economic difficulties, was particularly insistent on the urgent need for a change. Both Cripps and he, he wrote to Attlee, were terrified by Shinwell's 'sloppy sunshine talks' which continuously put the Cabinet in the position of being discredited by events. Nor did the passing of the worst phase of the crisis as the weather improved change his feeling. He continued to complain: 'If only there were a decent Minister in that job – Gaitskell or any other – I could talk to him as I do to my other colleagues frankly and constructively. . . . But with Shinwell all this is impossible.'

Meanwhile Cripps was writing in, if anything, even stronger terms: 'I have become even more convinced that it is *essential* that a change should be made at the Ministry of Fuel. I am sure this view is held almost universally by your colleagues and certainly it is by the country and by industry in particular.'

Dalton urged that James Griffiths, who had the confidence both of his colleagues and of the miners, should go to Fuel and Power, and that Shinwell should be moved to the Dominions Office. This latter proposal horrified Cripps when he heard of it. 'The more I have thought it over,' he wrote, 'the more unfortunate it seems. . . . It would be taken as a most serious slight upon all the Dominions. The protests, which would be loudly and vociferously made by the Opposition here, would not only be echoed in our own ranks but would be endorsed by the Dominions.'

Despite these and other criticisms Attlee was not disposed to move, in the middle of a crisis only partly of his making, a Minister who had the confidence of the miners: a matter of importance since much depended on their readiness to accept measures to increase output. And that there were other views of Shinwell's capacity than those of Dalton and Cripps was shown in a letter of 10 February from Lord Citrine, former General Secretary of the T.U.C. and at this time Director of the National Coal Board in charge of industrial relations. He wrote, 'He (Shinwell) has little to reproach himself with. Within my experience he has shown himself to be courageous, decisive, adept at his subjects. . . . The miners speak to me highly of him and quite evidently trust him.'

Attlee himself had a higher opinion of Shinwell's capacity in many directions than had either Cripps or Dalton, and although he realised a fresh momentum was needed to get over the fuel crisis, he met this by an emergency Fuel and Power Committee of the Cabinet under his own chairmanship. Not until the autumn did he move Shinwell, whom he then sent to the War Office, where, to many people's surprise, he proved highly successful, as he also did later when promoted to the Ministry of Defence.

Instead of replacing Shinwell at Fuel and Power by a trade unionist, as he was urged to do by several Ministers, Attlee promoted Hugh Gaitskell, who had originally been sent to that Ministry as Parliamentary Secretary 'in order to supplement the Minister's deficiencies in some directions' – a course Attlee often followed in his appointments. He thus set Gaitskell on the ladder which was to bring him to the Leadership of the Party when Attlee himself resigned.

A year which opened with the fuel crisis moved on from that to an exchange crisis in August, when the convertibility clause in the American Loan Agreement had to be suspended. It thereafter provided continuous economic difficulties and austerities, plus the incidental tribulation of the forced resignation of the Chancellor of the Exchequer, Hugh Dalton, as a result of one of the silliest indiscretions in recent political history. Such a year was not likely to enhance the confidence and internal harmony of any Government.

In an attempt to establish greater control over the unhappy course of economic events Attlee first tried the experiment of delegating to Herbert Morrison as Lord President of the Council wider authority over economic co-ordination and planning. This did not turn out very successful – partly because Morrison fell ill and had to go into Hammersmith Hospital to be treated for thrombosis, partly because it was not a task for which he was much suited. By September, Dalton, whose own policy and administration at the Treasury were now coming under increasing criticism, was writing to Attlee, 'Herbert just can't do it. No one who really understands what the problems are believes that he can. None of the Planners believe it.'

He urged that Stafford Cripps should be given 'responsibility as Minister of Production, or whatever the job is called for co-ordinating and directing all home production and export. He knows and you know that I will work with him, from the personal side and on the Treasury official level *with complete confidence and harmony.*' All those concerned with the carrying out of economic policy, he continued, would have complete confidence in Cripps. 'I beg of you,' he concluded, '*to insist on this.* Otherwise we have a very poor chance – or none at all – of getting through.'

The view that Morrison was wrongly cast as an economic co-ordinator was supported by other powerful Ministers, including Bevin. Bevin had once included both Cripps and Morrison in his general disfavour. But his opinion of Cripps's abilities had risen steadily with experience of working with him while his judgment of Morrison's had not.

Cripps however was in poor health. He had been compelled to go to a sanatorium in Zürich for treatment the previous year. This had seemed successful and he had written to Attlee full of hope:

30.8.46 Zürich

'My dearest Clem,

'Thank you so much for your most dear letter – it was very nice of you to find time to write.

'I have at last broken the insomnia and all should proceed well now and I hope to be quite fit to return on the 10th.

'I am afraid you have not had much of a time of rest with all the world in turmoil.

'Our dearest love to you all.

Yours,

STAFFORD'

He was, however, still obviously working under considerable strain and there could not but be some doubt as to how he would stand up under a still heavier burden of work.

While Attlee hesitated, Cripps let it become known that in his view something even bigger was required: the replacement of Attlee himself. Encouraged by his recently developed accord with Bevin, for whose personality and toughness he had acquired a very considerable admiration, he suggested that the proper course was for Attlee to step down as Prime Minister and make way for Bevin, taking over the Foreign Office in his place. Alternatively if Bevin did not want to leave foreign affairs Attlee could go to the Treasury while Cripps himself took over at No. 10 – the one essential thing was that there should be a Prime Minister who would inspire the country.

The idea of some such change gained a good deal of newspaper backing as it leaked out and gathered support among a number of M.P.s. In contradiction to the earlier attempt to displace Attlee, which had come from the Left, this latest move was backed by some younger members of the right wing of the Party and a number of trade unionists. Morrison, conscious no doubt that neither Cripps nor Bevin was very favourable to him, stood aloof. Nor did the idea gain the approval of any of the solid middle group in the Cabinet or in the Parliamentary Party. What was even more decisive was the contemptuous anger Bevin displayed when approached.

'Who,' he asked, 'do you think I am? Lloyd George?' Attlee, he added, was the best Prime Minister any Labour Government could possibly have and anyone who wanted to get rid of him was a fool.

Throughout these various moves, of which he could not help but be aware, Attlee remained unperturbed. He was prepared to step down if the Party wanted him to do so, and he let Bevin and others know this. But he had no intention of bowing to the desires of a minority or of letting himself be distracted from his proper job by troubling himself about intrigues. Still less did he concern himself with what the newspapers had to say. He was 'allergic to newspapers' and rarely bothered to read any but *The Times* and the *Daily Herald*.

Nor did the knowledge that Cripps would like to see him out of 10 Downing Street deflect him from his growing conviction that he was the right man to replace Morrison at the head of economic affairs. He bore him no malice and hard on the heels of the collapse of his Cabinet manœuvres appointed him to the new post of Minister of Economic Affairs with more extensive powers over the economic policy of the nation than any Minister in peace-time had ever before possessed. Six weeks later, when Dalton was compelled to resign the Chancellorship as a result of a few incautious words to the Political Correspondent of the *Star* a few seconds before beginning his Budget speech, he added further to these powers by making Cripps Chancellor of the Exchequer as well – a logical combination.

Cripps's own judgment of Attlee's place in popular esteem altered a good deal over the next two years. On the eve of the 1950 Election he wrote to him on 20 January to say, 'I am very worried about the broadcasting arrangements that have been announced and though it is nothing to do with me I do not think it would be right for me to neglect expressing my view. My main objection is to the wind-up, which I think you should do, not Herbert . . . Herbert has nothing like the same influence as you have . . . People will not pay attention to his answer to Winston as they will to yours.'

Not only did the attempt by Stafford Cripps to form a cabal against Attlee affect in no way their future relations, which in many ways became closer; it did not in any way change Bevin's attitude to Cripps, despite his normal hostility to those, such as Morrison, whom he suspected, rightly or wrongly, of 'conspiring' against the Leader to whom he had given his friendship and loyalty. His respect for Cripps's character and ability remained unaffected and the two continued to work together in increasing amity and regard. Together they went to Washington in September 1949 to try to negotiate a new economic and trading settlement to accompany what had by this time manifestly become unavoidable – a devaluation of the pound.

Subsequently a number of suggestions – and accusations – were made that devaluation had been forced on the British Government by the United States. In fact it was decided by the Cabinet before Bevin and Cripps left. The decision to devalue was communicated to the Americans at the first meeting in a statement which Bevin and Cripps drew up and which gave the reasons. But it was not made a subject for discussion. Immediately on getting back to the Embassy Bevin wrote to Attlee to describe the American reactions:

British Embassy,
Washington, D.C.
7th September 1949

'Dear Clem,

'Today we held our first meeting of Ministers, at which the Chancellor made a statement, a copy of which is also being sent to you. Because of the nature of the statement no actual discussion took place. It was, however, taken very seriously, and all subsequent approaches to the problem will, to a large extent, be governed by our decision, which will, of course, be kept very secret.

'We went on to discuss our future procedure. An agenda was approved and the Ministers formed themselves into a steering committee. The proceedings of this committee will be kept strictly secret and they will meet as often as required. There will also be a general committee of Ministers and leading officials and a number of working groups who will consider the whole problem in its different aspects. The exact terms of reference of these different sub-committees have not yet been agreed, but they will no doubt include commercial exchange (tariffs, customs etc.), U.S. purchases, establishment of a continuing organisation, overseas investment policy and oil.

'We met again in the afternoon . . . Acheson made a helpful intervention stressing the link between the financial problem on the one hand and the political and strategic problems on the other. I responded to this and I think my words went home. At the morning's meeting we had not failed to emphasise the importance of our decision from the point of view of maintaining peace.

'On the whole the atmosphere is very good, and I think we are going to get to grips with the problem very speedily.

Yours sincerely,

ERNEST BEVIN'

Bevin's hopes were justified – to some degree at any rate. The U.S. Administration accepted the fact that devaluation by itself could not improve Britain's international trading position to the extent needed. They accepted in principle the need for lower U.S. tariffs and more simple customs procedures and agreed that America should accept the obligations of a great creditor nation by increasing her investments abroad, particularly in undeveloped areas. In addition an alteration in the terms of Marshall Aid was approved, to enable Britain to buy Canadian wheat with American dollars. But it was devaluation that naturally made the biggest impact on public opinion. Its effect on Cripps himself was of considerable political significance.

This is Attlee's summing-up: 'Devaluation was, in fact, quite unavoidable. The pound was over-valued and we had extreme difficulty with the foreign exchange situation. I don't think anyone else could have done differently. But I am afraid Stafford did take it rather hard. He had a feeling that people were accusing him of something not quite honourable, particularly as he'd had to deny it right up to the last. He was rather a silly ass that way. There were an increasing number of rumours. They were affecting exchange rates and they had to be denied, you can't let that sort of decision be known until it comes into effect. Having to deny what was the truth was no doubt hard on a Christian like Stafford, but he wouldn't have let it worry him if he'd had any sense. As for devaluation itself, one just had to do it. Of course if the Americans had released some of the gold they had in Fort Knox, that might have changed things, but they wouldn't. We were in the position of playing a game in which all the chips were in the hands of one player – and he kept them in his pocket.'

The 1945 Parliament was now nearing the end of its life and it became necessary to think about the date of the General Election. There was a good case for holding it as early as possible in the New Year, but against this was the argument that the effect of devaluation on Britain's competitive position in world markets should be given more time to show itself. This was put forward by several of the younger financial experts in the Party, who claimed that electoral prospects would improve with delay. For a number of practical reasons, including the weather, Herbert Morrison, the chief party tactician, was also against an early Election. To postpone it until the middle of the year meant, however, having the Budget first, and to this Cripps was opposed. He was still smarting under the criticism that he had misled the country over devaluation, he felt that he had been put in a morally difficult position and would lay himself open to further criticism if he brought in a pre-Election Budget.

Attlee: He thought he would be expected to produce an Election Budget which went against his sense of rectitude. I sympathised with him. It is dangerous to play politics with the Budget. It opens the way to every possible kind of stunt.

Williams: I have heard it argued that if the Election had been delayed and the effect of devaluation in improving our export trade and our general economic position had been given time to develop you might have got a sufficient working majority in 1950 to make the 1951 Election unnecessary. In that case Labour would still have been in office when the terms of international trade turned in our favour after the Korean War ended and it became possible to take off controls and ease things all round – which might have altered the course of politics considerably, indeed there might still be a Labour Government.

Attlee: That's all very conjectural. Things were difficult and I don't see how we could have delayed an Election long. In my view it would have been wrong to bring out a Budget without first testing the sense of the country. It is true we hadn't lost a single by-election – a record, that – but the local elections had shown a strong flow against us and it was only right that the country should be given a chance to express itself.

What really damaged us was the redistribution of seats. We knew it was inevitable that a number of normal Tory seats, places in Bucks and Herts and so on, which had come over to us in 1945 would revert. But as a result of redistribution a number of constituencies in the East End of London and some of the big industrial centres from which there had been a big transfer of population because of bombing were done away with, including my own in Limehouse. The total number of seats in East and South-East London was cut by half – from eighteen to nine – and those that went had all been Labour strongholds. Elsewhere the result of redistribution in a good many cases was to transfer Labour votes from marginal constituencies to solid Labour seats, so that we got bigger majorities where we were already safe but lost Labour voters where we would otherwise have had a good fighting chance – often much more than a fighting chance.

'One vote one value is a good principle, but we probably pressed on with it too far before movements of population had really settled down – there was bound to be a flow back to Poplar, Stepney, West Ham and the rest, given time. We suffered for being too moral over that. But I don't think we could have delayed the Election. And even if we had, the effects of redistribution would have been the same.'

In the event, when the General Election took place in February Labour's total vote rose by more than a million and a quarter. But its overall majority in the House of Commons fell from 152 to 10.

15

To Stop a Third World War

Four months after being returned as Prime Minister with so meagre a majority Attlee was called on to meet a major international crisis – the invasion of Korea. He had no hesitation as to where national duty lay. 'Naked aggression, and it must be checked,' he told the House of Commons. British troops were already heavily involved in fighting Communist forces in Malaya, but United Kingdom and Commonwealth forces were the first to join those of the United States in Korea.

He was, however, much concerned lest the Soviet should use the Korean campaign to tie up American and British forces so as to give themselves greater freedom of action elsewhere. It was essential to think globally. Twelve days after the crossing of the 38th Parallel by North Korean troops he sent the following personal message to President Truman:

'Personal to President from Prime Minister. 6th July 1950

'I have been giving much thought to the problems which are likely to face us as the situation in Korea develops. These problems are of course primarily military but they are likely to have increasingly wide political implications.

'The implications will concern not only the way in which we should like to see the situation in Korea develop but also the likely reactions of the Russians as it develops. Russian reaction may be expected not only in the Far East; we have been giving some thought to other parts of the world where the Soviet Government may cause trouble for us.

'A particular aspect of the situation in Korea which is causing us concern is that the Russians have involved the Western

Powers in a heavy commitment without themselves playing an overt part, and there are other areas in the Far East where the same tactics are open to them. You have already made known your concern with Indo-China and Formosa. There is some reason to think that Communist-inspired activities in Malaya have already been stepped up in tune with the Korean affair. And we cannot ignore the possibility of a Chinese attack on Hong Kong.

'But further, we cannot be sure that these activities on the part of Russia will be confined to East Asia. I understand your military advisers have already expressed the view that Persia may again become a danger spot. We should consider whether the opportunity may not be taken of relighting the fire in Greece. And there may be other areas of potential trouble.

'No one can attempt to provide precisely in advance for every eventuality. But I hope you will agree with me that we should look ahead as far as we can and reach some agreement as to our common policy in these areas in the event of further outbreaks.

'I would like to propose to you therefore that representatives of our two Governments should meet to consider what courses of action are most likely to be adopted by the Soviet Government and should have an exploratory discussion of the plans we should adopt to meet them. Plans have already been concerted between us over a wide field but I think that the time may have come for extending the area to which our detailed plans should apply. Other Governments, in particular the French, may be concerned, but it will suffice if they are informed as and when the situation demands.

'I would therefore like to suggest to you that you should authorise the appropriate United States authorities to discuss these problems with Lord Tedder in Washington. If you approve this suggestion, I should propose to send a representative of the United Kingdom Chiefs of Staff to advise Lord Tedder on our thinking here.

'It seems to me that such talks cannot ignore the political implications. I should therefore be glad to hear whether you would propose that the Department of State should be associated with these talks. If so, I should of course arrange for Lord Tedder also to be supplied with appropriate political advice.

'My colleagues and I attach very great importance to reaching the closest possible understanding with the United States Government so that we can both plan in full confidence that we understand each other's approach to these weighty problems. I therefore deeply hope that you will be able to give me an early and favourable reply to this suggestion.'

The favourable reply came quickly and a series of confidential discussions between General Bradley and Truman's Ambassador-at-Large, Mr Phillip Jessup, on the American side and Marshal of the R.A.F. Lord Tedder, Chairman of the Joint Services Mission in Washington, and the Ambassador, Sir Oliver Franks, on the British, began along the lines Attlee had proposed. It was the first co-ordinated attempt to consider each of the potential danger spots of the world in turn, assess their order of strategic and political importance and prepare in advance for joint action in the event of Soviet aggression against any one of them.

Attlee and Truman both agreed that Korea had greatly increased the risk of total war. They were also agreed that it was essential for this reason to avoid as far as possible any action that might invoke or permit Communist attack elsewhere. One immediate result of the policy review initiated on Attlee's suggestion which has particular interest in view of some more recent events was that President Truman countermanded a plan by the U.S. Air Force to send high-flying photographic reconnaissance missions – 'spy planes' – over Darien, Port Arthur, Vladivostok, Karafuto and the Kuril Islands because of the obvious danger of a serious international incident if one crashed or was shot down.

By November, however, Attlee's fears, which extended throughout the whole of Britain and were shared by all parties, that the Korean campaign might become the springboard for a third world war were greatly increased by a turn in American policy which seemed to ignore the principle accepted as essential during the global strategy review in Washington, that an extension of the Korean War must be avoided.

After a brilliant initial advance towards the Manchurian frontier the United Nations forces under General MacArthur had suffered a reverse as a result of the intervention of substantial detachments of Chinese Communist 'volunteers' and there were widespread demands throughout America for a widening of the war. A request by General MacArthur for authority to retaliate against air attacks on his forces from Manchurian bases was passed to the British and other Governments with forces in Korea and was strongly opposed by all. But it was clear that there was a strong group in the Pentagon which was anxious for a showdown with Russia and that it was gaining in force. It also seemed to Attlee that the control exercised over MacArthur by the U.S. Administration was dangerously slight. Finally a statement by Truman himself, at a White House press conference, to the effect that the U.S. Government was determined to meet the military situation in Korea by whatever steps were necessary and that this covered consideration of all weapons, including the atom bomb, convinced Attlee that it was time to make it quite clear once more that Britain was absolutely opposed to any unavoidable extension of the Korean War and would not countenance the use of the atom bomb. He instructed the Foreign Office to send a telegram to the British Ambassador in Washington for transmission to the President informing him of his intention to fly to Washington. The telegram, dated 30 November 1950, read:

'Cabinet has now met and has decided that the Prime Minister should come to Washington as soon as possible for a meeting with President Truman.

'They feel that nothing less than a personal discussion with the President will meet the situation. The President's statement this afternoon has caused most serious difficulties here, and there is a strong feeling that it is essential to have a general review with the United States Government of the situation created by the Chinese intervention in Korea and the possible extension of the war in the Far East.

'We are deeply conscious of the burden which the United States has assumed on behalf of the United Nations in the Far East and the Prime Minister will come in no sense in a mood of criticism, but we feel that it will allay public anxiety, at all events in this country, if a meeting is arranged.

'The Prime Minister will make it clear that the United Kingdom is determined to resist aggression and to play its full part in this task. But in order to do so we must have a clear understanding of the policy objectives and of the role which each of us is to play.

'The Prime Minister would wish to discuss in addition to the Far Eastern situation
'(a) the raw materials position and its effect on our joint ability to play our respective parts
'(b) Western European defence.

'The Prime Minister would like to come at the earliest date convenient to the President.

'In view of the high feeling in Parliament and in the country it is essential that a statement of the Prime Minister's intention should be made tonight. We are trying to get clearance for this through the United States Embassy in London.

'Please act accordingly.'

By a fortunate coincidence M. Pleven, the French Prime Minister, and M. Schuman, the Foreign Minister, were in London on another matter and Attlee was able to see them before leaving.

To the King, who wrote from Sandringham in reply to Attlee's formal request for permission to leave the country, expressing his pleasure that Attlee was going to Washington and his confidence that he would put the case fairly and squarely before the President and explain to him the true picture of the world situation as it was seen by the British people, Attlee wrote:

10 Downing Street,
Whitehall.

'Sir, December 3rd, 1950.

'With my humble duty I thank Your Majesty for your gracious letter and for your kind good wishes for my success in the meeting with President Truman.

'I should have wished to have discussed these matters with Your Majesty, but although the idea of this meeting had been under consideration for some time, the actual timing was dictated by events. The unfortunate statements of the President required immediate action.

'The visit of the French Ministers was unexpected but in the result useful, though they have still some way to go towards meeting the views of the members of the Atlantic Treaty. I have the impression that French public opinion is in advance of that of the French Parliament and that the Ministers dare not go as far as they would wish.

'I agree respectfully with Your Majesty that I should put the whole position very fully and frankly to the President, pointing out that it is not possible for this country to do what it wishes to do in the field of defence, unless the United States Government makes its economic policy conform to the needs of the situation.

'I think that the Americans realise that to get heavily involved in the Far East would be to play the Russian game, and that we must have regard to the broad world strategy.

'Your Majesty's gracious letter gave me much encouragement to deal with the tasks confronting me.

'I remain, with my humble duty, Your Majesty's most faithful and devoted servant

C. R. Attlee'

Attlee flew from London on the Sunday evening of 3 December and reached Washington at 9.30 the following morning.

Attlee: I took with me Bill Slim, who was C.I.G.S. and who did a remarkably good job with the American military when we got over there, and some of our Foreign Office Far Eastern experts. It had always been our view, which I had made quite clear from the start, that the war should be confined to Korea and that it would be a most dangerous mistake to have large forces committed to a major campaign in Asia which would give the Russians exactly the opportunity they wanted for large-scale mischief elsewhere – an open invitation to commit aggression in other parts of the world while we were bogged down. I wasn't satisfied with the control over MacArthur. It seemed to me an odd thing that he had never been called back to Washington for consultations with the Administration and that the only time he and Truman had met was when the President journeyed to Wake Island to see him. I thought it a curious relationship between a Government and a general. Also I was much concerned lest American actions should seem to turn United Nations defence against an aggressor into a war between Europeans and Asians; I was in close touch with the Asian members of the Commonwealth and I appreciated their strong feelings. Finally there was the report of Truman's remarks on the atom bomb. I was much perturbed by that. So were we all – all sides of the House and in the country.

When I arrived in Washington Truman met me at the airport and we went straight to the White House. He had Marshall, who was the Secretary of Defence, Acheson, the Secretary of State, and General Bradley with him, and we got down to things without wasting any time. I pointed out that we were engaged in a global struggle against Communist expansion and it would be suicidal to allow our forces to be bogged down in China, fighting the wrong people in the wrong place at the wrong time. To try to attack China – a huge amorphous mass – was folly and to start bombing in Manchuria was bound to be taken as a form of aggression. Of course there were these so-called volunteers infiltrating, but we had been warned by the Chinese earlier that if we went beyond the 38th Parallel they would intervene. It was MacArthur who had insisted on going beyond and even apart from this initial folly I thought he had made an awful mess of the strategy in his attack and underestimated what he had to meet. Now he was keen on bombing Chinese industrial installations on the other side of the border. I was quite sure that was the wrong policy and that we must not allow the Korean War to develop into an aggressive, all-out war between China and America. South Korea was an outpost of UNO that had to be held. But it was a UNO force and not an American force that was doing the fighting and MacArthur had to be made to remember that.

The Americans raised the question of the threat of the Chinese Communists' claim to Formosa. I said, 'You must understand that this is purely an American opinion. You consider it an offence to American interests. But it has nothing to do with what we are doing under UNO, which is action against an aggresssor. The trouble was it was very difficult to make them see how the situation looked to other Asian peoples, which we knew because we have the great advantage of having Asian friends in the Commonwealth, which helps one to keep a world view. I pointed out to Truman that you couldn't expect the Chinese, particularly when they were feeling flushed with success, to be ready to settle for some principle announced by the United Nations, to which they were not allowed to belong. It seemed to me absurd not to face the fact that the Communist Government was head of the real China and get them into the U.N. However, it was very difficult to persuade the Americans on that; a democratic President or Prime Minister can't do just what he likes, he has to take into account the state of public opinion. Truman had to remember that there were a great many powerful groups playing about with the Republicans and raking up all sorts of prejudices against him for being too soft with Communists. The anti-Chinese lobby was very powerful and Truman probably couldn't afford to do more than he did.

Extraordinarily stupid, though, the refusal to recognise Communist China; it doesn't get you anywhere refusing to accept facts. One has to remember, of course, that the Americans have a great emotional feeling against this wicked Communist thing that has stolen their love from them in China. China had been their baby, they thought they were entitled to gratitude for all kinds of things. I daresay they were. But the Communists had come in and taken the show, and after the Americans had elevated China to a great place in the United Nations as a sort of American second eleven it had now turned round and become a second U.S.S.R. instead. Naturally it piqued them a good deal. Apart from that, they were having a general wave of anti-Communism at the time. I don't believe in that sort of emotional thinking but it affected American policy very much. It still does.

Williams: Do you think Truman appreciated how essential it was not to antagonise the whole of the Asian world?

Attlee: I think so. I was very insistent that whatever we did must not be just an American-British action, that we must have others in and particularly Asians. And we did. We got Indian support; India didn't send troops but she sent Red Cross. The Americans found it hard to realise that in the eyes of Asia they had become almost a spear-head of imperialism. They'd always thought themselves so pure and clean. They didn't realise that to a lot of people they were now Number One exploiter – even more imperialist than Britain – and how important it was that they shouldn't allow this feeling to be given further support by their actions. Truman himself was pretty open-minded and ready to look at facts as facts within the limits of his Constitution. But of course a President's not a dictator. Even if he sees the point you can't always be sure of delivery of the goods. He may get turned down by the Senate.

Although there were a number of sharp exchanges during the talks which continued the next day on board the Presidential yacht *Williamsburg*, and a good deal of frank speaking on both sides, the understanding that had developed between Truman and Attlee during their relationship over a number of years meant that both of them had never any doubt that, as Truman later put it, 'loyalty to principles and friends and also to treaty commitments is a British attitude and it's ours too.'

Attlee got the major agreements he had come for – that the

West must not get bogged down in a major war with China and that bombing of Chinese industrial centres must be ruled out. He argued strongly also against the view put forward by Acheson in these meetings that America and Britain and the other U.N. forces must be prepared to stay in Korea until they were forced out and should not contemplate any negotiations. We might well, he pointed out, have to choose between a shooting war with China or negotiation and it was more sensible to negotiate. To this Truman replied that they had to take into account the position of Chiang Kai-shek and the fact that for the American peoples his régime had become a sort of symbol. They could not allow Formosa to fall into Communists' hands. To this Attlee answered that, although he realised that American foreign policy depended upon keeping the American people together, it was also essential to keep the United Nations together and to remember that a policy which made Asian members of the U.N. turn against the West would be fatal. He knew that the President's Administration had to consider public opinion about Chiang Kai-shek and Formosa, but he should also remember that whatever was done in Korea would have to be done through the U.N., it could not be done by the efforts and orders of the United States and the United Kingdom alone, important though they were.

Later at a private meeting Attlee raised directly with Truman the issue of the atom bomb. Was the President's press conference meant to be taken as a hint that America was giving active thought to the use of the bomb? If so, he must tell him frankly that such a possibility had appalled British public opinion and, he believed, the public opinion of most other countries also. He received a firm assurance from Truman that this had not been in his mind. The press conference statement, said the President, had been a general answer to a general question and should not be taken as having any new significance.

It was the last meeting Attlee and Truman were to have while both were still in office. It was one of their longest and one of their frankest. On Formosa they agreed to differ. On some other issues they had sharp differences. But when it ended they knew that they understood each other's points of view on all the major issues involved and that by straight talking and close arguing they had done something to check and change policies that might have led to a new world war. And Attlee could feel also that he had forced the United States to take more fully into account the Asian viewpoint.

How strong this was and how vital it was not to discount it was made still clearer to Attlee on his return in a personal letter he received during the meeting of the Commonwealth Prime Ministers from Nehru, who, after declaring his conviction that every country in Europe and Asia wanted to avoid war, went on: 'But we are stuck because of this American attitude which I am convinced is completely wrong from every point of view.' The only result of an American policy that extended the war to China would, he said, be a break-up of the United Nations. The Commonwealth must stop 'this drift to inevitable disaster.'

Attlee had not been able to change the American attitude on China as a member of the United Nations. But as he came back from Washington he could feel that he had done something to stop the drift to disaster.

16

The End of the Labour Government

At home Attlee had to meet a situation of mounting strain as the attempt to govern with a tiny majority imposed new problems on his Cabinet. Neither Bevin nor Cripps, the two most powerful members of his Administration, were in a physical state to remain much longer.

Bevin had been seriously ill for some time. Even before the 1950 Election it had seemed inevitable that his health would soon compel him to give up the Foreign Office. However, a sea journey to the Colombo Conference did him some good and on board ship he scribbled a more hopeful note to Attlee, although the shakiness of the handwriting belied the optimism.

'Dear Clem, Jan. 2, 1950.

'We are nearing Aden, hence this note. I got your message in Paris, thanks. Had a tough time over Christmas but I felt I ought to try to do this job.

'I feel much better. Train and flying was a bit trying but the sea and good constant medical attention is making good headway.

'This morning I am much better, it is not the Swan song yet – Colombo will not be very strenuous, and a steady journey home will help.

'Keep me advised as to dates and coming events. I must be ready in Woolwich, it will affect my neighbours very much. I trust you are well.

Yours sincerely,

ERNEST BEVIN'

He was compelled to go into hospital for an operation before Attlee flew to Washington. Again he was hopeful, despite all that had been found to be wrong with him.

'Both doctors say I am nearly out of the woods so far as the angina pectoris is concerned and the treatment I have followed has been effective,' he wrote in the course of a letter from Manor House Hospital on 21 April 1950. 'I have some other trouble with the heart, fibrillations, or something of that kind, the cause of which I do not understand, but which seem to take the breath out of me every now and again. However, the rest here is helping that, and I am taking special treatment for it. Then I have the swelling of the legs, but they have something now which will take the place of the injections and so far the results have been satisfactory. The operation itself was a very nasty one, but the pain has died down.

'I am hoping that during the week-end the organs will be functioning correctly, and then I can go on with the other treatment, although the treatment for the other troubles will not necessitate my being away, although I will have to go slowly.

'I am giving close attention to the Atlantic Pact and all the other papers for the Acheson visit. I want to turn that into a success if I can.

'I have not given a detailed health report to anybody else except you, but I thought you ought to know. I believe I am going to make a good recovery.'

But by the time Attlee got back from Washington it was clear that no lasting improvement had taken place and that, despite his own determination to carry on, Bevin could not be left much longer in charge of Foreign Affairs.

Attlee says of Bevin's last months: 'He clung on. The doctors were often really quite hopeful and he hung on as long as he could, but he was suffering intensely. I don't think it affected his judgment, although some of the newspapers tried to say it did and kept up a bitter attack. They are more generous in such matters in America than they are here. When Dulles was ill they cracked him up and wanted him to stay on, but as soon as Ernie was sick the Tories started howling for his blood. He wanted to stay because he hoped there might be a chance to relieve tension with the Russians and he thought, if he was there, he'd know how to grasp the opportunity if it came. But it was a constant strain.

'Part of the trouble was there was no obvious successor. Herbert Morrison was anxious for it. It didn't really seem his line of country, but the others one could think of were all too young and inexperienced. It had to be a senior man and Herbert was the most senior. He seemed to want it badly and turned down every other suggestion I made to him, so in the end I appointed him. Rather bad luck for him as it turned out. It brought him a peck of troubles. It was heartbreaking having to tell Ernie he must move out but there wasn't really any choice. I made him Lord Privy Seal and gave him some jobs to do, but he was dead in five weeks. A terrible loss.'

Cripps also was finding the strain of work impossible. Early in the New Year he explained to Attlee that he did not want to fight another Election and would like to get away as soon as it could be conveniently arranged. Attlee replied sympathetically and Cripps wrote again from his home in Gloucestershire:

Frith Hill,
Nr Stroud,
Glos.

'My Dear Clem, Saturday (undated).

'Thank you very much indeed for your most kind and understanding letter in answer to mine. I am so grateful to you for seeing my point of view so clearly.

'I shall hope very much that there may be an election before too long and I am sure this is really essential for the country.

'I shall not say anything more about my going until the time comes at the election or at the end of the summer, whichever is the sooner. The best course will be for me to write you a letter that can be published when the time comes – probably the day after the end of the session – and just slip away.

'I presume you will tell the King a few days beforehand so that I can go and bid him goodbye. Apart from that, there will be no need for any formalities.

'I shall write and tell you how deeply I have appreciated your friendly kindness when the time comes for us to part!

Yours, STAFFORD'

By autumn it was plain that he could not continue. He was compelled to go to Zürich for treatment. From there he wrote to Attlee sending his resignation:

Privat-Klinck Burcher-Benner
October 4th, 1950. Sanatorium "Lebeudge Kragy"
'My Dear Prime Minister, Zürich

'My doctors here, with the help of an outside specialist, have now completed their examination and I enclose the short conclusion which they have reached and have submitted to me. The net result is, as you will see, that unless I now go off for a prolonged rest I shall probably do irreparable harm to my health.

'Under these circumstances I see no alternative but to hand you my resignation and to apply for the Chiltern Hundreds. This latter course seems to be essential in view of the narrow majority of the Party in the House of Commons. I should, naturally, have preferred to maintain my membership of the House of Commons, had it been possible.

'I am sending you these views at once so that I can come and see you on my return on October 16th, and then bring to finality the arrangements for my giving up my office and for the publicity connected with the change.

'You will know with what great regret I take this step but I am quite certain that it is the right and indeed the only thing to do.

'It will be sad to break the long and happy association I have had with you and my other colleagues, but I shall hope at the end of the year to be able to resume some activity useful to the country.

Yours, STAFFORD'

This hope of improvement was not fulfilled. Cripps died eighteen months later in the clinic in Zürich. He had been succeeded at the Treasury by Hugh Gaitskell.

On this, Attlee remarks: 'That was Stafford's advice. Gaitskell is very much an economist and of course some people have the idea that you don't want a man who understands finance. But if you have one I think you should put him at the disposal of the party. I don't think it would have done to put Nye Bevan in. I don't think he inspired much confidence in anyone abroad at that time and I don't know of anyone else one could have put in. I didn't think it advisable to bring Hugh Dalton back.'

Attlee still believes that the split in the Cabinet, and the resignation of Aneurin Bevan and Harold Wilson that followed Gaitskell's appointment and his insistence on cuts in the cost of the Health Services as part of the economies required to meet the increase in defence expenditure, might have been avoided if he himself had not been forced to go into hospital with a duodenal ulcer at that time: the long strain of responsibility during the war and on through the post-war years without a break was beginning to tell a little even on his constitution.

At this moment his absence was a serious misfortune. There were many who felt as did David Kirkwood, famous leader of the Clydeside Left in its stormiest day, when he wrote to the sick Prime Minister in hospital:

"Karleen"
Roman Road
Bearsden

'My dear Clem, 21.4.51

'Like all the other members of the Party I rejoice to learn that your health is improving.

'It would be absurd to pretend that there is complete unanimity in the Government, but in the House of Commons the loyalty to you is very strong and I feel sure that the feeling of tension will disappear on your return.

'Knowing how sadly we miss you, my greatest hope is that you may soon be able to be among us exercising that superb authority which everyone in the House recognises and admires.

'May I send my kindest regards to Mrs Attlee,

'Believe me to be

Yours sincerely,

DAVID KIRKWOOD'

But by the time Attlee recovered the split had gone too far to be repaired.

Attlee comments: 'It was unfortunate that I was ill just then. It oughtn't to have gone so far, but both sides dug their feet in and took up positions and wouldn't budge. One wants to avoid that sort of freezing of attitudes if one can. It's often a mistake to force the issue – better to let things take their time, let people blow off steam, without actually bringing them to opposite sides of the line where they can't go back. There's sometimes virtue in not allowing people to make up their minds too quickly. Nye was quite wrong, of course, in thinking that he could just say, "Hands off my old Department", but personal differences were involved too, and then the dispute was widened to cover the whole question of the economic consequence of rearmament. But Nye had fully accepted the need for an expansion in our defence expenditure and I had pointed out in public speeches as well as in our private discussions that the rate at which we achieved the defence programme was bound to be conditioned by availability of raw materials and machine tools and the level of prices, it wasn't one of those issues where you were left with no flexibility. One had time to see how things were working out and consider if adjustments were required as one went along. In my view, there was no real difference of principle between Nye and the rest of the Cabinet and I was sorry it was allowed to develop into one.

I was surprised when Harold Wilson took Nye's line. He ought to have had more understanding of the economic position. And John Freeman. As I say, I didn't believe there was any real clash of principles involved and I had hoped it could be handled so as to avoid letting it get to the point where it became a resignation issue.'

But to such an issue it came and on 21 April, only one week after Ernest Bevin's death, Attlee received Aneurin Bevan's letter of resignation:

House of Commons
'My dear Clem, 2.30 p.m. 21st April 1951

'In previous conversations with you, and in my statements to the Cabinet, I have explained my objections to many features of the Budget. Having endeavoured, in vain, to secure modifications of these features I feel I must ask you to accept my resignation.

'The Budget, in my view, is wrongly conceived in that it fails to apportion fairly the burdens of expenditure as between different social classes. It is wrong because it is based upon a scale of military expenditure, in the coming year, which is physically unattainable, without grave extravagance in its spending.

'It is wrong because it envisages rising prices as a means of reducing civilian consumption, with all the consequences of industrial disturbance involved.

'It is wrong because it is the beginning of the destruction of those social services in which Labour has taken a special pride and which was giving to Britain the moral leadership of the world.

'I am sure you will agree that it is always better that policies should be carried out by those who believe in them. It would be dishonourable for me to allow my name to be associated in the carrying out of policies which are repugnant to my conscience and contrary to my expressed opinion.

'I am sorry that I feel it necessary to take this step after so many years of co-operation in a Government which has done so much for the cause of Labour and the progress of mankind.

'I need hardly say that my adherence to the cause of Labour and Socialism is stronger than ever and that I believe that renewed efforts by all of us will result in another thrust towards the goal of our hopes.

'As is customary, I shall explain my position in greater detail in my speech to the House of Commons.

'May I conclude by wishing you a speedy return to health and vigour.

Yours sincerely,

ANEURIN'

To this Attlee replied in his own handwriting:

10 Downing Street
Whitehall

'My dear Nye, 21st April 1951

'I have your letter of today's date. I note that you have extended the area of disagreement with your colleagues a long way beyond the specific matter to which, as I understand, you have taken objection.

'I had certainly gathered that if the proposal for imposing charges on dentures and spectacles were dropped, you would have been satisfied.

'I must regret that you should feel it necessary to offer your resignation, but in these circumstances I have no option but to accept it. I note that you propose to make a statement in the House.

'Thank you for the good work that you have done as a member of the Government during these difficult years.

'Thank you also for your good wishes for my health.

Yours ever,

CLEM'

Attlee remarks: 'Up till then Nye had been a good member of the Cabinet, working as a member of the team. He was one of those horses who work very well in harness and he'd had six years of it with Stafford Cripps. Nye was much attached to Stafford, who could talk to him like an uncle. He always had a great respect for what he said and Stafford could argue him out of his attitudes and get him to see the whole picture. He cut loose after Stafford went. It was a great pity for him and the Party. And of course these splits didn't help us when we came to the Election.'

Before the election came, however, Attlee had another international crisis to face – this time over Persian oil.

Trouble had been brewing there for some time, for reasons which were well set out in two letters which Attlee received in September – one from Richard Stokes, the Lord Privy Seal, who had been to Teheran on a mission in search of a solution to the difficulties between the Anglo-Iranian Oil Company and the Iranian Government, thc other from the Aga Khan, who had written to Stokes and whose letter the Lord Privy Seal passed on.

The letter from Stokes read:

In Cornwall

'My dear Clem, 14.9.51

'Ever since I began to learn some of the facts concerning the oil business whilst I was in Teheran I have been very uneasy in my mind. This was brought to a head the day before I came away for my holiday by Sir William Fraser refusing to give me a copy of the A.I.O.C. 1950 balance sheet because it "had not been submitted to his Directors". I am told the fact is that in 1950 they made some £170 million profit, 60 per cent of it from Iranian oil.

'For many years I have known that Iranian oil is the cheapest to produce in the world. Twenty years ago I was told that it could be delivered and sold at a profit in America at a less price than the cost of production in Texas, this for geological reasons into which I need not go now. The Iranians no doubt know it.

'The 1949 balance sheet of A.I.O.C. showed £53 million written off £81 million cost, leaving the refinery etc. in at £27 million. The consolidated balance sheet shows more – £72 million written off £110 million – and £40 million written off £50 million in the Tanker Section of the business.

'Whilst I am not condoning the Iranian action in their unilateral revocation of a contract, this does all lend point to their feeling that in our asking for compensation they are being asked to pay twice.

'From all this I cannot help but feel that we are being rushed into insisting on an arrangement which is ungenerous to Iran having regard to all the facts, in order to maintain a 50–50 arrangement which may well be vital to America but is not vital to us where the cost of production is so much less – i.e. if as indicated in para 2 of this letter. If we do succeed in a 50–50 settlement how are we going to justify £68 million profit (3–5ths of £170 m.) on the sale of 30 million tons of Iranian oil last year?

'On the 50–50 proposal and compensation I think therefore we should think again.

'The next point that worries me is the insistence by our Embassy in Teheran that we cannot deal with Mossadeq. I think we could if some of the undesirable elements were silenced or removed – e.g. Fateini, Hassebi and Mahhi. It is important for us all to realise that the Shah and most competent Iranians I have spoken to consider the *best* settlement can be made with Mossadeq and that it is in the best interest of their country that we should attempt it. I don't believe myself that the old gang Zia – Jaram are any use, or could survive without martial law, which the Shah is loth to introduce. Although Zia has come out into the open, the Shah does not yet seem to be supporting him. Now comes the news of Mossadeq's message to Harriman. We shall be in a fix if Harriman comes out publicly saying we should resume negotiations when we have said we won't deal with Mossadeq. The sum total of all this is that I have *no respect* for Shepherd's judgement. His reactions so far as I have observed them are usually ungenerous.

'Finally I don't like what we've done with regard to shipments almost at point of arrival. Stopping further shipments from this end I do not disagree with, but to stop deliveries from ships already in the Gulf and at Basra seems to me very mean and I fear it will be so regarded whatever the money-collectors say.

'May I have a talk with you as soon as I get back next Friday?

Yours sincerely,

DICK STOKES'

'P.S. Half an hour after writing this the enclosed arrived from the Aga Khan. I think you ought to see at once. Much of what he writes would seem to endorse what I have said above.'

The Aga Khan's letter was as follows:

Hôtel Ritz
Place Vendôme
Paris

'My dear Lord Privy Seal, 10th September 1951

'Although I am not personally known to you, I feel it my duty to write to you frankly what I feel about the negotiations between A.I. Company, Great Britain and Iran.

'I have not stated my views to anybody and have no intention of doing so except to yourself and to Mr Harriman, with whose father and mother I had personal friendly relations for many years.

'You are probably aware that I have both British and Iranian nationalities, and I am one of the cases in which a man may have three nationalities: British, Iranian and Pakistanian.

'My Ismailia followers are numerous in Iran as well as in most parts of the British Colonies, such as Africa and Malaya.

'For these reasons, I naturally would like to see Great Britain and Iran relations friendly and, better still, intimate. Strained relations between England and Iran will undoubtedly be a cause of pain and worry in Moslem countries like Pakistan and the Middle East and in fact amongst Moslems all over the world.

'I was also in Teheran and saw everybody worth seeing, including the religious leaders, just before the assassination of Razmara. Naturally in that country people talk oil. What I feel is that, while a lot of other matters like management are being given great importance, the surest, shortest and most certain way of an understanding is not being frankly faced; all your proposals ultimately boil down to 50/50 participation between the Company and Iran. Other Near Eastern oil countries like Saudi Arabia are being quoted as an example. Even without nationalisation under the Razmara arrangement, Iran would have received practically anything between 40 to 50, so at 50/50 there is no great temptation for them to swallow questions like management etc. ... etc. *The Times* has had several leaders, but there was a very great and fundamental difference between one of its early leaders and the last one. The first one said that 50/50 would have no attraction for Iranians; the second one says that they will never get more than 50/50 and that they must be treated like any other Middle East countries.

'One thing I did find in Iran, even amongst my peasant followers in villages from north to south who came to see me, and the ordinary Iranian has a strong horse sense: they realise that Saudi Arabia from the very first got something like 30 to 40 per cent and, only after about comparatively few years of that rate, its 50/50. The Anglo-Iranian, whether through the fault of the Iranians or the power of the British – the cause is immaterial, the fact counts – for a generation never gave a regular and reasonable percentage like Saudi Arabia had, and they built up hundreds of millions of pounds of capital through Iranian oil at a ridiculously low percentage of payment.

'Whatever the legal aspect of the matter, the moral question is that they are not on all fours with a country like Saudi Arabia which, from the very first and in a short time, got vast sums and now starts with 50/50. Countries like Iraq, Bahrein, Kuwait cannot be quoted as examples. Bahrein and Kuwait are not independent international sovereign States and Iraq, when the oil transaction took place, was mandated territory and was in fact, if not in name, a British colony. Even now to the Iranians, their independence, which has gone on for several thousand years, is a totally different thing to that of a newborn state like Iraq, which is a British creation. Nothing more insults countries like Egypt and Iran than being compared to places like Jordan and Iraq which had no independence of their own for hundreds of years and are in fact (as I stated above), if not in name, protectorates.

'I cannot help feeling that the Anglo-Iranian should make a difference and give something for all the benefits they have had for over a generation at a very low cost and price. If 50/50 is to be the rate of the future, then all they have built in Iran, like refineries etc. (which they would never have built up and put so much money aside for had they from the very first been paying 30 to 40 per cent like the Americans did to Saudi Arabia) should in common equity be handed over without exception freely to the Iranians and then only stick to 50/50. If not, then certainly they should suggest something like 60/40 and be satisfied with small profit in future and thank their stars for having had a good run for more than a generation.

'From what I was told by the man in the street, whether a high priest or one of my followers in Ispahan or Kashan, there has been such a sense of injustice for over a generation that unless something right and proper in equity and obviously so is done on the British side, they would rather have no bread than half a loaf. Do not forget that Samson was an Oriental. The only people I met in Teheran who would be ready to come to terms on a practically 50/50 basis are the corrupt hated gangs of the sort that have taken their orders in the past, either from the British or the Russian Embassy, according to which way the wind blew. In London they seem to be waiting for that crew to come back but they forget that that is playing into the hands of the Communist Party, for these people are discredited. The poor Shah, for whom I have the greatest admiration and regard, and Prince Aly Reza and the Minister Ala, are the only honest persons in the Court circle. Arrangements made with the old gang above mentioned may look all right for the time being, but if there is a time of stress, you will see what propaganda value that will have for their northern neighbours and will leave with the nation feelings of despair and injustice.

'Now finally what I say is that if Anglo-Iranian honestly, and even generously, takes into full consideration the principle of unearned increment since the beginning, and this fact gets known to all Iran, then you will certainly get a satisfactory arrangement approved by Parliament, whether by the present Cabinet or a respected Ala or similar Cabinet without intriguing for the hated and corrupt old gang.

Yours sincerely,
AGA KHAN'

Bevin had been deeply disturbed by the oil position in Iran for some time before his death and about its possible effects not only on British relations with Persia but with the whole of the Middle East. But although he succeeded in getting some changes they were too small and came too late to prevent an explosion. In the closing stages of his administration Attlee, with a new and inexperienced Foreign Secretary at his side, found himself faced with a crisis as Mossadeq announced his intention to seize the Abadan refineries without negotiation and without any discussion or compensation.

This development, which set in motion a strong surge of nationalist emotion throughout the Middle East – as well as a different kind of anger in Britain – almost certainly played its part in the Egyptian decision to abrogate her canal base treaties which came in the middle of the General Election of November 1951.

There were in the Cabinet, as well as in the country, a number of strong voices in favour of immediate military action against Iran – the new Foreign Secretary's among them. Attlee, however, took a different view. Not only did he believe – as was later to prove the case over Suez – that quick and decisive military action on the scale required was in any event impracticable having regard to the disposition of forces immediately available, but also that it would put Britain in the wrong in the eyes of world opinion, including American opinion and might thus prove both militarily and politically disastrous. He was opposed in principle to the use of force by a big Power against a small Power except in so far as it might be necessary to safeguard the lives of British nationals if they were attacked.

Here is Attlee's view: 'I think if we had used force we would have raised the whole of Asia against us and a great deal of public opinion in the rest of the world too. And it would have been quite wrong morally and politically. It was impossible for us as a Labour Government to say that you couldn't nationalise the oil industry. The Persians had done it the wrong way – but one had to consider the situation, and the provocation. At this time of day it was quite out of the question to think you could revert to old form and act as a big nation throwing in its force to defend its commercial interests. Quite wrong, and certainly quite impossible for us, of all people.

It was hard on Herbert to have this on his plate when he hadn't been in the Foreign Office five minutes. It hurt his reputation all round. That was one of the reasons why I agreed to stay on as Leader after the Election. I wanted to go, but everybody said, 'No, you must stay, you are our biggest asset,' and apart from everything else it seemed a bit unfair, when I thought it over, to raise the issue of the Leadership when Herbert, who naturally had expectations, was in this position. Other things being equal, it seemed right to leave time for his reputation to recover. As it turned out, it didn't make any difference. When I did go in 1955, the Party decided it didn't want Herbert and chose Gaitskell. I hadn't anything to do with that. The Leadership of the Labour Party isn't an hereditary position, one doesn't choose one's successor. But Herbert's chance would have been even smaller in 1951 than it turned out to be in 1955.'

Morrison in fact had never succeeded in establishing the hold over the post-war Labour Parliamentary Party that he had over the Party in the 'thirties and, as he sometimes rather ruefully admitted to colleagues, never quite understood it in the same way. Although he continued to regard himself as Attlee's natural successor, and was so regarded by many, even as early as 1949

Arthur Moyle, Attlee's P.P.S., reported to him that 'it had become extremely unlikely that the Parliamentary Party would wish to see Morrison as his successor'.

When the Election was fought, Labour, torn by dissension following Bevan's resignation, gravely weakened by the death of Ernest Bevin and the illness and resignation of Stafford Cripps, and damaged in popularity by the Abadan and Egyptian crises, by the controls and austerities imposed by the Korean War, and by heavy defence expenditure, nevertheless increased its popular vote to just on 13,950,000, the largest received by any political party in British history and getting on for a quarter of a million more than that of the Conservatives and their allies combined.

But it was not enough. Labour's majority of 10 was replaced by a Conservative majority of sixteen. Attlee's Premiership was over.

As he packed up and made ready with his wife to take up their home in the cottage they had bought in Buckinghamshire, Cherry Cottage, near Great Missenden, one letter among the many he received pleased him particularly. It was from a fellow Prime Minister, Mr Louis St Laurent of Canada.

Prime Minister's House
24, Sussex Street
Ottawa

'My dear Attlee, Feb. 27, 51

'In spite of the detached attitude it is proper for us in the Commonwealth to observe in respect of the domestic controversial politics of our sister nations, I confess I was surprised at the outcome of your general election and, on personal grounds, I am genuinely sorry that outcome ends our official relationship as fellow Prime Ministers. I trust you feel as I do that the relations between the Governments of the United Kingdom and Canada could not have been easier or closer than they have been in these last few years. That has been the result in major part of your unfailing understanding and unreserved acceptance in spirit as well as in letter of the principles of complete equality of our national status.

The close and growing friendship which has developed between us in these last years has also been helpful to both our countries and my colleagues and I will miss you from Downing Street. Please accept for Mrs Attlee and yourself the assurances of my warmest regards and allow me to wish for you both some relief from the heavy strain of recent years.

Yours sincerely,
LOUIS ST LAURENT'

'P.S. I am enclosing a clipping from an Ottawa paper which, in spite of its Conservative leanings, has ventured to be objective.'

The clipping was a leading article from the *Ottawa Journal*. It described Attlee as not only 'in important respects a great Prime Minister' but 'in many ways a beau ideal of Prime Ministers.' As the pressure of State affairs grew ever stronger,' it concluded, 'many of his most valued lieutenants became ill or retired, but when foreign affairs went sour and domestic controversy intensified Mr Attlee stood firm by his duties and convictions. . . . He has played the game honourably and courageously according to the wishes of the team and in defeat he is not dismayed.'

Index